The Day Helicopters Flew Heaven on Stand By

Traumatic Brain Injury Through a Mother's Eyes

By

L. R. Athman

xulon PRESS

The Day Helicopters Flew Heaven on Stand By
Traumatic Brain Injury Through a Mother's Eyes
by L. R. Athman

Printed in the United States of America

ISBN 9781498455770

www.xulonpress.com

Table of Contents

—ɯɯ—

Derailed

—⚡—

Imagine your family and yourself on a train going 300 miles an hour with a goal for the end of the journey when suddenly it derails, head on, into a brick wall. My goals in writing this book are two-fold. I wanted to provide individuals and families of victims who have suffered a traumatic brain injury, hope, evolving to faith through the power of prayer for healing. I also ask that if you are reading our story, that you say a prayer for Matthew too. Without a doubt, every prayer said speeds up his recovery.

To understand the full impact of how the car accident affected our family, I need to describe how life was previously.

Kami, Matt, Brooke, Laura and Abby

Matthew, age seventeen, was our only driver. He would bring the girls to school, pick them up from after school sports, bring them to piano lessons, appointments, etc. Matt loved humor, always having a new joke, reading the comic section of the newspaper first and writing a pun on the blackboard before English class every day. Matt was a percussionist in band (drums, bells, and piano) and enjoyed being in pep band too. Matt loved to read and would spend any free time at the Pierz Public Library. He would play Call of Duty on Xbox live all the time, preferring this over going out on the weekends. Matt was taking three college courses, had a score of 30 on his college ACT, and scored one hundred thirty-four on his IQ test just two days before the accident. He was anxiously awaiting basketball practice to begin, as he would be one of the senior captains of the team this year. Matt was applying to colleges, his goal to play college basketball and to become a physical therapist. Matt was in Knowledge Bowl, youth group and varsity golf. He loved little children, especially his cousins, and would lift them up to touch the ceiling, much to their delight, being six feet, eight inches tall. Matt would always talk to elderly people, sitting next to them waiting for a seat at a restaurant, or when he would visit me at work. He loved animals, always stopping to pet any dog or cat if they would allow it. Matt took care of our pets every day at home too. The day of the accident, Matt was planning on going to the Pierz high school playoff football game and then to a Halloween party. He was on his way home after picking Abby up from dance practice when the accident happened a mile from our home.

Laura, age sixteen, had just finished tennis and the fall school play. She was super busy with her friends and boyfriend, always planning a social outing. She was waiting to re-take her driver's test, failing the first test after another car went through an intersection without signaling. Laura was in student council, band, choir, Knowledge Bowl, basketball, and active in youth group. She was always busy texting several friends simultaneously while doing homework and listening to her iPod with ear buds in. Laura was determined to have perfect grades, with the goal of being a doctor, lawyer, or orthodontist someday. She was a natural leader, bringing issues to adults and leading every group project. Laura had gone to her boyfriend's house after school the day of the accident since school had an early dismissal at noon.

Abby, age fifteen, was my helper around the house. She would help me with cooking, baking, gardening, and watching Brooke. Abby read on her Kindle every spare moment she had. Abby got straight A's in school without any help from Bill or me. Abby gave everything she did one hundred and ten percent effort. She had just finished tennis and the school play; however, was still busy with band (playing the flute), piano lessons, student council, choir, dance, and art club. Abby read the Bible frequently, was active in youth group, and volunteered several days each summer at Camp JIM (Jesus is Mine.) Abby made the varsity and jazz dance team in her freshman year and had just finished practice after school the day of accident when Matt had come to bring her home.

Kami, age eleven, was finishing her last year at Holy Trinity grade school. She was busy with piano, dance, and basketball. Kami loved to play piano, be on the computer, or read during her spare time. She would leave her coat, shoes, hat, mittens, backpack and clothes all over the house wherever they may land. Kami was very loving, always wanting a hug, writing Bill and I notes good-night if we went out, etc. Since Matt, Laura, and Abby were busy with after-school activities, Kami came home and watched Brooke. She argued with Brooke non-stop, never realizing that Brooke thrived on knowing "how to get her goat."

Brooke, age seven, delighted in being the "baby" of the family. She had six of us showering her with love since birth. Matthew still held her in church, and whenever she wanted a glass of milk, a spoon, a movie started, etc., she only needed to say the word and "voila" her wish was granted. Brooke loved first grade, was in dance, and spent her spare time coloring and playing with dolls. She would never go downstairs by herself, (where all her dolls were in the family room) afraid of being alone. Needless to say, a sibling would go down with her and watch TV or read to be with her. Little did she know that she would go from carelessly trick-or-treating one night, to being forced, by circumstances, to grow up far beyond her seven years the very next day.

I worked full-time at Country Manor in Sartell as an Occupational Therapist and the Rehab Coordinator, seeing outpatients for shoulder rehabilitation. I also worked every other Saturday in inpatient rehab at the St. Cloud Hospital, primarily with neurological patients. My days were absorbed with work, meals, and the kid's activities. I was excited for an overnight vacation for my Mom's birthday on November fourth (to celebrate her birthday on the sixth,) and my first-time "Girls Getaway Weekend" the following weekend. I was seeing my last outpatient for the day, Friday afternoon, when I received the phone call about Matt and Abby's accident.

Bill worked full-time at Trimpac (a millwork company) as a buyer. He made everyone breakfast in the morning, did all the laundry, and spent every spare moment bringing the kids to activities and appointments.

As busy as we were, I tried to appreciate these years, knowing someday I'd miss them. Little did I know how soon I would miss our "normal" busy life.

Having two of five children airlifted after a car accident is devastating beyond what words can do justice, however the extent to which it affects the entire family has been huge part of our journey.

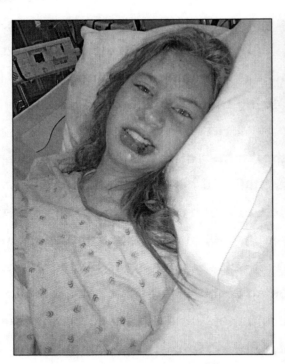 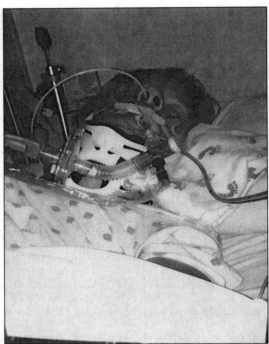

Abby and Matt in ICU

Feelings from Brookie Bear

Brooke (age seven)

—ɯ—

Dec 24, 2013

hi my name is brooke i love matt i want matt to come home right now this is brooke i want matt to come home right right right right right right right right right right right right right right right now i love love love love love love love love love love love love love love love love love love love love love love love love matt

Laura, age sixteen, wrote a poem about Matt that I didn't see until months after the accident, but needed to include.

This Can't Be Real

The elevator door opens, the hallway well lit
I gently walk off
I follow numbly behind a family friend
This is a sick place, they sneeze, they cough
My youngest sisters too little
To see what he looks like
The other an hour away with my dad
She is not well,

Yet none of us are well

At the time I knew his room number by heart

All I can think is this can't be real

My mother greets me with a sob

A long embrace

Her hair a mess, thrown all around

The little makeup left, smeared down her face

She pulls away, sobbing again

My grandma embraces, quiets her

Nurses come out, they open the door

I quietly walk in

Pull the curtain to the side

I took a glance and then I cried

This can't be real

His body was swollen

Cuts and bruises, purple, blue and black

Unrecognizable if not for being 6'8"

His hair greasy, pulled back

Fever is way too high

Yet his hands cold as death

Surely, this is death

This can't be real

Eyes slightly open, looking different directions

Bloodshot, sickly, crusty, unblinking

So yellow is his skin

This isn't even him

This can't be real

Cannot even breathe

A machine makes it happen

Tubes are everywhere

This is no sign of life, does God even care?

No movement, no reaction

His body is stiff, will not move a fraction

This must be a corpse

Not my brother

This can't be real

The doctor comes in

Puts a hand on my shoulder

"The damage is beyond repair"

My mom stifled a sob, I had to hold her

No more tears from me

I had to be strong

But this was his senior year

God, what did we do wrong?

No chance of a life

No chance of a dream

All his plans ruined

This can't be real

Whether you get a 30 on your ACT

Or flunk every class in school

Fate takes anyone by demand

Whether you were "popular" or "uncool"

The days have passed

The pain still here

It hurts going everyday

Still expecting him there

Every day I go to school

Not expecting them to care

Put on a fake smile for my friends

Worry about what brands I wear

Yet I still have a broken home

I know I'm not the only one who feels this way

So sad, so dark, so alone

Everyone has their daily struggles

Some so big, some so small

From brain damage caused by a car accident

To the other kids pushing you into a wall

These things make us human

Alive, make us feel

Many just cry

But like my brother, some fight

Please, Lord. . . .

This just can't be real

Laura read this to her Sophmore English class and received a standing ovation, but would have done anything to instead go back in time to how life was on 10/31/13.

Helicopter at the accident scene

The Day Our Lives Changed

—⚭—

On Friday afternoon November 1st, 2013, I was completing a new outpatient Occupational Therapy Evaluation when our receptionist, Kelsey, came into the clinic, visually upset, stating "You have an emergency phone call and he said no matter what you were doing, you need to take this call." My patient immediately said to go take the call.

My stomach dropped, my heart raced, my hands trembled, as I walked on jelly-like legs to the phone in the reception area. "This is police chief Eric Henneken. This is a phone call every parent dreads. Matthew and Abby were in a car accident. Matthew has been flown to the St. Cloud Hospital (SCH) and Abby was taken to St. Gabriel's Hospital in Little Falls by ambulance. They both sustained head injuries and were intubated. You need to get to the SCH emergency room immediately." I asked him what happened, and he said "It appears Matt ran a stop sign and was hit. You need to get to the hospital now!" I asked him where the accident happened—needing to understand, as I didn't believe it—a wonderful, sunny day, he had to be joking. He gave me the exact location of the accident, one mile from our home, then repeated "You need to get the emergency room as soon as you can."

My mind was spinning and I couldn't think—they couldn't have head injuries. Being an Occupational Therapist for 20 years, this was my WORST nightmare come true —having anyone I love sustain a spinal cord or head injury. I called my husband, Bill, on his cell phone, but he didn't answer. I then called his office phone and when he didn't answer, I had him paged. I told him what happened and very calmly he said, "I'll come get you."

I asked him if he was ok to drive and he said yes. He told his boss to shut down his computer, with no explanation, and bolted.

My patient had physical therapy after my evaluation at 4 pm, so I went to tell her physical therapist, Jenn, what happened and that our patient needed to wait for her because I needed to leave immediately. I went back to my patient and told her I was sorry but had to leave. I took my laptop and other papers from the clinic table, but didn't know what to do next. Thank goodness Jenn came in, helped me collect my thoughts, took the paperwork I wouldn't be following through with, and walked back to the inpatient clinic with me where my office was located. On the way through the clinic, the hospital emergency room called, (I worked at the hospital, so the number was familiar.) Jenn told me I did not want to take the call in the clinic, and led me into the clinic kitchen and closed the door, literally making me sit down for the phone call.

The nurse from the emergency room was calm, understanding and positive. I remember her telling me that Matthew was intubated, but alive, strong, and they didn't know the extent of his head injury yet. She asked how long it would take for me to get to the hospital and if I had a ride. I told her NO, he could NOT have a head injury or a spinal cord injury. Basketball was starting on Monday, he was to be captain of the team, this was NOT happening. Matt was going to the playoff football game that night and then to a Halloween party. He couldn't be in the hospital, hurt with a head injury. I prayed they had made a mistake—it wasn't Matthew, or they only thought he had a head injury. Bill arrived and I was almost hysterical, sobbing as we walked out. I remember Jenn taking my office keys, saying "You won't be back on Monday." It was completely surreal—I couldn't be gone, I had patients scheduled and many other projects to work on in my job as rehab coordinator. Bill was as strong as ever, without a tear, leading me to his car. On the way to the St Cloud Hospital, the emergency room doctor called from St Gabriel's Hospital and informed me that Abby was being flown to Hennepin County Medical Center (HCMC) in Minneapolis. She went unresponsive at the scene and had uneven dilation of her pupils. I didn't understand why she couldn't just come to the SCH as well, but he explained that if she needed neurosurgery due to swelling of the brain, St. Gabriel's in Little Falls and the St. Cloud Hospital didn't have a pediatric neurosurgeon. The doctor said they weren't going to spend the time to do a CAT scan, they needed to get her to HCMC as soon as possible in case she needed surgery. I got off the phone with Bill asking "What did they say? Why?" as I could barely choke the words out to explain. I called my sister who lives and works in the Twin Cities. She calmly said "They are perfect. They are healed in the name of God!" It brought me a wave of relief to hear this, but yet working in the medical field for so long, I knew there was a lot of unknown yet. She said she would meet Abby at HCMC, immediately leaving her job.

We arrived at the emergency room and security asked for my purse to check for weapons per protocol. I remember thinking he could just keep it. Didn't he know material things meant absolutely nothing to me? We were met immediately by two chaplains and brought to a waiting room to wait for the doctor, a pediatric intensivist. I was still sobbing and told them how Matthew couldn't have a head injury, and told them about Abby being flown to HCMC. When Dr. Joey came into the room, the chaplain looked at him and said "Mom knows too much." He came to me, knelt down before me on the floor, placed his hands on my knee and told me they had a tough time re-intubating Matthew, but he was young, strong, and we didn't know what the future would hold. "We know two things—we know he's going to make it, and we know he's going to get better."

They brought us to Matthew and he was semi-conscious, moving on the emergency room bed that was about two feet too short, as they tried to restrain him and give him medication for pain. The nurse came in and said we had visitors. I went out to the waiting area to find my best friend, Joan, and her son, Corbin, waiting for me. As we were talking, crying and hugging, I saw my boss through the glass security doors. My first thought was she must be visiting someone, as she was off work that day and wouldn't have known about the accident. She came in, gave me a hug, as I said "Are you here to see me?" She said "Of course I am, you goof." I replied "That's sooo nice," through my tears as we hugged. We all went with Matt as he was brought to the pediatric intensive care unit (PICU).

My parents arrived, Bill's brother and sister, and my friend and co-worker Jenn (PT). We made plans to go see Abby in Minneapolis at HCMC. I knew my friend Joan would stay with Matt and I needed to see Abby myself and know she was okay. Bill said one of us needed to be with each of them. They each needed to have a parent to provide any consents for surgery or procedures. In the meantime, we had called our daughter,

Laura, 16, who had gone on the bus to her boyfriend's house after school. We told her what had happened and she needed to go home right away to be with Kami and Brooke. I was immediately thankful Laura had taken the bus to his house and hadn't been with Matt and Abby.

I found out later my two sister-in-laws and our priest had also went to the hospital that night. Bill and his brother, Kenny, drove together in one vehicle and Jenn drove me to HCMC. It was the longest drive of my life. After figuring out parking, where we were to go, and getting to the emergency room, I was beyond frazzled. Abby was restrained to her bed, upset and kicking, with stitches in her lip, swollen about ten times the normal size. She had pulled out two IV's before being restrained, therefore the IV's were replaced in her feet. Abby had bitten through her bottom lip, requiring stitches for two hours, inside and outside of her mouth. Her nurse, Amy, was amazing, calling her sweetheart, telling her how pretty she was, how strong she was and putting her beautiful blood-soaked hair up into a bun. (Much to Abby's dismay, later it needed to be cut after days of trying to brush or comb through it.) We were fortunate to have family in the cities too. Bill's brother, Mike, his sister, Brenda, her daughter, Cindy, and my sister, Pam, were all there for Abby when we arrived. The chaplain was there too and asked if we wanted to say a prayer. As we all stood around Abby's bed and said the Our Father, I completely lost it. I had this strong feeling like we were praying at a wake (memorial) service. I helped Amy turn Abby as she vomited a huge amount of brownish blood. Amy was amazed I didn't freak out—it was all on the inside I guess. God was giving me the strength I needed without a doubt. I then received a phone call from my friend, Joan, at the SCH saying Matt wasn't waking up, hadn't had sedation medication, and may need surgery. Joan said the neurosurgeon couldn't believe there wasn't a parent there and we needed to get back as soon as possible to give permission for surgery if needed.

I was never was so torn in my entire life. I didn't want to leave Abby and "choose" Matt over her; however, Matt's injuries were far more involved and I understood the medical jargon much more than Bill. Kenny, Jenn and I drove back to St. Cloud, almost in complete silence. I told Jenn to speed—the police would understand; however, she said it would only take more time to get pulled over and she would drive as fast as safely she could. When we arrived, I was informed Matt's CT scan revealed he didn't have swelling of his brain; however, he was still unresponsive which meant his injuries were even more severe. He had a temporal lobe bleed on the left side of his brain, bleeding over the top of his brain, and a severe bleed with diffuse axonal shearing in his brain stem. He also had a swollen left forearm and lacerated spleen they would watch closely—but he didn't need surgery at this time.

Matt's nurse, Rick, was as laid back as could be that first night. He was on his computer and reading Laffy Taffy jokes to us. Matt loved jokes and it hit me like a rock that he couldn't hear, understand, or maybe ever enjoy a joke again. Rick said "Come on Matt, are you going to sleep your life away?" I gave him a look of pure shock and horror, as he added, "That's what my dad would say on Saturday mornings when we slept in too late." He also commented "At least he was wearing a seatbelt. You should see what they look like when they come in and haven't been wearing one." I wasn't ready for jokes, comparisons, or being told we "were lucky" at this time. All I knew was Matt wouldn't be playing basketball on Monday and everything would change—our family life, work, and our future plans. I slept about twenty minutes all night, sitting in a chair by Matt's bed as I held his hand. Kenny came back at four-twenty am to be with me. I vividly remember the youth group director texting me throughout the entire night "Praying for Matt and Abby." "Praying so hard." Every text gave me a little more strength to get through the most trying, horrible night of my life. I know she and her husband did not sleep at all that night either. God certainly was with all of us that night through the staff, chaplains, family and friends. It was the beginning of our journey of faith.

God's Love Continues

—∿—

Saturday and Sunday were a complete blur for me. Early Saturday since Matt still wasn't responding, Dr. Joey ordered an MRI. The RN called down to imaging and found out the test would occur in approximately two hours. Upon finding this out, Dr. Joey went back on the computer and changed the order to STAT (immediately.) I knew from that moment, Dr. Joey really cared and was on our side. The results were overwhelming beyond what words can describe. The area in Matthew's brainstem that was severely damaged controls the body's ability to breathe, to swallow, and to regulate body temperature. Matthew hadn't had anything to eat since Friday and it was time to make decisions. Dr. Joey said he would exabate Matt if I wanted him too, but if he didn't breathe on his own, since it had been very difficult to replace the breathing tube in the emergency room, it would be taking a risk. Due to Matt's severe head injury, he also would not be able to eat by mouth for "quite a while—possibly months," therefore we needed to decide on whether to place a PEG (abdominal tube) which would be more comfortable than a NG (nasal) tube. As I cried with my best friend at the results and the decisions required, Dr. Joey also had tear-filled eyes. I asked him what he recommended and he said "If it were any of my four children, I would have the tracheostomy and tube feeding placed. They can be removed with barely a scar in the future, but would allow Matt to breathe without the discomfort of the tube in his throat (that he was biting down hard on) and allow him adequate nutrition comfortably." That was all I needed to hear to make the decision, and I knew Bill would go along with whatever I felt was best. I had Dr. Joey call Bill and explain everything to him too and I remember vividly, asking him what Bill had said after the call. Dr. Joey said "He asked how you were doing." I couldn't have loved him any more at that moment, knowing how distraught he was over Matt and Abby, yet being worried about me. When I finally could stop crying enough to talk, I called Bill myself and within seconds, we just cried over the phone together. I asked if Abby could transfer to the SCH, but HCMC said she couldn't due to transportation, insurance, etc. Abby was "out of the woods" as far as needing surgery, however due to all the sodium they gave her intravenously to lessen the swelling in her brain, she needed to be closely monitored for any cardiac complications.

The visitors started arriving bringing baskets of snacks. One visitor from our town arrived with a basket of snacks, having experienced a similar situation when her son was in ICU after a cardiac arrest, saying "I know you won't want to eat even though everyone will tell you that you need to, but at least snack." I looked at her name on her shirt (security measure as the PICU unit is locked) and knew I should know her, but didn't remember for a few days. One man waited outside Matt's PICU room, waiting to see me, but didn't want to go in. I looked at his name and apologized for not recognizing him. He told me he was the radio announcer for all the Pierz sports. At every game, Matt would say "Hi Mr. Grammond" hoping (I think) he'd put in a good word for him during the game. I was so touched he would come to the hospital to find out for himself how Matthew was and to tell me how sorry he was the accident happened. He said he would keep Matt and Abby in his prayers. Matt's head basketball coach and junior varsity coach both came to see him the day after the accident. I felt like I needed to apologize to both of them that Matthew wouldn't be at practice on Monday. I sobbed as I hugged them both and told them Matt needed to wait three months for contact sports due to his lacerated spleen. He could play in February at the earliest and I was so sure that would happen—God wouldn't take basketball away from Matt. He had already visited St. John's University, Eau Claire, and Augsburg colleges and was planning on playing college basketball, hopefully on a scholarship. This year was his year to shine as captain of the team to earn a place on a college team. My greatest worry before the accident was that Matt wouldn't be close enough for me to make it to every one of his college games. Suddenly life and all our priorities changed and all I wanted in the world was for Matthew and Abby to be back to normal—safe, happy and healthy as it was two days ago. Amazing how we complain about our busy lives, taking for granted the blessings we receive every day, until a tragedy slams our world to a halt. I realized at this time and every moment since, a year later, everything is in God's hands. Man and medicine can only do such a miniscule amount as compared to healing God can and will accomplish through the power of prayer.

A relative of the other driver visited and asked for me to come talk to her outside the locked PICU unit. I looked at my friend Jenn and she knew I couldn't do it as I told her this. Jenn replied, "Nor should you have to,–I'll go talk to her." She came back later saying my brother-in-law talked her for a long time and she wanted to let us know how bad her family felt. I had absolutely no ill feelings or anger in any way towards the other driver. Matt had pulled out in front of him—that's why it's called an accident. I found out later the other driver was on the way to his Grandma's wake. My heart went out to him, as I can't imagine what a horrible day it was for him, too. I was too distraught to visit with her and didn't want to leave Matthew's bedside.

Over the weekend, my friends and sister stayed with me, keeping vigilance throughout the night as I slept for a few hours at a time. I slept in an empty patient room down the hall used as a "sleeping room" for families if the unit wasn't full. This in itself was such a wonderful gift—to be able to sleep in a bed, shower, and have privacy when needed. I had the night nurses wake me up every two to three hours for an update on Matt's status, even though they didn't want to. This way I could then sleep solid again, versus being in a light sleep, trying to get my body conscious enough to wake up and make sure Matt was okay.

I talked to Laura, Kami and Brooke at home and they were so torn and upset without Bill or me home. Brooke said "All Laura has us do is pray the rosary." I talked to Laura and told her Brooke needed to have a normal seven year old's life as much as possible—to play and not focus solely on the accident. After the accident, Laura immediately said she would stay home and take care of Kami, Brooke, our pets, and the house. This was such a huge undertaking for her at age sixteen, but she always was so grown up. After talking to Brooke, I knew she needed a distraction and not to be home, reminded of everyone being gone with Matt and Abby being in the hospital. Before I got the chance to call my sister-in-law to see if the girls could stay with them, she called and said, "Can I go get those little girls and bring them to my house?" It brought tears to my eyes as it was like an angel sent her the message we needed them. She immediately helped Kami and Brooke pack and brought them to her house. Laura, however, was adamant she would look after the house and pets and opted to stay home with friends staying with her. I was thankful their parents were willing to let them stay on school nights to be there for Laura. Our community was amazing in our time of need—just how much, I had yet to discover.

Matthew did partially become semi-conscious over the weekend when repositioned by nursing or receiving cares. He really did not like his mouth cleaned or suctioned. Every time coughing violently, showing how strong he really was as the PICU nurses said "Good cough!" I must have heard this no less than a thousand times over the next month. In hindsight, it did let me know coughing was good to prevent pneumonia, and to reassure Matt he was doing something good too. I can honestly say however, if I never hear "good cough" again the rest of my life, it would be ok with me. Matthew would respond to my voice, squeeze my hand or try to give me a "thumbs up" when repositioned or having pain. I was beyond thankful for this as it was my glimmer of hope, turned to faith, that Matthew would be okay one day. I could only imagine how scared he was. I met Mark, the chaplain, on Sunday I believe and he had such a welcoming, empathic, and caring demeanor, that I hugged him and sobbed as he held back tears of his own. I immediately told him that "Matt is so in there. I know he heard my voice and is trying to come back to me." Mark became one of my greatest supports and path to strengthening my faith over the next three months Matthew was in the hospital. I'm not sure how many chaplains the SCH has employed; however, we were very, very lucky to have him to guide our journey—another gift from God without a doubt.

One Day at a Time

—∞—

Nov 4, 2013

Abby had exceeded expectations, participating in physical, occupational, and speech therapy, progressing so well that she could transition home with continued outpatient therapies. Abby had a significant amount of pain due to her rib fractures and difficulty smiling, chewing, yawning, etc., due to the stitches in her mouth. Abby was dragging her left leg, I was told secondhand by Bill, and her physical therapist said it was a compensatory technique to avoid increased rib pain. It was so difficult not to be involved more in her care, talk to her PT, and watch her walk to determine if I felt she was ready to be discharged. I decided to leave it in God's hands and be grateful to have her and Bill closer and the girls all home together again. I was informed that if everything stayed on track, she would be home safe and sound tomorrow. We knew she had a long road ahead of her and would need to continue to work hard to regain her strength, but what a relief and gift to have her come home so soon. Abby needed to continue outpatient physical, occupational and speech therapy, as well as to have someone with her at all times, but I was SO thankful she didn't need surgery. Bill's sister stayed with Abby at HCMC on Monday so he could be with Matt and me during his surgical procedures.

I woke up Monday morning and sobbed, knowing what the day would hold. The mornings were the absolute worst time of day, realizing everything was real all over again, grieving for the losses Matthew had encountered, rather than simply having awoken after a bad dream. After showering, I texted one of my best friends from college, Carla, and told her about the accident. She immediately called me, said she was going to shower and would be at the hospital in about an hour. She was only working three days a week at this time, which was unusual for her. Another close friend who was an RN at the hospital came with her daughter (who was a friend of Matthew's and skipped school that day) to be with Bill and I too. As we were in the surgical waiting area, waiting for Matthew to have a tracheostomy (breathing tube through his neck versus his throat) and PEG tube (abdominal feeding tube) placed, two of my closest co-workers from the SCH (where I had worked two Saturdays a month for over twelve years) arrived. They brought a gift bag of several chocolates and gift cards for us to order food from local places who delivered, from many of the therapy staff. As we waited for the nurse to come in and let us know a procedure had started, then finished, and for each surgeon to let us know how it went, our pastoral assist arrived—rushing in breathless, not knowing if it was an emergency surgery versus a planned procedure. We said a prayer and he asked us individually what our prayer requests were. A few of us spoke up and others in the room avoided eye contact and looked at the floor in silence when Carla's cell phone began blaring music from a call. Everyone burst out laughing as she said "Well, leave it me for comic relief," and stepped out of the room. We would be talking about random things, until someone came in to update us on Matthew. I remember Carla saying "Wow, it just hits you in waves, doesn't it?" I couldn't have summed it up any better. The surgeons weren't as caring and empathetic as Dr. Joey, but that was fine—I needed them to be great at what they did in surgery. Everything went well and Matthew was visually calmer without the tube in his throat.

When the sedation wore off, Matt began to bite his tongue instead of the plastic tube. He bit so hard that that almost half of his tongue was purplish-black and we feared he'd bite it off. The nurse got a "bite block" to keep his teeth apart; however, we could not get it in Matt's mouth. They decided he may need to be sedated again. I begged Matthew to open his mouth at least 16 times to no avail. I asked my friend to go get Bill from the family lounge to see if he could help. Bill came in the room and said "Hey bud. We need you to open your mouth." Matthew immediately opened his mouth to Dad's familiar voice as I stood on the other side of the bed with my mouth wide open too. Matthew had begun to run a low grade temperature; however, this wasn't surprising since the brainstem controls the regulation of body temperature.

The doctors highly encouraged anyone who visited to have the flu vaccine. I called my Mom and asked her to bring Laura, Kami, and Brooke to the clinic for the vaccine so they could visit. She willingly agreed to do so and to bring the girls to see me at the hospital as I didn't want them to see Matthew yet. I called the clinic to set up appointments after school and was asked the typical insurance questions. I told them I couldn't bring the insurance card in, as she informed me how long it had been since we had been in and the information needed to be updated. "It's all about the money" I told her, beyond frustrated at this time. She replied "Yes, we do need to get paid for our services." I offered to fax a copy of our insurance card, thinking Grandma would pay privately if needed. When I told her Grandma would be bringing the kids to the appointment, the receptionist said "You're not even going to come in with them at all?" I then officially totally lost it. Sobbing, I told her about Matt and Abby both being in ICU and how the kids needed the flu vaccine to visit. Suddenly, she said the insurance card could wait and she was very sorry about the accident. I hung up the phone, sobbing, as Dr. Joey said "I'm so sorry you had to go through that." Upon reentering Matt's room, Bill thought something horrible had happened, confused as he had stayed with Matt when I went to call. I hugged him as I could barely talk, saying "They didn't have to break me to get flu shots." Bill said she didn't know or mean anything by it; however at that moment I wasn't as forgiving. Instead it multiplied my guilt and grief that I wasn't at home with the other girls.

Mom brought the girls to the cafeteria at the hospital so I could see them and have dinner with them. I got off the elevator and Brooke immediately said "Why does Grandma have make-up on and you don't?" The answer was easy—I had cried mine off again. Laura was allowed to see Matt, turning pale and crying, however strong and brave as she held his hand and talked to him as if they were sitting on the sofa at home. Kami was very upset she wasn't considered old enough to see Matt, saying "I'm his sister too. It isn't fair." Brooke was more upset about not being able to stay with me, or to have me leave and go home with her after our visit. I did find out they had a child life support consultant available for children or siblings that needed to understand what all the tubes were for so it wasn't scary when they saw a loved one. I decided we would schedule this prior to Kami and Brooke seeing Matthew.

Abby's Home

—∽—

November 5th, 2014

Tuesday was an amazing and absolutely overwhelming day in the best way. Abby was able to come home after "passing" her two physical therapy sessions yesterday to ensure she was safe with stairs and balance. After being discharged from HCMC, Abby continually asked for McDonald's French fries. Bill told her he wanted to get out of Minneapolis before stopping, but Abby just keep asking repeatedly when she could have French fries. To this day, Abby has no recollection of wanting the fries and laughs at the story. Bill brought her to the SCH to see me and I expected her to walk in and look great, but she came up in a wheelchair, tired and sore, worried about homework, and the knot in her hair. Abby did not want to see Matt and that was ok with Bill and I, as we didn't think she was ready for anything more. We were so worried Abby would feel guilty because the accident happened after Matt had picked her up from dance practice. Abby had called and asked Matt to come get her. He was playing X-box and said he had two more rounds in the match. Abby said she could probably find a ride, but Matt replied, "No, I'll come get you. I can play this game anytime." I've wished so many times she had found a different ride home, or Matt had finished his game, so the accident wouldn't have happened, but we cannot change the past. Kami said later "Why didn't I go talk to him? He would have left later." I told her if she had and the accident still happened, she'd blame herself for stalling him. It wasn't anything she could have prevented. This seemed to certainly make her feel better.

Abby was worried about homework, band, the school play, and when she could return to varsity dance. It was difficult convincing Abby to allow herself time needed to heal. We were so thankful she was alive, home, and had no significant cognitive deficits. All the prayers said by so many people made this happen—allowing our family to be closer together, versus in three different cities.

On Tuesday morning, I woke up wanting to see or talk to the mom of a traumatic head-injured boy I had worked with for two years at Country Manor in Sartell several years ago. I thought about e-mailing, googling, etc., to send her a message or to call her, knowing she'd understand and help me feel better (her son was athletic, captain of many high school sports, and loved by everyone too.) I was pretty down in the dumps, thinking of having popcorn with Matt someday, among many other things, when Fr. Popp, our priest happened to come to see us (even though on vacation.) He spent almost 2 hours talking, having breakfast and coffee with me. I so needed Fr. Popp to strengthen my faith and believe everything would be ok. We then went to see Matt and he became more alert—giving me a "thumbs up" on his left, then right hand. God is SO good.

I was elated and went outside for a break. After being outside approximately 2 minutes, the mom of my previous head-injured patient I wanted to talk to earlier that morning, drove up about 10 feet from me. I asked her how she found out and she said "about what?" She was at the hospital to see her son and knew nothing about Matt and Abby. She said "I even went to the other parking lot, but it was full, so I came here." I knew at that moment that God was so present, listening to my every thought, and Matt was going to be okay.

Matt slowly decreased how much support he needed from the vent to help him breathe and was able to monitor his body temp better as the day went on. He began physical therapy and occupational therapy with therapists who are friends and work at the hospital with me, which was very reassuring. Matt had a sedative prior to physical therapy, but was able to wiggle the toes on each foot and give her a "thumbs up" though before he became sleepy.

The driver of the other vehicle visited today, giving me flowers with shaking hands. I felt so bad for him when he told me how sorry he was. I explained to him we had no ill feelings, it was an accident, and really didn't know how much or how fast Matt would recover. His wife and another family member who had visited earlier were with him. It was draining to try to cheer them, when all I wanted to do was crawl in a hole and sleep for years. I was trying to convince myself as I was reassuring them. I cannot imagine how difficult it was for them to visit.

The basketball team and three coaches came up in the evening and needless to say we were told we were exceeding the number of visitors allowed per fire code (more than once.) The team brought Matt's jersey (#51), cards and a signed basketball. It was overwhelming to see and find out what everyone had already done for us, without asking. The generosity, caring, love and prayers were beyond what anyone could imagine. It was almost as emotionally overwhelming as our situation. We knew someday everything would turn out awesome—with so many caring people, nothing else could be possible.

Matt became very alert before the last team members left. He was wiggling his toes, lifting his legs, giving a "thumbs up" and opening his eyes part way. It was wonderful and brought tears to many of us. My mom called to tell me so much food was brought to our house that both of our refrigerators were full. She needed to bring some food to her house. Knowing Bill and the girls had pre-made food when I was not able to be there was so comforting. The support we were shown kept me going, giving me the strength I needed, along with the knowledge God would heal Matthew.

All emotions with God at my side

—∿—

Nov 6, 2013

Matthew's doctor woke me up this morning to say good-bye—he was going to be off for 10 days. He came into the sleeping and I immediately said "Don't turn on the lights—you cannot see my hair." Anyone who has seen me first thing in the morning can attest to this as he probably would be so devastated he wouldn't return. I was so sad to see him go, but he assured me he would check on us no matter where we were when he returned—"even the cities." (Disappointment)

I got ready, tried the make-up thing again and was doing pretty good when my cousin, Karla, came to visit after her night shift as an RN here. The new doctor met with me and discussed medications, oxygen, tube feedings, body temperature, and finally the discharge plan including insurance criteria for hospitalization. "Catch 22" as Matthew was not awake enough to tolerate an inpatient rehab stay now (really? no-kidding, as he would need to actively participate in three hours of therapy a day—I wasn't surprised) and for him to stay at the SCH, it needed to be medically justified. The tears started to come and wouldn't stop. I began to have friends and family visit, call and text as God knew I needed them. The head football coach arrived and said the team would be wearing lime green ribbons on their helmets with Matt's name for the play-off game Friday night. Ok, NOW tears are completely justified. (Frustration and gratitude)

Matt became more responsive around eleven-thirty am, lifting his right arm over his head, wiggling his toes, moving his ankle and giving us a "thumbs up." Happy Birthday to Grandma— having Abby home and Matt respond to her were the only birthday presents she wanted this year. In the afternoon, my boss brought my leave of absence paper-work to sign for my job at Country—now everything became even more real. (happy/sad combination)

Matthew slept through his OT, PT and rehab consult in the afternoon. I've known Dr. Anderson for fifteen years. He gave me a hug and told me "Lynn, you know as well as me, it's a waiting game. He is showing positive signs and we just need to wait." (Encouragement and relief)

Laura, Kami and Bill came up at night and Matthew was sounding a bit congested with secretions. Laura said she didn't like the sound of this and asked the nurse to suction his tracheostomy site. The two nurses were at the head of the bed, and Bill and Laura by his feet. Matt coughed so hard that he literally sprayed Laura. Some of this was the water of the humidity from the trach mask—versus all secretions, however the look on Laura's face was priceless. It's called sibling payback. Bill looked at me like "Stop laughing. It's not funny and Laura is traumatized," but I had to just go with it. It was the funniest thing I had ever seen. My friend, Jenn, was holding her breath laughing beside me, and Laura, after the shock subsided, was laughing right with us. Laura said "I didn't think he could get me from four feet away" as Jenn adds "or three feet over his head." I laughed until my stomach ached. (humor)

The evening was so amazing. After putting Matt's hand on a basketball, he rolled it with his hand, which began to slip off the ball. He then voluntarily used his right hand to bring the ball back to being balanced under his hand at least six times. As we were video-taping this, I was hopeful and relieved as this was a learned skill and he remembered it. (amazed)

Jenn and I went to the family lounge for something to eat later that night. I went to get us two glasses of water when Carrie, the nurse, came by and said "Matt followed his first command for me." I'm thinking he squeezed her hand, lifted his leg, etc., then she adds "He snapped his fingers for me." The RN who was with Matt told her to come look as Matthew was snapping his fingers over and over. He stopped and she asked him to snap his fingers again and he did. Earlier that day Matthew's friend and I were reading the card from the adoration at church and many of the band class had commented about how they missed him in band, especially Mr. Blinn telling Matt to not go too fast on the drums. Five hours later he snapped his fingers—I knew he was listening to us talk. I am very grateful for all the years of piano, drums/bells, etc., Matt had participated in. I was crying tears of happiness when I walked back to the family lounge, scaring Jenn something bad had happened in the past five minutes. Matthew being able to snap his fingers (which I can't even do effectively, which requires significant fine motor coordination) is HUGE. (elation)

I had started to journal last night, however fell asleep three times typing so had to wait until the morning. (exhaustion) We were so thankful for all the prayers—having Matthew's name on prayer chains, church groups, and the prayer candles that were lit for him–even in Brazil.

Mom of 5

—m—

November 7, 2013

As I was thinking of what to title this entry and how the day went, I struggled. Good news initially—Matthew was able to stay in pediatric ICU through next Monday because of his new trach. They would possibly transfer him to an acute hospital bed on the pediatric floor after this for "maybe another week."

Abby came up to see Matt today and really didn't show much emotion. When I asked her how she felt seeing Matthew—was she sad, confused, etc., she replied, "Not really, but it might be the drugs I'm on. I could really go for a blueberry muffin." I was speechless at her reaction. We went to the cafeteria in search of blueberry muffins. I asked a girl working if they had any and after taking one look at Abby's face (swollen with stitches) she went to check the freezer, returning with muffins. We went to the family lounge on the PICU with visitors as Abby ate a muffin. She commented the muffins at Coborn's grocery store were much better and they should stop on the way home. We had bought four small muffins and the other three were on a plate in the center of the table. Suddenly Abby looked at the plate, the people sitting around the table, and put the entire plate in front of her so no one else would eat them. I will never forget this. The "not so good muffins were not so bad after all."

Abby walked into the hospital today rather than being in a wheelchair which was wonderful, but had several episodes of loss of balance, laughed, and said, "I wasn't going to fall." She complained her left foot dragged at times, but my friend, Lisa, (a PT who also sees Matt) said it looked like she wasn't bringing her hip in due to rib pain, and reassured us it would get better. Abby had been taking pain medication which may have been a huge part of her behavior. She didn't remember much of being at HCMC which worried me. The nurse from HCMC called and said that speech, occupational, and physical therapy wanted Abby to have outpatient therapy, hopefully the following week and she would make the referral. Abby had wanted to go back to school for a couple hours a day starting next Tuesday. After seeing her, I really felt she should take another week off and start therapy first so we knew better how she would do as well as any modifications needed. It was amazing to have Matt and Abby with me, yet I didn't feel like I could do enough for either of them individually, much less at the same time.

Matthew had a good day overall. They took out his catheter and he's keeping his body temperature down without the cooling blankets. He's getting oxygen, but continues to do well without the vent, breathing on his own. In physical therapy, he sat on the edge of the bed with the help of Lisa (PT), the student PT, the respiratory therapist (just in case we needed her) and the RN standing close by. Matt couldn't hold his head up, pushed his legs out, (but not his entire body), and opened his eyes one third to one half of the way. I was kneeling on the floor to see his eyes and I KNOW he was looking at me. He tolerated sitting for about five minutes, with his oxygen level going down just a bit, and his heart rate increasing above one hundred and thirty beats per minute (which is between fifty and sixty bpm when resting). Matt worked so hard, it broke my heart thinking of all the patients I had worked with to sit on the edge of the bed after a stroke, the very first time. You have to start somewhere though and it was a wonderful thing to see, bringing me hope.

The speech therapist explained in detail about Matthew's need for rest so his brain could heal. It was best to only stimulate him with music, talking, touch, etc., for about ten to fifteen minutes at a time (ok–I'm guilty of doing way more than this, so I'll back off.) Dr. Anderson told me yesterday "I know the therapist in you wants to work with him 24/7, but he needs time." How did he know I wanted to continually work with Matt? I did, but also knew and made sure he had rest for healing too.

Matthew was turned every two hours, so had therapy right after this when he was most alert. OT at eight-thirty am, a rest from nine to ten am, speech at ten-thirty am, a rest until noon, nursing cares at noon, and two pm, PT at two-thirty pm, then a rest from three to four pm. The speech therapist said if Matt was alert we should limit stimulation to one of the senses only (ok-I may have been not following this either.) Matthew couldn't smell with the trach in, so we needed to talk to him, play music, touch him, or show him pictures when his eyes were open, one at a time, so he could concentrate on only one of his senses without being overloaded with stimulation. This was tough as the mom in me needed to talk and touch him at the same time. She also said to only have Matt hear one or two voices at a time. Listening to several voices, or a conversation in the room was just too much for him at this time. We would certainly follow her recommendations without a doubt to allow for a quicker recovery. It made me remember how often I'd be talking to Matt while he was watching TV, on the Xbox, or iPod, and he could repeat my words verbatim when I thought he wasn't listening at all.

The visitors continued, texts and responses from our friends and family posting on the Caring Bridge website. Each act of kindness I had been shown brought tears to my eyes. New drum sticks were brought by a band member—signed by all the percussionists tonight with a note for Matt when he gets better. I never imagined when people would talk about all the support they received after an accident, death, etc., (in a small town especially) and still have a tough time comprehending the magnitude of prayers and support we have been shown. Laura told Bill to "start with the upstairs refrigerator." He made enchiladas for Abby's friends last night and put in a hot dish for them tonight that were brought over. Knowing how much everyone cared, praying constantly, was so huge in getting us through each day.

A relative of the other driver visited me again since her mom was in the hospital after surgery. She told me about her mom's medical and psychological problems. I was empathetic of course, but had way too much on my plate to give her any support and encouragement, but I tried. She went with me outside after I told her I had to call Brooke. I had told Brooke I would call her last night and then realized it was too late when I remembered after all the excitement with Matt "snapping" his fingers.

Brooke read me every card the entire first grade gave and then wanted to begin with the second graders. She wanted to know what day I'd be home, and became angry, saying "Why do you like Matthew the best?" I tried to explain to her that Matt needed me the most right now, however she was crying and having nothing to do with this theory. I told her I'd call her before the bus came in the morning and she said, "No you won't. You don't even know what time the bus comes." I told Brooke she could get out of school and spend the afternoon with me tomorrow. After finding out Dad was going along with the plan–she then was happy and said "love you whole bunches." It's a lot for her to deal with, but what do you do? One day at a time. I didn't even get to talk to Kami today and only texted Laura twice. I know this isn't fair to either one of them, but being older they understand more. After running between dance, piano, tennis, school play practice, art club, Spanish club, student counsel, band, choir, basketball, etc., for five kids for years, I never felt so torn as a Mom until tonight. I was completely exhausted by the time I hung up. The relative of the other driver was still with me, listening to my conversation the entire time, and said "My five year old misses me too because I need to stay with my Mom." Oh my gosh! She had no idea how different our worlds were at this time. In my opinion, she could have gone home to her daughter and didn't need to stay 24/7 with her mom. I had talked to Brooke for forty-five minutes and was exhausted. I had nothing left to give her, which was unlike me—I was always giving to my patients, their families, the kids, etc. I was completely drained and running on vapors. As I thought about my physical fatigue and my state of mind, I had such a strong, strong vibe of the story of "footsteps in the sand"—never having a cross so heavy you can't carry it, and when it is, God then carries you. Thank you God for carrying me at this time.

The Great Unknown and Mr. Potato Head

—⚬⚬—

Nov 8, 2013

Bet I've peaked your interest with my new title. Today was an exhausting day. I got up before six am to shower and get ready for the day and had company from six am to nine pm with the exception of twenty minutes when I met with the neurosurgeon about the results of Matthew's repeat MRI.

The MRI wasn't near what I'd been hoping and praying for. The brain stem damage was even more extensive than his last MRI; however, there wasn't any swelling to speak of and the blood in various areas of Matt's brain had already begun to be reabsorbed. We went over the areas that were affected and what these areas control. Matthew MAY have the following: Difficulty staying alert and attending, expressive aphasia (meaning it would be difficult to say the words he wants to,) difficulty having both eyes focus together to see, difficulty with recognizing faces and people, weakness in his left shoulder and hip, and he may be able to read, but not understand what he reads. Matthew had been reading college level books for many years and was very proud of his reading scores; therefore this was actually the most heart wrenching for me. Recognizing the look of someone being defeated, the surgeon then went on to say that we have no idea what will happen, but the journey will take months and months and a lot of patience. After we calmly went over the results and questions, I called Bill to tell him, and then my parents and Brooke arrived and I cried and cried. However, as I thought about how Matt doesn't move his left leg much, it's like "miracles" keep happening. Matthew began to straighten and bend his left knee and then proceed to lift his whole leg straight up toward the ceiling like a dance kick, seeming to me as if he wanted to say "see Mom, I got this."

Brooke stayed most of the day today which was wonderful and exhausting to stay positive and cheerful as I was falling asleep in the chair, waking to her saying "Are you even listening?" It's amazing how five days (oops, seven days if today truly is Friday) in a hospital allows you to forget how important pushing the elevator button is. As we left the locked PICU, with me holding Brooke's hand in search of pea pods on the salad bar, the relative of the other driver in the accident was waiting for me to ask how the MRI turned out. I was still so upset, I said "It was worse." and left on the elevator. I know she meant well with her big smile, but I didn't have anything to smile about or that I felt I needed to discuss at this time. In hindsight, I should have been kinder and have regretted this many times. It was really bad timing. Brooke and I had lunch together and played Mr. and Mrs. Potato Head on the floor in Matt's room (yes, the floor, even though everyone who knows me knows I'm a germ freak). Brooke at one point did say "Do you need to go by Matt?" which I'm sure helped in her understanding of why I'm at the hospital. She continually rattled off what his heart rate was on the monitor.

Matt had his eyes open more today and was a bit more congested, therefore started chest percussion therapy three times per day today. This did help him to breathe more easily and at one point he even seemed to enjoy it. The doctors and nurses on our unit are fabulous—willing and wanting to do everything possible for him. It's been a week with several different nurses; however, his every need is not only anticipated, but taken care of with a smile.

Not a whole lot to say, but it has been a great day with Matthew moving his legs around, opening his eyes more and occasionally giving us the thumbs up. Keep it up honey. I know you're a fighter.

Hope, understanding, and "thumbs up"

—m—

Nov 10, 2013

I slept better last night than I have so far—the RN woke me up at two am per my request to let me know how Matthew was doing, and then I slept until five-thirty am. Waking up is the toughest, remembering once again that it's all real. I was teary thinking how afraid I am I'll forget all the memories of Matt over the years, then teary because I knew I'd never forget anything. I decided to help myself more than anything, I'd include a memory a day in my journal. When Matt is better, he will be say "gosh mom, this is worse than your 'tell-all' Christmas letter." (I know he'll understand.)

When Matthew was little and we went trick-or-treating, he didn't want to just get candy (and probably would have been fine just visiting everyone without any candy involved), he wanted to "check-out" everyone's house. He would begin walking into other rooms, check out whatever TV show was on, look at pictures, etc. It was semi-embarrassing, but made all my family, friends and neighbors laugh. Needless to say, whenever I had him go get something from the basement refrigerator or freezer, it was the same. He'd check out the TV, a book along the way, etc., and it would take quite a while for him to return after some encouragement. Then the *Incredibles* movie came out with "dash" (who was superfast of course) as one of the characters. I began to call him dash when I needed anything and would literally time how long it would take for him to get me the requested item. He loved it and it was efficient for me too, lasting for at least two years, I would guess. Lately, (oh say like the past five years as obviously I haven't let this go and it was a joke between us) if I said, "come on dash" when Matt was stalling with the computer,

41

TV, iPod, or phone when I wanted him to get me something, and he would shake his head and say, "I can't believe I fell for that."

I went to Matthew's room pretty teary this morning and Dr. Moore was already waiting outside his room. She came and talked to me, saying she was going to wait, but since I was already teary she decided "to just get it over with." She said "I thought about it last night and because Matthew's oxygen levels go lower and his heart rate increases (up to one hundred and fifty bpm) when he coughs, I want to put him back on the ventilator for a couple of days to rest." She said if he didn't have the trach she wouldn't re-intabate him, but since he does this will let him be more comfortable without struggling to rest and heal. It felt like a giant step backwards, however after the respiratory therapist put the vent back on, I could see what a good decision this was. Matthew relaxed and truly looked comfortable and as if he was just sleeping for most of the day—it was a relief to not see him upset and to finally relax his arms and legs.

Dr. Derr from inpatient rehab came to see Matt in the late morning. I bragged about the things he has done for us so far while he checked out Matt's reflexes, muscle tone, and pupils including reaction to light. Dr. Derr opened Matt's eyes and told him to look at the light on the left and he did. Matt wouldn't look to the right, but maybe tomorrow. I felt much better after talking with Dr. Derr as he explained the MRI just shows water flow and we really have no idea what kind of nerve damage there is. He said due to his age and how incredible the brain is, if one area is damaged, another area may take over that function for it, even if it never did this before an injury. How encouraging to think all those "maybes" I wrote about yesterday really are "maybes." Dr. Derr said "I'll keep checking in with you Matt," and Matthew gave him a "thumbs up" two times, bringing a smile to both of our faces.

The rest of the day was more relaxing for me today. Bill came up in the afternoon and we went to the chapel at the hospital with Fr. Popp, three friends, and the girls (except Abby who is with her aunt.) After mass Bill was smiling and said "I just feel so much better now" and insisted we go out to dinner to get me away from the hospital. We were gone just over an hour and it was nice, but dificult not to feel guilty. I have learned more than I've ever wanted to about guilt since the accident; sobbing for days now unnecessarily above and beyond our situation. Despite what someone close to me may speculate about why the accident happened, sins that are preventing Matt from being completely healed instantly, etc., with Fr. Popp and my family and friend's support, it is crystal clear that the accident wasn't because of anything I or anyone did or didn't do. God doesn't punish anyone on this earth for what someone else has done–he saves that for our judgement day after death (only God can and should judge us, versus us judging others on this earth) and his healing is WAY above this. I no longer feel like I did something wrong to have this happen, but know it did happen for a reason we will hopefully find out someday and good WILL come out of this somehow. Amazing how much stronger I feel after a few hours of sleep, mass this afternoon, a good dinner and time alone with Bill.

Laura is staying with me tonight and we were able to talk for quite a while about how things are going for her–good and bad at school. I am so thankful to all of her friends and the teachers for being there for her–to talk, to allow her to cry, to use her phone for updates, and even sleep in class during quiet/study time. As difficult as this has been for Abby and Matt physically, I know it's been way more difficult emotionally for Laura, Kami and Brooke. I can't express how thankful Bill and I are for helping them during this time too.

Abby is only allowed to be on electronics for fifteen minutes at a time, complaining that all she does is eat and sleep. She had a massage with healing touch on Thursday (I think) and will again on Monday to help with all her aches and pains. Abby will start therapy next week at to further assess her balance, any oculomotor dysfunction (movement of the eyes, visually focusing, tracking, etc.) and higher level abstract thinking/reasoning skills to make sure everything is perfect, and if it isn't, to speed up her recovery.

Guess that's enough information for just one day. I've always written a bit more than I've needed to with any assignment or even my notes at work, but it's therapeutic for me to do so,—-so just hang in there with me.

Waiting

—Ɱ—

Nov 10, 2013

As I went for a walk tonight outside after Bill, the girls and visitors left, I thought about how difficult it is to just wait now for Matthew to wake up. Then I thought about all the good things we wait for—peas to ripen in the garden, a birthday or vacation, in line for the rollercoaster, dinner at a restaurant, the grand finale at 4th of July fireworks or a concert, etc., and began to think that the more we have to wait for something, the more it's appreciated. Matthew is waiting to heal so he can make that entrance all the more wonderful for all of us to appreciate. In the meantime it gives us time to renew and trust that God will make this happen. I walked towards the south entrance of the hospital and noticed the Christmas lights were up on the building and instantly warm tears streamed down my face wondering what this Christmas will be like for Matthew, Abby, and our family. As quick as I had this thought, church bells began to ring (for six pm mass I assume) and I knew I had yet another sign that God is hearing the cries of my heart and will answer all of our prayers. The tears were still of sadness, but also combined with being so thankful in knowing and feeling that it is in God's hands and He has it all under control.

My memory today is of Matthew playing Tee-ball at age four I believe. He always was an emotional child overall and sensitive which is why even today he often will carry an Asian beetle or spider outside rather than kill it—he is too kind to hurt anything or anyone. Anyway, Matthew wanted to be the only one to bat, as well as to play the entire outfield. He would be playing a shortstop position by third base, and if the ball was a foul by the first base line, he would run to go get it and then cry "Mommy! Mommy! Mommy!" when another child picked up the ball. He wanted to do it all. They had asked me to be an assistant coach to be out there with him, and this seemed to help, but all the other parents would laugh uncontrollably when he did this. I was never so glad to have the season over. Now I wish it was yesterday and I could go back in time.

Today, was a very mellow day of healing. Matthew doesn't have his arms restrained since he went back on the ventilator and is much less agitated now without having to fight to breathe and cough. The doctor said he has right lobe pneumonia, but his chest X-ray looked better today than yesterday. He looks like a teenage guy relaxing. Matthew needs more oxygen when he's on his left side due to the right lung being higher than the left, therefore his breathing isn't as efficient. When he is lying on his back, or right side, Matt is visually way more comfortable. The nurses are so wonderful and sit at his bedside approximately 90% of the time, even though they could be out by the desk and wait until an alarm goes off. Matt's heart rate has barely gone over 100 bpm all day and he started a low dose of medication to decrease his blood pressure as well as a "water pill" (diuretic) to decrease the fluid around his right lung.

Matthew had OT and PT today and did follow quite a bit of assisting the therapists with range of motion or commands they asked. When Matthew became so tired he couldn't move his leg or shoulder as they asked, he did not fight the passive movement by the therapist, which is huge. His PT was very happy Matt hasn't had extensor tone the past two days—meaning straightening his arms and legs rigidly, but rather allowing us to bend up his knee and to put the CAM boot on to help maintain his ankle dorsiflexion (bringing his ankle up toward his chest) as Matt has super tight calf muscles even before the accident.

Abby was here most of the day too and is looking SO much better. Laura and her friend went shopping and he bought her a new jacket which really brightened her day—especially since all her clothes were cut off at the scene of the accident. Abby is still taking pain medications and isn't herself. She is very focused on food of all things—obviously MY daughter. Grandma made sidepork and brought it over for her, Bill made her favorite pork links this morning, and she had lucky charms yesterday that "were the best she's ever had." Abby would live on cold cereal if we let her, typically having up to 5 bowls a day. Abby is asking for blueberry muffins and wants to go out to Mongo's to eat. I'm not sure if this is how she's dealing with all the stress and changes, but as Laura said "it's better than her not eating." Laura can be so rational.

Kami and Brooke stayed overnight with my best friend last night and are doing much better emotionally—especially with seeing Matthew so comfortable today. Kami was teasing him and was very encouraging. Kami went to a movie today with my friend to "just do something normal" and Brooke decided she wanted to stay with me rather than go with. She did make them promise to bring back cotton candy though—as she needed to get something out of the deal.

I find myself making Matthew so many promises that I should be making a list. I told him he could grow his hair for the entire basketball season like he wanted, could get a smart phone for Christmas, and that when he wakes up I won't call him "snookems" ever again. I just miss him so much—with his daily hugs and "love you moms," but know it'll just be that much more appreciated when he's awake. Give all your kids an extra hug for me tonight—they are so precious.

Cream Filling

—៣—

Nov 11, 2013

When I think of my situation now, I compare it to getting to the cream filling center of a bismark, the caramel filled chocolate candy, ice cream in a dreamsicle, etc. The outside is ok, but what's really good is the inside. I was super busy working full-time at County Manor as the rehab coordinator and at the St. Cloud Hospital two Saturdays a month prior to Matt and Abby's accident. I did work at home in addition to bringing the kids in several directions for every activity possible on any given day—often cooking on Sunday for leftovers between school and dance, youth group, tennis, art club, etc. I had lost being in touch with my best friends for months at a time. Now I've seen and/or talked to each of them pretty much on a daily basis. Prior to the accident, much of our interaction with our family and friends was on an as-needed or incidental basis due to our very busy lifestyle. The accident was like the bite into the bismark, candy or ice cream in my thoughts today, bringing out the amazing good that we often forget about, in so many people for our family. We have received cards, visits, calls, texts, food, etc. from so many people every day that I can honestly say I have never felt so loved by my closest friends, family and cared about in my entire life. There is good that comes out of everything and as I analyze my life being flipped upside down, I know I would have never known all the goodness in the center of so many people out there if it hadn't been for the accident. I have been told by several people that it's ok to be angry that this happened, however, I have NO anger—just sadness and extreme hope. I know that God would never want Matt or Abby to suffer or be hurt in any way (they both are very religious and kind to everyone), but things happen in our lives and God will be there even more so because of their faith and all the prayers being sent up in their behalf.

I pondered today's memory, as I have so many to share now, but as I look at the number of people who are following Matt and Abby's story, that many of you don't know about Matthew being born at home, New Year's Eve, on our living room floor. I thought this would be a good story for today.

Matthew was due on 1/26/1996 and decided to make his grand entrance into this world on New Year's Eve, 12/31/95 with two cops, two paramedics, and one chihuahua present. I wasn't feeling right the entire day, but had diagnosed myself with a bladder infection. I had called the med-help line about six pm and told them I was having pain every five minutes, lasting for about thirty seconds, but wasn't due for close to another month. The doctor agreed with me and ordered an antibiotic for my "bladder infection." Bill was eating pizza and watching Star Trek, in no hurry to drive to White Bear Lake for the prescription (the closest pharmacy from Roseville that was open twenty-four hours a day.) It took two and a half hours for Bill to return as apparently everyone had been sent there. I was near tears when he returned and after taking the medication, Bill and I, and our dog, Buddy, rested in the spare bedroom upstairs, hoping after a little rest I'd feel better. At 9:50 pm, I couldn't rest at all, calling back to the new on-call doctor and telling her "it hurt to breathe." She said she had been updated about my earlier call and that she would order a medication to numb my bladder and if it wasn't better in two to three hours, to come into the emergency room. Bill was going to leave again, however I adamantly informed him that was not going to happen, nor was our neighbor going to come stay with me. He then decided we were going to the ER, put on my shoes, and went to pack a hospital bag. We had planned for months what all needed to be included in the bag and also looked at car seats multiple times, without making any decisions or final preparations, and now needed to pack in a hurry. Bill came back upstairs and I had already kicked off my shoes and said I wasn't going anywhere—we were going to have the baby. This was at approximately 10:10 pm. Bill called 911 which I would never have thought to do and was repeatedly told "Sir, you need to remain calm" which only irritated him and increased the volume of Bill repeatedly telling him we were both calm and to quit telling him to be calm. He did not know that the dispatcher had help in route already. Needless to say, by the time the police and paramedics arrived, they knew we weren't going anywhere too. A large policeman tried to kennel Buddy and that didn't go over at all. I don't remember any pain with Matt's delivery, but rather Bill and I laughing as he tried to coach me with the correct breathing because nothing in our prenatal classes accounted for Matthew being born "under the Christmas tree" at 10:28 pm that night. Everyone said "Oh, you didn't get the New Year's baby" and we would reply "we needed the tax deduction more." Matthew, Bill and I all went to the hospital in an ambulance, Matt wrapped in a foil blanket. I think I didn't sleep for approximately two days, opening my eyes to make sure he really had been born (as now that the accident is real and actually happened) and it wasn't one of my famous dreams. About a year ago, Matt said "when you say I was born under the Christmas tree, you don't literally mean 'under the Christmas tree,' right Mom?" He knew the answer with one look and a smile.

Matthew had another relaxing day for the most part with stable vital signs, no restraints, and resting most of the day. His pneumonia seems to have improved, with his oxygen levels remaining higher and his temperatures lower. He didn't have a chest X-ray today as the doctor said she "wouldn't change her treatment right now no matter what an X-ray revealed." Matthew was groggy during OT and PT sessions; however, then would complete some of the motions asked of him after the therapist has left the room. It certainly makes me wonder if it's delayed processing and/or motor planning. Matthew started on a low dose of medication for arousal/ increased alertness today–sure praying that tomorrow he will fully open his eyes and remember me.

Treading Water

—∽—

Nov 12, 2013

Today was a "status quo" day—no big changes to report. Dr. Moore had decided a chest x-ray wasn't needed due to knowing that the results would not change anything she was doing right now for treatment. She did change her mind; however, as Matt hasn't been able to decrease his oxygen as much as she would like. The x-ray didn't show any significant changes from two days ago—which was good. The brain stem regulates and tells our body to breathe and how often. It also regulates our body temperature. Matthew has been breathing up to fifty times a minutes when upset, but typically thirty to thirty-five breathes per minute at rest, with and without the ventilator. Normal respirations would be anywhere from twelve to seventeen per minute for an athlete at rest. Even with changing the respirations per minute and his oxygen levels on the ventilator, Matthew "overrides" the CPAP of his vent and breathes too frequently. The doctor said it's good that his brain is telling him to breathe, but that it hasn't figured out the correct rate yet. Matt's temperature has been much better—ninety-nine to one hundred degrees for the past two days with Tylenol and morphine as needed. Sure beats cooling blankets and ice packs though. Matt is still catching up from all the energy he was using when off the ventilator to breathe prior to last Saturday. He tried to help with bending and straightening his arms during OT this morning, (while bending and straightening his foot pretty much in rhythm,) and slept through PT completely despite calf and hamstring stretches which are very tight and somewhat uncomfortable for him.

Matthew had just a few times of wiggling his toes, giving a "thumbs up" and squeezing my hand today. He had his eyes open almost half way this evening, but I have no idea if and what he's seeing. He is trying so hard to become awake, it completely breaks my heart. If he hears my voice being sad at all, I see a tear roll down his cheek which of course adds to my feeling sad in the first place—what a vicious cycle, huh?

I feel like I'm treading water—not moving a whole lot in any direction, but staying afloat. I know the day Matthew becomes awake doesn't determine how he'll do long-term. He needs time to heal right now and I need to be patient. I'm worried about going through the grieving process all over again after Matthew wakes up if he's not one hundred percent like he was before the accident, then ask myself "how can he be after all he's gone through?" (again I pray for patience) Brooke asked last night if fish sleep at night and how can they sleep if they can't close their eyes. I told her that would be a good question for Matt and we should ask him when he wakes up. Her response, as she points to her head is "He might not know. Remember he had bleeds in his brain?" Oh how I wish I could forget. When I told her the first time she came to the hospital to see me, not Matt, that she couldn't see him yet because he looks different, she immediately said "Doesn't he have any hair?" Overall I think she's doing pretty well for this traumatic change in her life.

Abby had physical therapy today at the Plaza (SCH outpatient adult rehab) and did very well. Her PT felt that she was dragging her left foot due to compensating for her sore ribs on that side, and didn't find any areas of concern with her strength and balance. What a relief. He still wants to work on strengthening and establishing a home exercise program for a few more visits. Abby has OT and speech evaluations tomorrow morning to further look at her vision and cognition. She was more herself today, wanting to bring a present to a girlfriend tomorrow at school. That's the caring Abby I've missed over the past eleven days. (Can you believe it's been that long already?) She has quite a long road ahead of her, but I know it'll be a downhill coast versus an upward battle.

Today's memory is sparked by all the cards Matthew received mentioning how smart his is, how no one else wants to read in class, and missing him having the answers in class. I wanted to share with you his quest for knowledge has been since he was about two years old. At age two, Matthew went to bed (naps or for the night) with a Bible, calculator, dictionary and a calendar. He loved words and numbers as a small child, labeling the magnet letters on the refrigerator without difficulty. One day, we went for a walk and there was random chalk on the sidewalk. Matthew stopped, stepped off the curb to look at the chalk more closely, walking on each side of the chalk to figure out what it was, he proudly said "J!" He was then content to continue on his way. As a teenager however, Matthew needed reminders to feed the pets both food and water, and to replace the liners in the wastepaper baskets. He simply retains very detailed information when he deems it important. If you asked him, or Bill for that matter, how they golfed this summer at Eagles Landing on hole fifteen, they could tell you, including which clubs they used and more than likely the direction of the wind and the ball they were using. I, on the other hand do not retain information very well anymore, blaming it on trying to remember shoe sizes, dentist appointments, activities, information at work, etc., justifying this by saying my brain is full and unable to retain a lot of new information unless I deem it really important. I even went into Matt's room yesterday and was informed by the nurses that my shirt was inside out. The nurses are so caring and wonderful to Matt and now even help me muddle through the day as well. It took me three days in the sleeping room I stay in on the PICU, after wiping up water on the floor each morning, to realize there was a shower curtain the entire time. In my defense however, I did try to adjust the shower nozzle and flow each day to limit the amount of water.

I continue to read everyone's comments over and over, gaining strength from all the encouragement. I was pretty down this afternoon, as I was sure upon waking up this morning that today would be the day Matt would be super alert, when a friend stopped in and had me laughing within minutes. It seems like I always have a friend or family member call or visit just when I need it. I asked Father Popp tonight if we could have another Eucharistic adoration to help Matt become alert and make a full recovery as I know these prayers were HUGE in getting where we are right now. Please keep the prayers coming and coming as Matt's recovery is completely in God's hands.

Sandy Beaches

—◊◊◊—

Nov. 13, 2013

Abby had OT and Speech therapy evaluations today. The speech therapist said she found "higher level cognitive and attention deficits" and recommended Abby not return to school part-time next week as we had thought, as she still needed time to heal. I didn't get to talk to the OT that saw her, but all three therapies want Abby to come back tomorrow, as well as an additional speech therapy session on Friday. Abby was smiling more today and laughing more than usual or would even be typical for her, but it was SO good to see her happy again. I have NO doubt she will return to one hundred percent, but needs more time in addition to therapy, massages, healing touch, chiropractor appointment and many prayers.

Matthew had a better day today. After posting on Caring Bridge about his respirations being too high last night, they have improved for the first time today since the accident (another sign of the power of prayer.) He had been between thirty to fifty respirations per minute, however today even was down to fourteen respirations at one time. He has been in the low to mid-twenties most of the day. Matthew has also improved his oxygen levels from sixty to eighty-five percent over the course of the day which was his doctor's goal. He was more alert, opening both eyes about half way several times today too.

A friend, who is an Occupational Therapist and has worked with head injury patients for many years, visited today. She shared a story about a past patient who had been unresponsive for a long time. When she woke up, she knew who had drawn a picture in the room without being told and without any name on it. She said her patient knew everything that had been said while in a coma. She felt like she was resting on a beach with her toes in the sand and the warm sunshine in her face, being so comfortable she just couldn't get up and come back. This made me more peaceful about how Matthew feels at this time, however I did tell him it was "probably long enough time to spend checking out the babes on the beach" and I needed him to get back to me when he was ready.

In OT, Matt did follow bending and straightening his elbows and fingers with extra time to process commands, depending on how tired he became. In speech therapy, he was given a swab (like a sponge on a lollipop stick) and he held it–even adjusting his pinch without assist. The speech therapist was very excited about this–as was I of course. Matt moves his toes and ankles often throughout the day, however did so minimally during PT today, as he was super tired. He still has chest percussion therapy three times per day to help to get rid of secretions. This morning Matthew held my hand and actually rubbed my hand with his thumb in a soothing manor as if he was comforting me—oh my gosh. It was a wonderful gift to me.

Matthew had friends visiting this evening and all of them told Matt how band wasn't the same without him playing the bells. "We followed your lead and now the song sucks." Each of his friends told him how much they missed him. It was awesome to know he wasn't forgotten, but also sad. His friends talked about band, school, sports, etc. Matt gave them a "thumbs up" a couple of times, as well as when they left, saying they would be back next week. The nurses always comment on what wonderful, nice friends Matt has.

My memory today of Matthew is when he was about one and a half years old. Matthew was in one bedroom and Bill and I were in another room across the hallway. In the middle of the night (approximately two am) our bedroom lights turned on. Bill and I have no weapons and immediately sat up, expecting the worse. As soon as we were sitting up, Matthew smiled and said "Hi!" Needless to say, he moved from his crib to a real bed the very next day. Matthew always was Mr. Sociable. When we would go to Perkins, Walmart, or the grocery store and if he ever saw an elderly person or a little child sitting on a bench, he'd sit down and strike up a conversation for as long as time would allow. Matthew wanted to be a physical therapist to help others with his huge caring heart. I never thought he'd pick the medical field, but surprised me on the way home from a basketball game last year, saying "Mom, I think I want to go to college for physical therapy." I couldn't believe it, but strongly encouraged him to do so and he hasn't veered from his desire since. Now he'll just have first-hand experience to share with future patients.

I know Matt and Abby's recovery would not be anything near what it is without all the powerful prayers being said on their behalf. I have friends/family/and even strangers tell me they are praying constantly and during the middle of the night, having dreams about Matthew, etc., and know all of this is a result of God's healing for our entire family.

Lifetime Lessons

~m~

Nov 14, 2013

I t's a quiet morning and I slept the best I have yet last night—your prayers for the entire family obviously helping me out physically in addition to emotionally and psychologically. The night nurse came to see me before she left this morning and told me about Matt's "good night." He was snapping his fingers (probably because his friends were talking about band last night,) giving the old thumbs up, and pushing his feet into her hands on command. She said they also worked on pointing, but that was more difficult. Anyone who knows Matt, knows he isn't someone to "point fingers" at anyone. I was telling some visitors about how Matt would never feed into a conflict, no matter how much he wanted to. He'd tell me what he really wanted to say or do in particular circumstances, and then what he actually did do, which was usually "I said nothing, or walked away."

After a basketball game about a year ago, one of the other players came over to Matt and said, "your team needs to re-load their guns." Of course after Matt explained to me what "guns" were (as that's the sort of thing he always did for me,) he said "Mom, I just wanted to punch him." I asked him what he did, and he said, "I stepped back, folded my arms and said; 'well that isn't a very nice thing to say, is it?,' in the calmest voice ever and he didn't even have a reply." Matt then said, "Well Mom, you know—do onto others as you'd like done to you." One night I was downstairs on my computer and Matt was playing Xbox live with some guys he didn't know who were talking smack. Matt had his headphones on and was super quiet for a long time. Finally, I heard him say "yeah, I'm still here, I just don't need to talk bad about anyone's mother. That's not why I play Xbox."

I asked him about it and he said the guy was saying mother jokes, such as, "your mother is so fat" and other more awful things." I was never so proud.

We can learn a lot from Matthew in the way we treat our friends and family that's for sure. I think about the labels we put on people—even here, such as the TBI patient (traumatic brain injured), saying someone is a perfectionist, lazy, stupid, etc., even in the adult work place as well as in school for the kids. I think of Bambi being Matthew's favorite movie for years as a child and that Thumper the Rabbit had something to do with this. "If you can't say something nice, don't say nothin' at all." That movie was a good investment for a lifetime lesson. I know when I return to work, I will be more patient with my co-workers, other departments, insurance representatives, and family members. Not that I was awful before, but saved 99.9% of my patience for my patients during the day and sometimes ran out for everyone else.

Matthew was helping with arm range of motion (movement/exercises) during OT this morning, and in speech held a toothbrush, even turning it over to brush his bottom teeth when asked. Just another sign of how much he understands and is receiving God's healing. To be able to hear a command, motor plan it and follow through with the task, is huge.

The Wooden Cross

—∿—

Nov 15, 2013

The first two days after Matthew's accident are rather a blur as you can imagine. I remember the chaplain coming in and giving us four hand held wooden crosses. We have two in the room. My Mom and a friend have the other two. As the day went on yesterday, Matthew became more and more inquisitive about his trach, bringing his right hand up to feel for it. The nurses really do not want to restrain his arms, so stay right at his bedside, not stepping outside the room, afraid Matt will pull his trach out. Anyway, back to my story, I put one of the crosses in Matthew's hand last night, and he was trying to feel and figure out what it was. He brought his thumb over the cross and felt the rounded areas, then switched to his pointer finger and felt around the cross as well, switching his finger and turning the cross on his own.

The nurse came in this morning to give me an update on how Matt's night was, saying Matt was awake from two to three thirty am. He had his eyes partially open and was "trying to figure things out." He found his trach and was feeling the plastic on the suction tubing (rolling it in his fingers), finding the elastic on his briefs, snapping his fingers loud enough to have her turn around to figure out what the noise was, and then after she gave him his basketball, he rolled it forward and back on the bed until he was tired and went back to sleep. What a way to start the day.

As close as Matthew and I are, you find out things you never knew when a tragedy happens. To my surprise, Matt would write a pun on the chalkboard before class in College Composition class every day. One particular pun that Matt wrote I think is super funny.

"Automatic toilet flusher, I appreciate your enthusiasm, but I wasn't quite finished yet." Well, as many of you know, there are automatic soap dispensers in the hospital, located in some of the most inconvenient places. Last night Kami stayed with me and as I went to turn on the light in the room, the soap dispenser dripped on the blanket I was holding. I said "Got me again" in a monotone voice and Kami laughed so hard she had to lie on the bed. She said, "It's not what you said, it's HOW you said it." The soap dispenser on the side of the sink where the electrical outlet is in the bathroom, gets me frequently as I reach for my curling iron, brush, etc., both of which are not optimal placement in my opinion. It makes me think, "at least I have a room with a soap dispenser and a shower to be thankful for." I know many of you have heard the saying, when you have dirty dishes, be thankful you have food, when you have laundry to do, be thankful you have clothes, if your house is a mess, be thankful you have warm shelter. Whenever the kids were absolutely driving me crazy when they were little–screaming, jumping, etc., Bill and I would look at each other and say "at least they're healthy." Sure beats all those days when they were sick, wanting to lie on the floor, so I would instead be thankful for their energy and that they were happy.

I went for a walk and thought about the soap dispenser of all things. I had the analogy that our family is waiting under it similarly for God's love and blessing to drop down. We pray so hard and wait, and then unexpectedly we receive a dose of hope, comfort, love, a sign from Matthew, a visit, card, or note to give us strength. Everyone says, "you are so strong," but really I'm not. I'd be curled in a ball crying without an end in sight if it weren't for all the love and support that I feel every minute of day from all of you.

My memory today is one of my favorites. When Matthew was 3 years old, Bill and I took him, Laura, and Abby to the Morrison County fair. Bill took Laura and Abby, a newborn in the stroller, to get something. Matthew and I went to look at the animals. There was a huge turkey in a cage and Matthew wanted to check him out. I told Matthew not to go too close because the turkey can be mean, as he continued to step just a bit closer. The turkey stuck his head through the cage and bit his nose! Now I should have been devastated, but Matt held his nose jumping up and down, saying "the **turkey bit my nose, the turkey bit my nose!" super fast, and I could not stop laughing. Bill came back, making a good point that if he had been with Matthew when this happened, I'd have been very upset with him for letting him get that close, and that it wasn't funny. (Believe me, it was hysterical.) When he moved his hand, there was a perfect triangle of skin off his nose from the turkey's beak. I was then relieved it didn't go for his eye. Even funnier was Matthew telling the story to everyone with action to boot. He would say, "I went closer,. . . . and closer, ...and the turkey bit my nose!" stepping closer, holding his nose and starting out the sentence slowly then as fast as he could say it by the end (increasing his volume too). We have this videotaped–someday we'll look at it again and be sure to laugh. At Thanksgiving that year, Grandpa Cliff asked Matt if he was eating the turkey that bit his nose to get even, and Matthew didn't know what or how to respond. It was priceless.

Brookie Bear

—⚭—

Nov 15, 2013

Today was a busy day with visitors as Pierz was off school. Matt did help with arm exercises in OT–he will resist straightening his elbow, but then when I tell him to "do a curl" and count the reps or tell him to stretch his arm and reach the bed, he listens to me more so than the therapists. He's knows my voice and he's always been "a Mommy's boy." It gives me comfort and reassurance that being here is the right place for me now. When I was talking to my friend about how good he did last night, even though he looks like he's sleeping, he gives me a thumbs up from across the room. The night nurse who tried to get Matt to "point" his finger would have been happy as he was making this gesture, snapping his fingers, tried to grab the sheet, pillow, etc., or take my hand. He is SO in there, just needs time and prayers to come back to me. Matt doesn't smile though, no matter how often I ask. Matt would always joke and say, "I'm laughing inside Mom, but I show no emotion" when I told him something was funny. I usually did get at least a smirk. Matt's friend, Cole, was here and Bill picked up a Kosh ball for Matt to hold (better than grabbing at his trach) and I told him to throw it at Cole by the window. Matt picked it up, lifting his arm and bending his wrist back and then dropped it on the bed. It made me teary for the wonderful fact that he tried and also because of all the effort he needed to do so.

Physical therapy helped Matt into a Biodyne chair today. It's like a big recliner that is able to be positioned flat and then brought up in increments. We had three PT staff, myself, the nurse and the respiratory therapist helping and it went very smooth. Matt was up for about fifteen to twenty minutes and had company during this time. It was difficult to keep his feet on the footboard as his ankles/calf muscles are tight and he didn't want to stretch them to ninety degrees, so would straighten his legs and lift them off. It was wonderful to see him out of bed and with his new glasses on.

Matthew has four younger sisters and has always wanted a brother. When Laura was born, he didn't comprehend the whole brother/sister option being under two years old, but he sure did for Abby, Kami, and Brooke. He used to say, "Mom, can God change her into a boy?" or "Can she grow into a boy?" or "Can we buy a boy instead?" By the time Brooke was born when Matthew was ten years old, he expected a girl and wasn't disappointed. He said, "I guess it just makes me special because I'm the only boy." Matt would come home from school and ask to hold Brooke (better option than chores or homework) and would rock her, watching TV of course, for hours and hours. I was able to make dinner, wash clothes, etc., because Brooke was totally content. I'm not sure when, but Matthew named her his Brookie Bear and it just has stuck with her. He'd give her piggy back rides, and still did until recently it seemed inevitable that she would hit her head on the doorframe, ceiling, etc., (with Matt being 6'8") so this took a smidgen of the fun out of it for her. She loved his "underdogs" on the swings, which Matt always was very willing to leave the garden to do when she yelled for him.

In church on Sundays, Matt would want to hold Brooke (all of the kids fought over her) and when he finally had his turn, holding her, he would turn around toward the back of the church and show her to the people behind him. I would tell him to turn back toward the front of the church, but remember how proud he was to show her off and the fact that he was holding her. He used to say for several years she was his favorite sister, but I know he loves all of his sisters. Lately, Brooke would chime in every time he'd try to talk to me, several times, and this really irked him, as he'd say "I get to talk to Mom too." It always made me think we just didn't get enough time for just us. When Matt had his away basketball games, we would talk about everything on the way home. I hope we'll be able to go to quite a few of them this year yet and have quality time together.

Matthew has been off the vent all day, still maintaining great heart rate, blood pressure and respirations. The power of prayer and healing is amazing. He's on the vent now for the night as he usually has a time where he needs more oxygen during the night and his doctor wants him to rest well. The doctor and nurses feel his pneumonia is improving and isn't in his lower lungs any more, but working it's way up and out. Matthew is starting to swallow spontaneously more often, which is super important for weaning off the trach in the future. When he's really sound asleep he may drool out the side of his mouth, but Bill and I as many of you I'm sure have done this at some time or another too.

My aunt came today and asked what specifically she and her church group should pray for. I told her to pray for Matthew to be able to open his right eye more, that he can focus his eyes together, and for healing in his brain stem—for the swelling to go away and the nerves/axons to connect. Quite the wish list, huh?

The Team

—∞—

Nov 16, 2013

Today, Dr. Joey returned with a hug and afterwards we discussed the "plan" for the next few days to couple of weeks. Matthew can stay on the pediatric unit for at least another week or ten days, most likely changing the status of the room to progressive care. If Matt can then tolerate inpatient rehab–OT/PT/ST for two to three hours a day, he can transition there at the St. Cloud Hospital. If he's not able to be awake enough to tolerate this, he'll need a longer term setting until then. They've mentioned Children's Hospital and Bethesda Hospital in St. Paul; however, my first choice would be Country Manor in Sartell where my job is as the rehab coordinator. He could have intense therapy there, his sisters and friends could continue to visit him, but he would need to be accepted. The nursing ratio is of course lower in a subacute setting then inpatient rehab which has four to six patients per RN. Medically I'm hoping he can go to inpatient rehab at least first for a while, but it will depend on God's timing. I've thought about it a lot today, and either would be ok, so I'm just putting it all in God's hands for the time frame it takes for Matt to be more alert for longer periods of the day. I was hoping he'd open his eyes further today and smile for me, but he didn't, so my mood pretty much matched the gloomy weather today for the most part.

Matt did participate more with arm exercises today, following commands to open and close his right hand in occupational therapy, and did take the wash cloth off his face, pinching it for the first time today. This afternoon, Matt was up in the Biodyne chair for about thirty minutes with PT and even was trying to help with some of the leg exercises

64

in sitting. Matt would pretty much do the opposite movement the PT asked of him as far as straightening and bending his knee—most likely due to delayed processing with the command, trying to figure out which leg and which muscle group to "fire" to perform each movement. But, it WAS movement none the less. Matthew was so tired after, sleeping for about two and a half hours.

Matt's basketball coaches and the entire team came to see him after having a scrimmage in St. Cloud today. I could not wake him up and it tore at my heart to see such sad, stoic faces initially. My friend Jenn, who is a PT, happened to be visiting and graciously assisted me in waking Matt with a stretch to his ankles and hamstrings per my request:) Matt then straightened his arm, squeezed my hand, and had his eyes about half open. He was more alert for quite a while. He squeezed our hands, his Kosh ball, moved his feet, and gave us a "thumbs up." Jenn did let Matt know that it was "all Mom's fault" and he squeezed her hand and attempted a "thumbs up" for her too. We put the new basketball jersey over Matt and took a picture of the team with him. We asked Matt to give us a "thumbs up" for the picture and he did. It was the coolest ever and made my whole day, and I think the team's too.

One day Matthew asked me if I would quit work if I won the lottery. I said "of course I would—or at least work very part-time or on-call." Matt said "but I thought you really liked your job", which of course I agreed that I did. He then says, "but you love your patients and they love you and they need you." I told Matt we didn't need to worry about it because chances were very good that I wouldn't win the lottery. I thought about this many times since. Rather than say, "yay, you'd be home with us all the time, we wouldn't have to take the bus, etc." he instead was worried about the patients that I might not continue to help. Matthew has a heart of gold. His plan always had been to be a marine biologist and play basketball for the Miami Heat. When he told me last year that he wanted to be a physical therapist, I was completely surprised and proud that he would choose a profession similar to mine, being an Occupational Therapist. I think it was in God's plan that I chose this path so I could be here and him Matthew through this journey.

I am so thankful after seeing the pictures of the van, that Matt and Abby survived the crash. First of all, that Abby is doing so much better and home, Matt didn't sustain a C1 or C2 spinal cord injury with paralysis from his neck down, and for everything he's progressed with medically, physically and cognitively thus far. I also thank God every day for our family, friends, community, supportive jobs, and everyone's prayers.

When Bill and I moved back to Pierz after being in the cities for nine years with tons of privacy—only knowing two of our closest neighbors, I had a huge adjustment living in a small town again where everyone seemed to know even the smallest details of our life. "I see you planted a tree in the yard yesterday" I was told one day at the grocery store and wanted to say, "really?" Then as time went on it hit me like a cement block, being in a small town, people actually CARE that we did plant the tree and more than likely were already praying it'd grow. I realized very quickly I entirely got the better end of the deal giving up some privacy for tons of caring and love. Everyone has been overwhelming good to us—couldn't imagine this journey without the support we've been receiving.

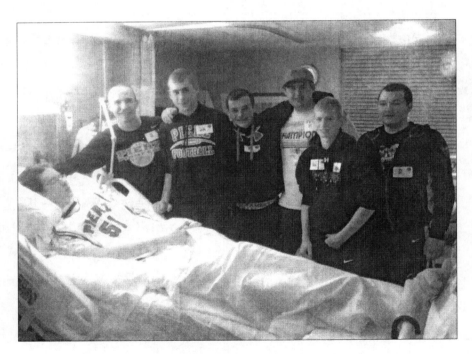

Basketball team in ICU

Snap On

—〰—

Nov 17, 2013

Matthew's nurse today titled my journal. When I came into Matt's room today, he was much more alert. He participated in OT for forty-five minutes, giving her a "thumbs up" right away, opening/closing his right hand, bending and straightening his elbows, helping to raise his arms up, etc. He did amazing. My first thought was that there were many prayers from my post, asking God to help him become more alert so he can transfer to inpatient rehab in a week. Matthew is very much enjoying his Kosh ball. This morning, unbelievably, he began to dribble it superfast against his chest. He tried to give it to Grandpa today too. I asked Matt to snap his fingers for Grandpa and he did–loudly. Grandma quickly came over and asked him to do this for her too, and he did again. It was just those two times, but clear and distinct. The nurse said Matt pointed at his trach a couple of times today and she explained he needed this to breathe and not to touch it, and so he brought his hand back down to his side. He also has been grinding his teeth today, but every time he did, she'd ask him to stop and he would. He is understanding so much and following what we ask or tell him to do, and then becomes so tired, he sleeps with his mouth wide open.

In physical therapy today, Matt was in the Biodyne chair for about thirty minutes and did help with leg exercises some, the best being to move his ankles up and down. He coughed really hard, tried to dive forward in the chair, and his eyes flew wide open. The widest I have ever seen them since the accident. I tried to have him smile for me when he was more alert—but he's saving that I'm sure to combine with a hug, or "love you Mom"—so I'll patiently wait.

Today's memory for me is about Matthew's "crazy day" this summer. Having a driver in the house has been wonderful, as Matt caters to his sisters and felt very important bringing them places. I'd be making dinner and Laura or Abby would text Matt to pick them up from tennis. I'd say, "Why didn't they ask me? They knew I was home?" and Matt would say "Because they just know I'm always available—I'll go get them." Often Matt would take Kami to piano lessons for thirty minutes on Wednesday nights. He would stay with her and read, then bring her home, always saying "sure Mom, no problem." What an awesome big brother.

So on with my story. One day this summer Matt needed to pick up Laura from a friend's house, take Abby and Laura as well as himself for dentist appointments, return movies we had rented, and take Kami and Brooke to/from swimming lessons—to catch the bus in Pierz. I came home from work and Matt said, "Mom, let me tell you about my crazy day. I took Abby to the dentist at ten-thirty am, and went to get Laura. I couldn't find Katie's house, so called her for directions, but there wasn't a house there, she told me to take a right versus a left. I called her again and she finally went out to the end of the driveway and I found her after about fifteen minutes. Then I realized that I forgot the movies. I went home to pick them up and Brooke came in the house with me. I went and dropped Laura off at the dentist and then went to bring Kami and Brooke to the bus for swimming, and found out that Brooke had brought her swim bag in the house and forgot it when we went back home for the movies. So I took Brooke back home, we got her swim bag and then got back to the bus again at 11:02 am—Kami had them wait for me. I then went to the dentist and Abby's there, already finished with her appointment, saying, 'there's a baby that won't stop crying and two boys who don't listen to their mom and it's giving me a headache—take me home'. So I get back in the van and took Abby home and went back for my dentist appointment. After that I ate lunch and played Xbox for a bit, then fell asleep. Abby then came downstairs at two pm and asked what time I needed to pick up Kami and Brooke. So I hurried back to town (he was one hour late) and they had played on the playground and walked to Grandma's house. Mom they were happy as a clam, smiling and just fine. Is this what it's like for you and Dad, Mom? It was just crazy."

Matt would get stressed out if the gas light came on in his van, not wanting to ask for gas money, despite taking the girls everywhere. I'd reassure him he could go to St. Cloud and back with the gas light on, but he'd still worry. I would give him my credit card to pay at the pump, but often he had put his own money he had earned this summer. Bill and I agreed that Matt shouldn't get a job this year because he was taking four college classes and would have basketball the majority of the year. I told him to apply for scholarships instead of trying to get a job and he was ok with this. I just wanted him to completely enjoy his senior year. Now I'm so glad he wasn't working as we were able to spend more time with him, although the responsibility would have been a good experience for him.

I've received many cards with family and friends who have sent in for prayers at various churches, healing masses, prayer chains, etc. I know we must have over a thousand people praying for Matt and God will hear our prayers and has shown his loving, caring, healing ways already, every day.

Abby was visiting tonight and looking much better, but still pretty sore. She walks very slow and seems to be more herself. She said tonight "my memory is good." Abby was supposed to be in the school play this weekend and went to watch it today. The director had her go up on stage for a picture with the entire cast and of all the freshman cast too. Abby seemed embarrassed, but obviously thought this was really cool as her eyes just lit up when she told me about it. She has another chiropractor appointment tomorrow and therapy every day this week. Abby said that the speech therapist will re-assess her at the end of the week to see if she can go back to school next week. "But I think she will let me."

Bill plans to return to work half days this week to have some normalcy I think more than anything and to save some vacation time. I'm able to use sick time I've accrued for the past seven years, since my maternity leave with Brooke, so I'm very fortunate at this time. Our jobs have been very understanding, telling both of us not to worry about work at all. We are lucky to work for such wonderful people, companies, as well as such caring coworkers.

Matt appears to be resting up for his middle of the night sixty to ninety minutes of being awake. I know he needs to rest to heal and we heal the most while sleeping so I won't disturb him. I know this will be a week filled with gifts of healing for Matt and Abby.

The Patient in Room 311 and Freddy the Leaf

—w—

Nov. 19, 2013

I took the day/night off yesterday from writing and now have so many thoughts, I don't know where to start. I received a post today stating "When you should be relying on others for strength, you are giving us hope, faith, and strength in God through your journal entries." How incredible is that?

It made me think of the sermon in church here at the hospital a week after the accident about "Freddy the Leaf." To be honest I literally fell asleep off and on during the homily (and also once when standing and had to quick regain my balance) and so after mass, Bill recapped the story for me, saying, "What a good story it had been." The ironic thing is, as I had taken walks outside that first week and even after, watching the leaves blow in the wind with no control over where they would end up, I thought of this being Matthew, Abby and our whole family at this time—it's all in God's hands. The shorten version of the story was about how the leaf was so worried about falling from the tree as other leaves were dropping to the ground. Over the winter, with the snow, rain in the spring, the leaf had to decay to bring nourishment to the tree to help it bud again in the spring—thus helping the tree and all the many, many leaves on it. This made me again think of how Matt and Abby's accident, as horrible, tragic and seemingly unfair as it is, has helped many, many people turn to God and will undoubtedly help them in future situations that arise in their personal life. Abby spent the day with me at the hospital and said that one of her friends wrote her a letter saying she never believed in God before, but prayed to him for the first time the day of the accident. How powerful is that?

Abby is still not quite herself in my opinion, and I probably would know. She laughs more than normal at things until her ribs hurt, gets easily frustrated at things that never would have bothered her before (such as twirling spaghetti noodles on a fork at lunch) and interrupts conversations often, which is not her "norm." She has another massage tomorrow and two healing chiropractor appointments this week, in addition to PT/OT/ Speech therapy. She says "all I can do is sleep and eat" so that's why I talk so much. That's a pretty good rationale, so she'll just need time and prayers, however it makes me a bit hesitant of how frustrating school will be when she returns.

Today, believe it or not, I had a weak, overwhelming moment. I went to Target with my friend and Abby to pick up a few things, including some for Matt to stimulate his level of awareness. I felt we had done a good job, purchasing another Kosh bracelet ring that can go on his left wrist (for awareness of his left arm which he doesn't use much), maracas, bells on a hand held dowel, and a Nerf basketball and hoop so he can raise his arms in OT and feel for the rim for a slam dunk. Matthew was up all night last night and pretty much slept through the day today. He was up in the Biodyne chair two times today as sitting up is better for his heart and lungs and he wasn't following leg exercise commands. I tried to have Matthew shake the maracas and he did try one time only, and did not attempt any of the other things I brought for him, excluding rolling a strand of the Kosh ball in his fingers. I suddenly had this overwhelming denial and almost a panic attack that this person in the chair COULD NOT BE MY MATTHEW. It was simply the patient in room 311 that I was seeing today. I turned away and just as quickly, I thought of all the hope everyone has, myself included, that he will recover with more time to heal and my fear and panic went away. I texted my boss back about this who just happened to ask how the day was going, and she told me to focus on today and look at the awesome things Matthew has accomplished in the past two weeks. He will have his ups and downs like we all do, but with God's healing, we will both be strong and get through this. Well, that kicked my butt and I did not wallow in self-pity as that's fruitless anyway.

They had team rounds again this morning and said Matthew needs more time to completely wean off the vent. I think it's God's way of giving us more time for him to wake up. The doctor said it probably wouldn't be until next week before he was off the vent completely and then he needs to be monitored "for about three days" afterwards to ensure he's ok without it. I did check with **Country Manor** and they accept "stable trach" patients, so I know either way the future will be ok with excellent care. Matt is swallowing spontaneously all the time now and rarely needs his saliva suctioned which is a huge step towards eating and getting off the vent in the future. He coughed so hard he literally got the care chalk board with mucus this weekend, which is on the wall about two feet away from the foot of his nine foot bed. I'd say we have the powerful cough mastered.

As I thought about things while being out today, it's amazing how my perspective on everything has changed. Who cares in the grand scheme of things if we have to wait in line at the grocery store, gas pump, for a green light, a slow driver in front of us, or a restroom to open up—especially if you have the time, but as a society we get irritated with waiting? I now know what it's like to wait in a way no one can understand, except maybe my family and close friends. I don't think someone chewing with their mouth open, chewing ice, or tapping their fingers on a table or desk will raise my blood pressure anymore, as it's not what matters in life. Think of the irritating habits your family or coworkers may have, and re-analyze what really counts.

Matthew has had such excellent care here in the pediatric intensive care unit. It's almost as if the nurses are part of my family. They care beyond a job and are triumphant with every gain Matt makes. One of nurses wrote a letter last night as it was the first night I didn't sleep at the hospital, saying how he was up all night—later than me, working his Xbox fingers, etc. and how much he loved me and wanted me to have a break from taking care of him and everyone else. The letter was signed, "Love Matthew." At first I was in complete shock reading the letter, then almost in tears as I want him back so much, then overwhelmingly thankful God has put each nurse into our lives. My friend read the letter and said "It truly is from Matthew. God just sent it through an angel which happens to be his nurse, Erin." Oh my goodness. I had goose bumps down to my toes. It always makes me teary when the chaplain comes in for prayers and I see/hear the nurses praying right with us.

Matthew did do something that may seem trivial to you, but made me very happy tonight. While my sister-in-law and I were doing healing touch with Matt on the sides of his head, he yawned. Not a little yawn, but a huge, open-mouth yawn as if to say, "Yeah, I'm still sleepy, give me a little more time, but I'm thinking about waking up and getting back to normal." Another sign from God that he will be ok, I just need to jump on board with God's time frame. I changed my goal for Matt to be home by Thanksgiving to being home by Christmas.

The social worker then came in and is filing for long term care disability with social security, to be pro-active, but took the wind right out of my sails. I can understand the reason behind it, but of course it puts doubt and fear of Matt not getting better long term—until he does something amazing like yawn and snap his fingers.

My memory today of Matthew is about our dog, Buddy—yes the one present during Matt's birth at home. When Kami was almost two, Abby five, Laura six and Matthew eight, I took the kids for our first springtime walk, pulling Kami in the wagon. Buddy of course went with and was walking in the ditch, sniffing and minding his own business. He had been with us for eleven years already that spring and his hearing and vision were beginning to fail. A black truck was coming on the other side of the road where Buddy was in the ditch. Matt yelled, "BUDDY!" and without looking, he came trotting across the road to Matthew, only to miss the front tires and be killed by the back tires a few seconds later. Laura, being so kind-hearted, began to cry as hard as I was, seeing me so upset. It wasn't anyone's fault, Matthew was worried about him being away from us with the truck coming. He still blames himself for calling Buddy, stating, "It's really my fault Buddy died." I tried to explain to him of course it wasn't and that Buddy was starting to lose his vision, hearing, and walk slower and just loved him so much he wanted to come to him. Having died so suddenly was probably a gift to Buddy, as he was older and didn't have to suffer. Matt never accepted this theory and I think with his kind heart (as he couldn't even shoot a sparrow with his brand new BB gun he got for his tenth birthday) he probably never will. Matt would never intentionally hurt any person (or animal for that matter), as this is just who he is—my gift from God.

That's what happens when I take a day off writing and Matt's sleeping—you totally have all my thoughts and analysis of our situation. Thank you for listening and being there for my family. God will show his healing power of prayer with the great number of people gathered in his name each day asking for Matthew to recover. I just know it.

Why our family?

—⚹—

Nov 20, 2013

Today was "scribbly" for me. Tons of different emotions once again; however, I feel my hope and faith for Matt's full recovery has reached a higher level today. Let me tell you why.

I woke up in the hospital this morning from a wonderful dream that Matt was running, with a "CODE BLUE" page over the intercom. Excuse my language, but what a hell of a way to start the day, instinctively listening that the room number announced wasn't Matt's. . . (again, as I find myself worrying even when I'm in the room with him—must just be a motherly response.) I went to Matt's room and found out he once again had been up most of the night. He was pretty tired and had trouble following leg exercises in PT, so my friend Lisa, PT, said "Let's get him sitting on the edge of the bed to see if this wakes him up." It certainly did. Matthew did so much better than we last tried this about ten days ago. His heart rate, blood pressure and oxygen levels remained stable and he tolerated sitting for twelve minutes. Different than last time, he didn't push his legs straight out into extension, or push his body backwards. Matt did use his right hand on the bed automatically to help keep his sitting balance and did show some trunk and neck strength/muscle activation too. Matt wasn't pushing with his right hand as many neurologically impaired patients do, and let me easily take his hand. I had Matt try the small Nerf basketball and the hoop I bought yesterday with his left hand and he did try to raise his arm some and also dropped it quickly with cueing to do a "slam dunk." All four of us cheered.

Later this morning, we helped Matt slide into the Biodyne chair, bringing the flat chair into a near seated position for speech therapy. Melissa, our speech therapist is incredible. She brought flavored ice for taste stimulation—lemon, and orange. She started with lemon and Matt chewed and swallowed quickly with less than a pea-sized ice portion on a spoon. She then put a spoon with nothing on it between his lips and he had no reaction. She was ecstatic that he knew the difference, trying this a few times with one hundred percent consistency. When asked to give her a "thumbs up" if he wanted more, he did this too. I was SO happy as this will help him to eat again in the future—remember, I am waiting to have popcorn again until Matt can have it with me. After all this, he pretty much slept through OT in the afternoon, but that's ok, you just can't have everything in one day.

I had company this afternoon and was discussing the medication Matt gets for increasing his alertness at eight am and eight pm. The nurse working with him immediately said "maybe that's why he's up so much during the night" and she called the pharmacy requesting to move his pm dose earlier which was then changed to five pm. That's how all the nurses are with Matt's cares and our needs—doing everything humanly possible to help his recovery.

I took Abby to OT today and that was an enlightening challenge at best. After her OT noted I was literally falling asleep sitting up and offered to find me a bed (how embarrassing) we continued to look at Abby's vision. She had Abby lie on a mat on the floor and visually track a swinging tennis ball, forwards, backwards, diagonals, side to side and circles both directions. Abby had a very hard time with this, keeping her eyes tracking and presented with jerky eye movements. We were given several eye exercises to complete at home which was great. I told her therapist about Abby only wanting to wear loose clothing, due to her rib and left shoulder blade pain with reaching. I had shown Abby a modified technique for putting on her shirt (as I have worked with stroke and shoulder patients for over twenty-four years) however she wanted nothing to do with this. Her therapist confirmed this was a good idea and Abby reluctantly tried it, stating, "at home I'm going to do it my way anyway." Abby does not lift her left arm any more than she needs to as this irritates her left rib fractures. Her OT suggested having her right arm assist with a wooden dowel to hold onto, and we also tried holding her hands together and bringing them over her head, but this was uncomfortable too. I suggested sliding her hand on the wall and she did with less pain, however; Abby was really upset with my ideas, stating, "Who's the OT here anyway?" Well, it wasn't or maybe it was her lucky day as she had two OT's in the room. I explained to Abby I was trying to help and if I didn't love her, I wouldn't be trying to have her do these things. She seemed ok with this and said she wasn't mad at me—WHEW.

I came home today for the first time with tears in my eyes the entire drive, thinking how much I wanted to be home for the girls, and being "pre-sad" knowing Matt wouldn't be there. Brooke wouldn't let me even take off my coat, asked if I was going to cry, and dominated my attention the entire evening, giving me the silent treatment if she asked me a question without an immediate response while I was talking to Bill, Laura, Abby or Kami. I took Kami to piano lessons and Brooke said "I miss Matthew" on the way. She asked if he'd be home in November or December which made me happy she understood it would be a while, but also teary thinking of the holidays. I told Kami and Brooke about our amazing day— how once Matt was more awake, but we really had no idea how long he would be in the hospital. They both understood, but what a tough load on their shoulders too–wish I could shield it from them, but in time it'll all be ok and they won't remember how much sadness they felt at this time.

I picked out boxers, and shorts for grandma to adapt with velcro, so Matt can wear these at the hospital, along with T-shirts that have larger neck holes, realizing he doesn't even own a V-neck. It was one of the toughest things I've done yet, looking through his Comets (AAU basketball team he did for the past four years,) Pierz band shirts, St. Cloud State, and other sports teams that he loved. The flood of memories was devastating. I wanted to scream, and at the same time, knew getting him in real clothes for therapy is a positive step for the future. We also had Matt's favorite meal, spaghetti, at Brooke's request and this was tough too, to see his empty chair at the table. Then I thought of the flavored ice today and that he will be eating spaghetti again with us, hopefully by Christmas. Matt had applied to Augsburg and Eau Claire colleges the week of the accident and Abby said, "The colleges called again today–what am I supposed to tell them?" These were the colleges interested in Matt to play basketball. I don't need to again express my sadness.

I thought of a patient I had many, many years ago who was diagnosed with cancer. She went to her oncologist and in her denial and anger, told me that she asked her doctor,

"Why ME?" She said he replied: "Why not you? What makes you so special that nothing bad should happen to you and should happen to someone else?" I remember telling her how angry I'd be and asking her if she yelled at him, or got another doctor, etc., and she replied, "No, it ended my self-pity as I couldn't come up with a good answer why it shouldn't be me." It made me today think of our situation and as wonderful and religious as Matthew and Abby are, I cannot answer this question either as to why this should happen to anyone else instead, nor would I ever want another living soul to go through this.

My memory today brings tons of hope for Matthew's future accomplishments. Matt began piano lessons around age eight and would get upset if his teacher corrected any key played incorrectly as he wanted to master everything immediately and make his instructor and me proud. As he progressed in his skills over the next year or two, if the instructor corrected his beat, or timing, he would get so upset the instructor almost quit teaching him if his behavior didn't improve. I told Matt if they didn't find anything for him to improve on, why were we paying for lessons. Matthew took piano lessons up until he was about fifteen years old, stating "there wasn't a song he couldn't teach himself at this point." I was so proud when he played the theme song of the Titanic at a piano recital a few years ago. In swimming lessons too, when Matt attended classes at the YMCA, he started in the nice warm pool. After passing all the classes in this pool, he then transitioned to the large, cool pool. Matthew knew that where the flags were above the pool, the depth was over his head, and would grab the side of the pool or the floatation dividers between swim lanes and cry almost hysterically. The instructor assured me he needed to keep coming to lessons and the fear would go away, stating she was like that as a child and now she's an instructor. True to her prediction, Matthew surpassed all expectations and was at the level just below lifeguard by the time basketball consumed our Saturday morning swimming lessons. It makes me think as scary and challenging as this all is, he will surpass my greatest hopes. Matt's basketball coach texted me after the second MRI, finding out through Laura how upset I was, stating "Matt has exceeded expectations his whole life and will again. Keep the faith." I will end on that note, asking that everyone reading this will KEEP THE FAITH for any trials you may encounter in your life.

It's the getting there that matters

—w—

Nov. 21, 2013

I received a card with a turtle that had a band-aid on it's shell. The card said "It's not the speed, it's the getting there." I love this card as it reminds me in a positive way that Matthew will get there with lots of time, love and prayers. So many cards we have received are so inspirational I know it took a while to find "just the right one." With encouraging notes, bookmarks, etc., knowing how much people care for our family—I just feel showered with love from all of you. It has changed our whole family's life, like the accident has. The difference, however is when Matt is back to normal (or his new "normal") say a year from now, the good we have experienced in people through this tragedy, and power of God's healing will change our life forever rather than short-term for the better.

Matt slept most of the night last night with the change in medication from eight to five pm. He was more alert for all of his therapies, both eyes about half open most of the day, and didn't need us to "try to wake him up" today for therapy, a doctor's visit, etc. We have a new doctor today, Chris Johnson, who will be here for ten days (thankfully there are only three doctor's total that rotate for pediatric intensive care.) I liked him right off the bat. That's a bonus for everyone—including my readers I'm sure. Dr. Johnson changed Matthew's morphine to as needed versus scheduled and consulted with Dr. Anderson to begin Ritalin for arousal two times per day. Dr. Johnson wanted to try Matt not only off the vent, but off the CPAP that gives him extra breath volume, for four hours with only oxygen through his tracheostomy. Matthew did great with his oxygen levels and his heart rate; however, fatigues quickly due to the effort he needs to put forth to breathe. After three hours with his respirations increasing up to forty a minute, he was put back on the CPAP this morning and will be on the vent during the night yet.

Dr. Anderson came in today to see Matt and look at his therapy notes and "is planning on having him come down to rehab." This was so wonderful to hear. Dr. Anderson threw Matt his Kosh ball when he was in the Biodyne chair and he immediately picked it up, but decided not to throw or drop it when asked as he wanted to check it out.

Today in OT, Matt's therapist brought in a weighted bean bag for deep pressure sensation to help with arousal, but also calming–both to his arms and legs. I'm not sure if Matt liked or disliked it–guess we'll see how tomorrow goes. She also brought in a six pound weighted ball and Matt held it against his chest with his right hand and arm. I plan to continue to work on this sensory stimulation; however, with the changes in his breathing assist today and three therapies, I let him off today.

Speech therapy, Matt didn't open as much, but I think he doesn't like orange or raspberry flavored ice as much as the lemon he had yesterday. Matt did bring a washcloth partially up to his mouth to wipe his lips with his right hand, brushed part of his teeth with assist to hold his arm up, (but pushing the toothbrush in and out himself) and when she said good-bye, he raised his wrist and "waved" with his index finger extended. She was so excited about this.

In PT today, Matthew sat on the edge of the bed for about ten minutes, but was only on oxygen and so this tired him more quickly. He again used his right arm for support, but didn't want me to take his hand off the bed today. He demonstrated increased head control–only needing one hand on his forehead to guide him, versus needing total support. Matt also demonstrated increased trunk strength. I think all the coughing he does, bringing his head and shoulders off the pillow, is making him stronger as difficult as it is to watch. The coughing and swallowing are needed in preparation for eating and weaning off the trach, so it's all good. It sure is a juggling act between medical versus rehab status. Both want to progress him, but both effect the other immensely. Now that Matt is hopefully turning his nights and days around, this will help his participation in therapy, however weaning off the vent and CPAP makes him tired, thus limiting his participation. It's a fine line of what to do with either side to meet our goals in each area while avoiding limiting the progression of the other.

Today's memory is about how Matthew didn't complain or ask for things, even when it was no big deal to do so. He would wait until his feet hurt to tell me his shoes were getting too small—even though I told him many times he needed to tell me sooner if they were getting tight. Matthew was water tubing July 3rd, about three or four years ago when I was working. I came home and he told me he had hurt his pinky finger tubing "I probably jammed it." I thought no more of it and he didn't mention it again until six weeks later. Matt said, "Dad and I were waiting for the swelling to go down first, but does my finger look normal to you?" Matt held out his hand and the middle joint on his right pinky finger was angled out the side at a forty-five degree angle. I immediately yelled "Billy!", and made an orthopedic appointment the next day. The hand surgeon questioned my friend, Carla, who was a hand therapist, working at St. Cloud Orthopedics (who "got us in sooner" than the six week, first available appointment.) "They just didn't notice his finger was broken for six weeks?" the hand surgeon asked. Matt ended up having surgery three days later, requiring bone grafting and a pin placement. He's just not one to complain. If Matt hurt himself during a basketball game—falling with a floor burn, an elbow to his eye, etc. he would look at me and then rub where he was hurt to make sure I knew he was in pain. I knew he needed my caring and he knew he'd get it. When Matt made a really good play on the court, he would look at me and raise his eyebrows as if to say "see what amazing thing I did?" It was adorable and often had many other parents smiling as well.

Matt's favorite foods are spaghetti, pizza, popcorn, and spicy nacho Doritos. He would easily eat two or three bags a week. One day we were out, and rather than ask us to pick some up for him, he drove to the gas station to buy a bag himself. Well they happened to be four dollars and ninety-nine cents at the gas station. When I came home, Matt said "I never knew Doritos cost so much. If that's what you and Dad have been paying, you don't need to buy them for me anymore." I just melted as this is one of his basic food groups. I told him we always buy them at Walmart/Target or where ever they are on sale, two bags for five or six dollars. He said "Well, then you can buy them, but only if they are on sale." Bill and I chuckled as we felt he had his first reality check for what college would be like, finding out about the real world in so many ways. Matt would say, "If I don't have money for food at college, will you send me some?" I always reassured him we would help him out and he could come home at any time. Ironic how as I sit here eating Trix cereal in the hospital lounge, I'm waiting for him to come home now, months earlier than I had ever envisioned, and waiting/wanting him home even more than I would have been when he was coming home from college next fall.

Matthew's Faith

—⚊—

Nov 22, 2013

As I was thinking about what to focus on today, I was thinking about Matt's faith. Abby was baptized when Matt was three and a half years old. I'm sure Grandpa has it on video, but when they said the gospel reading was "according to Matthew," Matt yelled out "ME?" with everyone laughing of course. In Matt's school masses on Friday mornings, he would answer every question Fr. Jerry or Fr. David would ask. They would call on other students too, but Matt always had the right answer. His arm would shoot up to answer the question before it was even asked, thus the reason he was called upon so often—curiosity if he would really know the answer. When Matt was graduating from Holy Trinity, Fr. Jerry said, now his sisters needed to answer the questions, which they did too, but without as much enthusiasm.

In the past year or so, Matt and I were driving through St. Cloud on Division Street and were running late to get to four-thirty mass on Saturday afternoon. I couldn't believe it, but we hit every light green through town (ten lights I'd guess.) When I commented on this, Matt said, "Mom I said a prayer that we'd hit the lights green and so did"—he had NO doubt we wouldn't. It made me realize Matt prayed more than I knew and how strong his faith was. One day Matt burnt his finger on hot pizza sauce, right out of the oven. Rather than swear, he put his finger in his mouth and said, "Oh Sweet Jesus." I'll never forget it, as more than likely, that wouldn't have even been my response.

This morning I was really worried about Matt. He had his second dose of Ritalin and seemed more upset, even at rest. He was holding both legs completely straight and raising them off the bed—pretty good leg strength though. In OT, she did the deep pressure tapping with the bean bag and also brought up a vibrating massage roll to encourage calming alertness which worked great. His heart rate even went down to fifty beats per minute by the time she was finished with her session. She left this for me to use too. I'm very lucky, as the OT's have left equipment for me to use in the room, which may not be the norm, but know I'll return them, know where they are, and want to do anything possible to help Matt's recovery.

Matt was up in the Biodyne chair when the "medical team" came in for rounds. The dietician and case manager left and the social worker stayed behind and said she called the business office and said the total amount of our bill thus far. Matthew heard this and became so upset that speech had to end her session. His arms went straight and crossed, legs straight out, heart rate higher than it's been in weeks, one hundred forty to one hundred fifty beats per minute, and respirations in the forties. I told Matt it was all ok, and all we cared about was him getting better. I went to get his nurse to have him go back to bed, or give him morphine to calm him if he was having pain. Just then Fr. Popp came in with Michael (pastoral assistant from Buckman) and his nephew, Jesse, who had played traveling basketball with Matt last year. Jesse went over, said hi and talked to Matt, and he began to relax immediately. (I was afraid more visitors would further upset him at this particular moment but it was the complete opposite.) I asked Matt to give Jesse a thumbs up, and he immediately brought his thumb up faster than I've ever seen yet. He held onto Jesse's hand and squeezed it hard, increasing his grip when asked to if he understood Fr. Popp or Jesse. My mom and dad were visiting at the time and mom and I needed to get out the tissues as you could tell how much having him here at this moment meant to Matt. Another angel sent to us by God. When they mentioned leaving, Matt again began shaking his legs, putting them straight out, with his heart rate and respirations again increasing. When we asked Matt if he wanted Jesse to stay, he pulled Jesse's hand in closer and it was very difficult for him and Matt to have him leave.

In PT today, Matt didn't do much for leg exercises in bed, but did sit on the edge of bed again for approximately ten minutes, able to help hold himself up some with his left hand today as well as his right with help. Matt's eyes were open in sitting and he didn't get as tired either. Matt tolerated being on oxygen for five and a half hours today, increase from three hours yesterday, and he may try this again later this evening.

It is so reassuring to know Matt is understanding us and trying his best to "wake up." I think how fortunate we are that he survived the accident. His bucket seat was pushed against the passenger front seat, buckled, and tipped back into the second row for protection. If his seat wouldn't have moved, I have no doubt he wouldn't be with us. God still has great plans for Matt and I know he will continue to touch people's lives. My prayers go out to families that have lost a child as I can't imagine how it would be. I may have a pretty good clue though from the night of the accident, but thankfully we didn't experience this. God will answer our prayers.

Real clothes

—⁓—

Nov 23, 2013

Today was a very good day. Matt slept all night last night, so he was awake the majority of the day, excluding a good nap. He kept his eyes about half open and gave several "thumbs up" for the things he wanted or if we asked him a question where the answer was "yes." Matt was only on oxygen all day today. He'll be on the CPAP tonight, which helps to give him extra breath volume if he needs it. The goal is for him to only need oxygen by Tues to transfer to inpatient rehab here at St. Cloud Hospital. I'm so excited he qualifies—thank you for all the prayers for God's healing to make it to this new step in Matt's recovery.

Matt worked with OT this morning, reaching with both arms, with assistance, for him to put his Nerf basketball in the plastic rim. He doesn't use his left arm as much, so doing this was really nice to see. In PT he sat on the edge of the bed with Bill and I, the PT and only one nurse today, progressing to only needing three of us and holding his balance way better. Matt uses his right hand for balance and also to help some pushing up from being on his right elbow. When sitting up for a while, he had his right eye more open than his left for the very first time. The nurse today gave him a weighted beanbag and asked him to bring it up to her hand and he did. She was pretty excited. The nurses are so on our side, wanting Matt to get better, excited about each baby step. Matthew's skin is perfect (actually better than when he came in) due to his excellent care and repositioning.

Abby stayed at her friend's house today versus coming to the hospital as she's here every weekday already. I'm sure she enjoyed this and it was a wonderful "normal" day for her. She is able to go back to school on Monday, but only for about two or three hours to start with. Mrs. Keith (the high school social worker) brought Laura and Kami to the hospital yesterday after school for us and discussed Abby going back to school. She said she will have Abby only make up the "must know" assignments initially and anything she needs to turn in, she'll have until the end of the quarter to do so. I so appreciate this and it will help Abby from getting too frustrated and overwhelmed as she eases into school after being off for three weeks.

As I think about my life and how God planned for me to be here for Matt, it's amazing. I wanted to be a veterinarian in early high school (until seeing a cow's stomach cut open on the farm) then a beautician (until the art teacher told me I wouldn't like touching dirty hair with lice) then decided I wanted to be a nurse (until the HIV scare came out and I wanted nothing to do with blood) and just happened to talk to the career counselor who suggested therapy to help people but not doing all the medical cares. I said "ok, that sounds good" and went for my 2 year Occupational Therapy Assistant degree, only to begin classes for the registered program within a year. I took many classes on vision, neurological rehabilitation, and shoulder rehabilitation. Within the last 2 years, I took courses on healing touch or "energy techniques" for healing. I often use this with any of shoulder patients who are having pain, with excellent results. My sister-in-law, Diane, and I have worked on Matt's recovery with healing touch almost every day since the accident and I know this has helped him hugely. We have been fortunate to have Diane provide healing touch and be a wonderful emotional support with her never-ending faith and optimism that Matt will make a full recovery.

Typically with a closed head injury, there is a period where the patient will be agitated and often aggressive. Let me tell you why I don't believe this will be a phase of Matt's recovery. When Matt was little (two, or two and a half years old) he never "fought" to get a toy back that Laura would take away at home, or the kids at daycare. He wouldn't cry or become upset, but rather would shrug his shoulders as if to say "Oh well, it's not worth the fight or effort to keep it. I can find something else to entertain myself." One of his daycare settings in the cities would tell me, "I tell Matt to fight for his toy and it's NOT ok for anyone to take what's his, but he doesn't put up a fight." One day last year Matt came home from basketball practice and said they had a team meeting, where the team players may express any issues they may have about other players. Matt said "I looked down, but I knew they were going to say something about me." One of the player said, "Matt, you need to be more aggressive" and Matt said "I knew that was coming, and then other players said this too." Matt said, "Then Coach Dahman said 'Matt, how many sisters do you have?', and I said four. Then Dahman asked me if I was allowed to punch them, and I said, 'Oh no'. He then asked if I could yell, pinch, or shove them. I said, No, I'd be is so much trouble." Matt said that Dahman then said, "Most of you have a brother to rough house with, Matt doesn't with four sisters. Being aggressive just isn't in him." Matt said he was so glad the coach had stuck up for him and knew why he didn't feel right being aggressive. When getting his graduation pictures taken at the end of October, Matt would raise his eyebrows for every picture, happy or serious and we had to remind him not to do so. Matt said, "I feel so mean making a serious face with my eyebrows down."

I feel like Matt is slowly coming back to me and I'm beyond thankful for God's healing through everyone's prayers. Today Matt wore his Comet's basketball shorts and T shirt and actually didn't sweat as much as when he's in a gown. He looked so much more normal with clothes on, I could have cried for happiness. One day at a time and I see a flicker of the light at the end of the tunnel already.

When I walked into Matt's room this morning, his heart rate and respirations were high and he was more awake and aware than before. The nurse said she gave him his basketball and he only could open his right hand to put on it, but tried with both hands, stating "I wanted to cry." Matthew will let me open his left hand, especially if his left elbow is extended, but doesn't try to open it on his own. He did give a "thumbs up" with his left hand today, which I haven't seen in a while though. I know he will continue to improve, however I hate to think of him having to struggle and be frustrated with this.

Matt was only on oxygen all day again and the plan is for him to trial this during the night tonight for the first time. His oxygen saturations have been one hundred percent the majority of the day so I think he'll be just fine. The goal is for him not to need the CPAP to assist with breathing at all, then to decrease the oxygen to needing only humidity, and then deflating the balloon in his trach to allow him to breathe in through the trach and out through his nose. Matt will then try a valve that will allow him to talk when it is plugged.

Matthew is swallowing well and needing less and less suctioning. They have changed his CPT (chest percussion therapy) to only as needed today, and he hasn't needed it.

Matthew did some nice things today in therapy and with his nurses. He took the drumstick in his right hand and hit the balloon his nurse held in front of him. It took about a minute for him to process and respond to the request. Matt had visitors this afternoon who brought him "a band in a box" which was super cool with a drum, cymbals, a triangle, etc. Matt tried so hard to hit the triangle with his right hand and finally did lightly three times. In PT Matt sat on the edge of the bed with help of the PT, Bill and I and the nurse suctioning his mouth two times I believe. He worked on flexing his trunk forward and straightening his arms to roll a ball. When weightbearing through his left elbow, I asked if he could give me a "high five" and he immediately raised his right hand with his fingers extended. Matt needed assist to bring his right hand up for "slam dunks" in OT, but did let go of the ball better today. Bill and I, my parents and girls went out for lunch today. When we came back the nurse said Matthew had been crying, stating, "I think he was sad, realizing more as he wakes up." She said, "I told him it's ok to be angry and sad, and it's ok to cry." What a wonderful gift she gave him with her permission to do so.

I received a post that the Brooten-Belgrade-Elrosa and Howard Lake Waverly basketball teams are praying for Matthew. I can't imagine how they found out, but it made me tearful to know our "rivalry" teams are praying for my Matt—stating it puts into perspective how basketball is only a small part of our life when something like this happens. I have had other posts from parents of Matt's AAU teams too. I hit me like a cement block tonight as I thought about this, that maybe Matt's basketball "career" thus far was all in preparation for having so many extra prayers to help his recovery after the accident. Matt got his first basketball and adjustable hoop at eighteen months and has loved basketball ever since. Previously before the accident, it was all about being 6'8" and senior captain this year and which college would potentially accept him on a basketball team. As many of my friends and family know, Matthew's goal from about age eight was to go to college for basketball—preferably the Miami Heat.

Initially after the accident when Matt's CT came back ok, I was told no sports for three months with a spleen laceration. I thought, "Well it'll be ok, he'll be playing by January or February." Then the MRI revealed the brain stem injury, and suddenly basketball didn't matter at all. I look at all the games I've been to with screaming parents not only encouraging their children, but at times upset with how they have played (even in other sports) and I've always wondered if the child really wanted to play him/herself and "how the car ride home would be." I always tell the kids that the most important thing is to have fun with your friends; however, I did tell Matt what he should work on (the little advice I had) and he always wanted "Dad's opinion" too after each game. When I was told the Pierz High School National Honor Society is having a boys and girls basketball fund raiser in Matt's honor on December 21st, it made me first of all so sad as Matt wouldn't be able to play, then so overwhelmed because it will make Matt so happy to have other kids playing for him. I just hope he can be there to watch, even for the night.

Today's story has been ongoing for Matt his whole life. Being so tall for his age, from about age ten on, whenever he went anywhere he'd get asked how tall he was, followed by, "Do you play basketball?" Matt would always answer "6'8" (recently of course) and "why yes I do." We went shopping before school started this fall and at every store at least two people would ask these questions in sequence, making the girls burst out laughing. Matt would just patiently answer, never becoming upset as this was a way to talk to new people. He would say "I should just get a shirt that says I'm 6'8" and I play basketball to save all the questions." At Kohl's this year, Kami went behind a clothes rack Matt was at and said "Excuse me sir, but can you tell me how tall you are and if you play basketball? She tried this twice and Matt was a good sport about it too.

I believe that all things happen for a reason. Even though having our children hurt really "sucks," we are so lucky to still have them with us. Without a doubt, unconditional love has taken on a new meaning at a much higher level, as does the power of prayer. God's healing, as well as knowing there is so much good in everyone, brings a new gift each day to our family. God bless you all for caring.

Jesus take the wheel

—⚬—

Nov 26, 2013

Good thing God has everything under control, because I feel like I have no control of the steering wheel or accelerator right now in my life. Matthew continues to make slow, but continued progress. Yesterday and today were good days in therapy for Matthew. He is able to answer yes/no questions with a "thumbs up" more consistently with speech therapy. Yesterday the speech therapist asked Matt if he was born in China, and Matt did not move his thumb, I said to ask him if he was born under the Christmas tree, which the speech therapist did, and Matt did in a split-second. In PT Matt trialed an E-Z stand yesterday which is a hydraulic lift which brings a person from sitting to standing; however, we were unable to stand him completely because his heart rate increased too much and in all honesty I think his head would have hit the ceiling. Today, with the help of Matt's head basketball coach, we trialed the tilt table which Matt can slide over onto when lying down and it then transitions to standing. We were almost upright; however, Matt started coughing, leaning his entire upper body and head forward (remember when he is standing, we are reaching over our heads to hold him upright). He became sweaty, increased heart rate, and wasn't as alert, so needed to lie back down, but did tolerate twelve minutes. In OT Matt is reaching with his right hand with very little assist, to put his Nerf basketball in the hoop with increased speed and releasing the ball about seventy-five percent of the time without cueing to do so. Today he even held onto a weighted dowel and lifted both arms overhead with assist, and worked on elbow flexion and extension, progressing to verbal cues only to initiate the movement.

Medically, Matt trialed being without the CPAP or oxygen last night, but did need to be put on oxygen again. Dr. Anderson came in and said he wanted a chest x-ray to see why his oxygen saturations dropped before having him go to inpatient rehab. The plan is for Matt to go to rehab on Friday, if he's medically stable. Matthew's Ritalin dose (to increase alertness) was doubled and a sleeping medication was ordered to allow Matt to sleep more restful. I told Dr. Anderson that Matt was sleeping good, and then he asked me if he was having dreams, or was it a deep sleep? OK, he had me there—it'd only be a guess, and Matt will do better with a good night's rest.

Matt is keeping the nurses on their toes and he is listening at all times. When the nurse had her back turned, but still in the room, Matt took off his oxygen and decided to remove his trach dressing. Today, when they were washing him up and had him on his left side after standing, (planning to change to his right side,) one of the nurses said "He looks so comfortable, I hate to turn him," and Matt gave her a thumbs up, making them all laugh, and getting his way. How could you not give him what he wants after that?

I went home for the adoration at church last night and was touched by the number of families and friends who attended for the sick of the parish. The absolute toughest part for me was seeing the basketball coaches and team kneeling with heads bowed in prayer, and seeing my parents and Bill's parents there, knowing how tough it is on all of them. As I wish I could take Matt and Abby's pain and worry away, I'd include our parents in this wish too if I had my way.

This morning, I was told I needed to pack up as the census on PICU was getting high and they needed the room. I packed everything up, called the Gorecki house about availability as it's across the street and fairly reasonable; however, they were full. I planned to stay with my best friend until they had an opening, but then the charge nurse came and said I could stay another night as they had a bunch of discharges they didn't know about. I'm on the waiting list for tomorrow if they have an opening and my plan is to be close for at least a week while Matt transitions to inpatient rehab. They do have a sofa that folds out into a bed in the rooms on rehab, but the nurses would call a code if they ever saw my hair in the morning. So, like so many things right now, it's out of my control as to where I'll stay for now. If Matt does great sleeping at night, I will go home instead. I do feel somewhat guilty as I haven't cooked now for almost four weeks, except for spaghetti one night.

Tonight was the boy's first basketball game—I'm guessing that may be why one of the nurses Matt has frequently, commented that "I seem a bit down today," which of course made me teary. I listened to the first half and then the computer I was using lost connection. I have to admit, I felt angry tonight, as well as sad, that Matt isn't able to be out there with his team. My friend who was here with me said "God knew how much Matt loved basketball. He must have a really cool plan for him now and I can't wait to see what it is." It's going to be so awesome. I went to tell Matt the half time score and he looked great in a new t-shirt, hair washed, etc., and his heart rate went up as I told him. It seems so unfair, but when I step back and think of basketball as just being a game and the most wonderful thing to me right now would be for Matt to smile and give me a hug, it no longer matters. It's our faith that matters and the baby steps forward every day. I need to stay focused on this and prayer, and Matt will be ok.

To lighten the mood, I thought I'd share a good memory I have about teaching Matt how to clean the toilets. You never quite know what I'll write about, do you? I'm not sure who decided this should be Matt's job, but I decided to make this a "fun" chore. I took all the supplies to clean the entire toilet as well as the toilet bowl cleaner and brush. I instructed Matt, doing a little dance with the motions, hula hoop motions with making the circles with the brush, knee squats to brush into the toilet hole, and officially "how to inspect" under the lid, around the toilet at the floor, etc., to make sure all was clean, with a very serious inspection list. Matt told me about the flow of water which he knew I absolutely knew nothing about, but humored me none the less. Matt was laughing and repeating my demonstration and after we were finished, said "I don't know why this is such a big deal. It's not hard to do or a bad job after all." Matt never really complained about having to do this chore again. Procrastinate, yes, complain, no.

Baby Steps

—ɯ—

Nov 27, 2013

All day, every day, from the nurses, friends and family, I hear "baby steps", as Matthew continues to make small gains. I hope for a huge stride, sprint, lunge forward; however, Matt will heal at the pace his mind and body can endure with never-ending assistance from God, family, nurses, therapists, and friends. I was thinking a lot about when Matt was a baby today. When I was on maternity leave with him, I literally was getting tender, red heels from rubbing them on the foot stool as I rocked him non-stop for three months straight, needing to put a pillow under my calves for pressure relief. I never put him down, even to switch clothes from the washer to the dryer. As a result, and due to his long torso, Matt didn't sit up on his own until he was six months old after being sick when Grandma visited so I could go to work. He learned how to "army crawl" at Grandma and Grandpa Athman's house, wanting to get to a half full bottle of Mountain Dew that I put on the carpet—he was so intrigued with the movement of the soda in the bottle. After that, he would crawl so fast to get to every piece of lint on the carpeting to get it into his mouth. It was like The Amazing Race to beat him to the piece of lint before he got there and his vision was unbelievable. (Good thing he was the first born when it was easier to keep the house clean, or the girls would have been throwing up lint balls.) Matt didn't walk until fifteen months, at his own speed again—why walk when you can be carried?

As I watch Matt work on reaching for the bed rail to roll, pushing up from his elbow into sitting, and on his sitting balance, etc., I know he is trying his absolute best and will accomplish all these motor skills again in time. I need to look at it "as getting a repeat of those wonderful childhood memories back" as I appreciate each little thing he does so much more than I did almost eighteen years ago. Of course this is different as I analyze his vision, the use of his left arm/hand, and constantly being concerned for his respiratory status.

Today, Matthew did much better using the weighted dowel in OT with both hands and less resistance. He appears to have less tightness in his arm overall, and has given me a couple of "thumbs up" with his left hand the past couple of days. Matt did have a chest X-ray today to find out more about why he again needed oxygen last night. They wanted a side view of his lungs so positioned Matt facing a bar to hold onto with his hands that was over his head. The nurse said he took this opportunity to pull his entire upper body up off the chair. She said, "He is so strong. We had to tell him to relax." The X-ray results revealed "no acute changes since the last X-ray on 11/16, and residual pneumonia," meaning it wasn't any better or worse. I didn't talk to the doctor after this to see what this means medically—if he'll need another antibiotic or not, but Matt isn't running a temp at all. Dr. Johnson said anyone who has pneumonia can cough "gunk" for up to six weeks easily. Matt requires suctioning less often and is swallowing regularly if he's not sound asleep.

In speech therapy today, Matt worked on more "thumbs up" and "thumbs down" for yes/no questions. Matt didn't answer as well today, but was tired from OT, his chest x-ray, and being up in the Biodyne chair. He stayed up for three hours today, not wanting to lie down–telling me "yes" to staying up in the chair and "no" to getting back into bed. It's better for his heart and lungs to be up sitting, so this was great. Matt's speech therapist said as he progresses to level four of the coma scale (which increased from level two out of seven last week), he will have a shorter attention span, trying to take everything in and process information.

In PT today, Matt worked on sitting on the edge of the bed with three of us for fifteen minutes, demonstrating better trunk and head control, but this was still tough and scary for him. I had Matt try to put his hands on my shoulders to help him lean forward, but he didn't relax enough to straighten his left elbow. I did almost get my hug this way so it was therapeutic for me too.

I moved out of my room at the hospital and rented a room at the Gorecki house across the street from the hospital. I plan to stay until Matt gets settled and I know he's doing ok during the night on the inpatient rehab unit. It's a nice room with two twin beds and an enclosed shower–no more mopping water up every morning. There isn't a TV in the room, but that's ok–no time anyway when I write so much these days. There are two kitchens, a laundry room, living room, library, play room, exercise room, etc., and no food or beverages are allowed in the rooms. I may or may not have had a candy bar and a Diet Pepsi while writing this anyway. It was tough to leave the room on the PICU after almost four weeks, but it's a step in the right direction for Matt's upcoming move to rehab.

Despite encouragement, I don't plan on going home tomorrow for Thanksgiving. I just cannot leave Matt on the holiday. I don't feel I need Thanksgiving this year as I am constantly reminded of how thankful I am looking at Matt, the cards, posts, and texts. Remember to look at the many things you can be thankful for in your life. I did find out that Matthew is prior authorized to go to inpatient rehab when he's ready medically. What a gift that is–I am so thankful.

Abby had her follow up at HCMC in the cities yesterday and she is doing great. She can add another class each week, but is not able to participate in phy-ed or Industrial Technology (IT) yet. My understanding is that IT requires welding and saws for wood-working which are dangerous and loud, so we'll wait to resume this class, or find another class if needed. I see Abby changing every day to her normal, caring ways. Initially when she saw Matt, she didn't really go near to him, talk to him, or show any emotion, simply asking for food. She now is worried about how his head is supported on his pillow, wipes his mouth if he needs it, and talks to him often. I love to see this.

Bill is busy taking Abby to and from school and to appointments, (not going to work the past two days), visiting Matt, washing clothes and keeping things as sane as possible at home. He literally fell asleep sitting up in a chair in Matt's room tonight as he wakes up constantly every night. He is very positive and continues to tell Matt to relax and take the time he needs to get better. I know he worries about Matt too, especially when Matt is upset, sweating, has a high heart rate, or if his legs begin shaking. Typically this means Matt is uncomfortable, too hot, has pain, or is upset by something he hears–like my end of the conversation when I'm talking to Brooke who is either screaming, crying, or giving me the silent treatment when I call home. I can have two guests at the Gorecki house, so she can stay overnight with me over the holiday. This will give her some quality time she needs with me. It'll all work out I just know it, and in time she'll understand. Kami watches her after school every day and told me Monday night that she "has used up all her patience with Brooke." I told her to pray for God to give her some more. This was not the answer she wanted and as I said it, I thought this was exactly like something my mom would say. I know all the prayers being said is the key to helping us all get through this time until things are "normal" again. My niece (through marriage) told me that she shuts off her alarm in the morning, grabs her phone, and reads my post before she gets out of bed. I'm so touched by how much everyone really cares and have never felt so loved by so many people before—which I know is a part of God's plan and another one of the gifts he's given to me since the accident.

The Best Thanksgiving ever

—⚏—

Nov 28, 2013

I've never had a Thanksgiving when I have been as thankful as I am today. I'm so thankful for Matt and Abby surviving the accident, their progress to date, all of our friends, family, excellent medical care, all the support from our community, jobs, and far beyond with the circles of prayers across several states and even to other countries. I know I wouldn't be as "strong" without all of this, and even though I certainly still have my moments, I also have SO much hope.

I slept fairly good last night at the Gorecki house except from two to three am, then unplugged the night light which helped. I then overslept my alarm and got to Matt's room at 8:35 am and his OT was already working with him. He had a bath already, and his friend had already visited and left a signed basketball and a giant poster from kids at school. Matt had a really good day, continuing to understand a lot of what we ask or tell him, and to respond quicker. His new thing is to wave good bye when asked, raising an opened right hand. When I went out to get something, I asked him for a "thumbs up" that it was ok and I'd be back and then asked him to wave. He literally waved to me with only his thumb. THAT MADE MY DAY. It is so Matthew's personally.

Matt didn't have speech today with the holiday, but did have OT and PT. He worked his arms and hands in OT and in PT went onto the tilt table again. Matt was able to tolerate increasing the degree of incline in ten degree increments, tolerating fifty degrees well, and sixty degrees for a couple of minutes before having his heart rate too high at 146 beats per minute. Matt tolerated a total of twenty minutes however and his blood pressure remained stable. He wasn't as anxious and even gave a "thumbs up" for yes to go higher. I told him he could handle this if he could handle power tower at Valley Fair. I remember watching a movie a few months ago that had the view point like you were moving in an airplane over cliffs–which gives me motion sickness. I asked Matt if he still was apprehensive about high heights, like he used to be, and he replied "Yeah, like every time I look at my feet." I thought this was a pretty good come back and partially wondered if maybe that's why he no longer gets motion sickness on the rides at Valley Fair like he did when he was younger.

I had three friends visit this morning before going to their Thanksgiving meals with their families, several posts and texts wishing me a Happy Thanksgiving. This is incredible to me, that we are thought of even on Thanksgiving Day. Maybe even more so as I believe many people are even more thankful for having their families and God's love in their lives due to Matt and Abby's accident.

Another "gift" in a way was finding out yesterday (from my brother who talked to someone who works with the driver who was behind Matt at the stop sign where the accident happened,) who said Matt DID come to a COMPLETE stop. When I received the call about the accident initially I was told that "It appears Matt ran the stop sign;" however, this was before the investigation, but it's good to know it was simply an accident. He was one hundred percent sure Matt stopped completely, then pulled out as the truck was in a blind spot, or he didn't see it. The reason this was a gift to me is because initially my first thought was "the kids have seen me go through this stop sign so many times—being an open intersection in the country a mile from our home–thinking it was partially my fault for setting a bad example." Matt was too smart to follow my ways and this is a relief to me and my family.

Today, one of the orderlies who is like a big teddy bear, giving me hugs when I need it, always asking about Abby, and visiting even when he doesn't have to stop with a quick hello, came in and said, "I'd like to buy you and your husband dinner today." He said to "look him up when my husband comes in." I knew I wouldn't do that, but thought it was so nice that he offered, confirming what a wonderful person I already knew he was. He came back later this morning and brought me a twenty-five dollar gift card to the hospital cafeteria that he bought himself. Another angel, huh? He came back later to care for Matt and said "I'm coming back to see you in that tilt table." True to his word, he came back with another orderly and they helped Matt transfer onto the tilt table, stayed the entire time and to return the tilt table. What an amazing man who really cares.

Bill and the girls came up this afternoon and we went to Perkins for dinner which was nice. It was so out of the norm for us on Thanksgiving and I could tell they felt it too, except for Brooke who was ecstatic she was spending the night with me. She just finished playing tic-tac-toe and card games with Matt's nurse and is coloring as I type. I think it's time she really needs with me and moving to the Gorecki house where she can stay was meant to be.

Dr. Anderson will assess Matthew tomorrow for inpatient rehab and I'm fairly certain it'll be a go as Matt didn't need oxygen at all last night and has been tolerating close to two hours of therapy a day already. It will be difficult to leave the nurses as they seem like family to me now. The nurses say, "It's okay when we know you and your family, but when you know ours, we know you've been here too long." I already know most of the staff on the rehab unit here, so it won't be like starting over when we move, but switching to a new group of friends. It won't be a secured unit, so other than his therapy sessions, he can have visitors, but will still need good periods of rest. He is doing much better with the medication changes, sleeping at night and being awake most of the day so I think he's ready for a change.

Mom Versus Therapist

—⁓—

Nov. 29, 2013

Today was a quiet day—the first day with only one visitor, Father Popp. We had a nice talk and he said "the people keep asking me what the outcome will be—what's the prognosis?" I told him we really have no idea. The neurosurgeon said it would take two years to know how Matt will be. It's up to God's healing in answer to our many prayers.

The night with Brooke was good for both of us. We have two twin beds, and when neither of us could fall asleep, she read my mind and said "Can I come snuggle for a little bit?" About two hours later I needed to abort ship and take her bed—after getting flung at across the face several times. She then woke me up around four am saying "Can you please not snore so loud?" I snore when I'm really tired, so I do believe I woke her. The days with Brooke have more spirit, but require a bit more patience on my part. She wants Matt to play basketball all day long and to proudly show each nurse or therapist what he can do. She continually says, "Squeeze my hand if you love me a whole bunch." Matt doesn't get much of a break unless we leave the room, but I'm sure between the two of us, he knows he's very loved. Brooke still has questions such as "Is Matt's heart still beating? Will he be home for Christmas? If not, will you come home for Christmas?" I told her I would, and if Matt isn't home by then, maybe he'll be able to come home for the day. I'm sure we could lift a wheelchair up three steps if needed, or Bill would carry him.

Matthew seemed a bit down in the dumps today and had tears several times. It's as if he understands too much and is sick of everyone asking for a "thumbs up," to snap his fingers, wave, or play with his basketball—I can just imagine him thinking, "Okay Mom, you know I'm smarter than this." Dr. Anderson came in and said Matt will move to rehab on Monday now because they have a patient discharging tomorrow and he'll have as much therapy in this room as in rehab over the weekend. Dr. Anderson also ordered Matt's trach to be changed to a fenistrated trach without the cuff, allowing him to have some air go through his mouth and nose. He will be able to cover the trach hole with his finger and talk too. I cannot wait to hear his voice–it's been four weeks today.

Matt did something new today–straightening his left arm with his right hand, wanting to stretch them both. The therapist in me is ecstatic because he's attending to his left side. I gave him his Xbox controller today and it broke my "Mom" heart to see him holding onto it with his right hand and trying to figure out why it wasn't working with both hands.

Matthew was able to sit on the edge of the bed for fifteen minutes with his PT, Bill and I. He continues to require less assistance for balance. The PT said, "It's so nice to have another therapist to work with, we can do so much more." When Matt was up in the Biodyne chair today, he was able to keep his feet on the foot board much better (the stretch and weight bearing through his feet and ankles in the tilt table yesterday made a huge difference with his ankle range of motion). I placed a transfer belt around his shins padded with a towel to keep him from kicking his legs out and rubbing his ankles on the board. I struggle as the therapist in me knows this is a good thing to do, yet the Mom in me wants to let him put his feet up comfortably using the sofa chair as a footrest. I caved and let him put his feet up after about forty-five minutes. As I sit here in Matt's room, he's crossing his ankles, a typical position at home sitting on the sofa or the floor. I think I should go correct his positioning to avoid tight hip adductor muscles, but the Mom in me says "Oh heck, leave him alone, it's one thing he can do by himself now." I helped Matt change shirts today lying down in bed. When I helped him to put on his left sleeve, before I knew it, he had put his right arm in and then began to push up his right sleeve with his left hand. I was so excited–both the therapist and Mom in me:)

I bought a book at the Book Fair here at the hospital a couple weeks ago. It's called "This Too Shall Pass" and is about getting through tough times. I found a saying in this book I wanted to share tonight.

It is difficult in troubling times to imagine that any good can come from deep suffering. We are so caught up in our negative state that we cannot comprehend the idea of a silver lining. But some of life's greatest challenges lead to life's greatest lessons, lessons that bring about wisdom, maturity, and a newfound faith that did not exist before. Just as a lump of coal is transformed into a beautiful sparkling diamond only by submitting it to tremendous outer pressures, a life can be transformed into a joyful experience only by submitting it to opportunities for growth disguised as obstacles and challenges.

How's that to think about? It confirms that something very extraordinary will become of Matt's life by having experienced this. Definitely the wisdom and newfound faith is in full-gear for our families as for many people who have followed Matt's story. We surely have joyful experiences every day that we wouldn't have appreciated before, and definitely have faced the obstacles and challenges. I continue to pray for Matt's vision, left arm/hand function, for him to begin talking, to no longer need the trach, and for that smile I've been waiting for. That would be my Christmas wish list for the next century. Amazingly, this is the first year I can remember my Christmas list not containing any materialistic items.

New hand gestures

—⁓—

Nov 30, 2013

Matthew is coughing much less and I'm hopeful that he'll soon not need the trach over the next couple of weeks. Matt was able to go to the family lounge in the Biodyne chair today. It was fun to get him out of his room for a change of scenery for about a half hour. God's healing for Matt never ceases to amaze me. He was able to do hand signs of "peace," "okay," "thumbs up, and "high 5" all consecutively without hesitation. I've been so happy, near tears each time he has shown this to us. Matt was more relaxed in the tilt table today, even doing his new signs in standing. The nurse said she was adjusting his pillow and asked him if it okay, and he clenched his hand closed, she adjusted his pillow again with the same response, and after the third adjustment, he quickly gave her a "thumbs up." She said "He just knows so much."

Brooke stayed another night with me, waking me up a couple of times again, saying, "Do you have to snore your head off?" but asked to stay again, so it couldn't have been so bad. She was with Matt when I was in the lounge with my parents today, coming in and every few minutes to tell us Matt's heart rate. It was a bit high, so we went to check on him, and here Brooke was taking pictures of Matt with our camera in the room. She said, "Look at this picture with the thumbs up he gave me." Sure enough, Matt had been humoring her with proof on the camera. He doesn't get a break from the love of his four sisters, and as usual, Matt was a good sport.

Matt is moving his legs more today too, lifting his legs and bending and straightening his right knee throughout the day. He has been more awake all day with his eyes open.

Several times, when I ask him a question, he points to his trach, so I remind him that soon he'll be able to talk. Matthew's nurse lets Brooke crawl up on the bed and help move his right leg over to get on/off the Biodyne chair. She is SO committed to this, saying "When is Matt getting into the chair? You know I get the leg." She gave him his drum and drumstick and asked him to hit the drum, saying "All I want for Christmas is for you to hit it Matt." She's grown up well beyond her 7 years in the past month.

Bill just brought the cards from the mail at home and it's amazing to me how the cards still continue. I did tear up when he received a card from the ladies at the Pierz library. Whenever Matt had any extra time, it would be his place of choice. He was as content with a reference book, a magazine, or a book. When we went to mid-semester conferences about a year ago, what really touched me was how all the staff told us how much they enjoyed Matt–from the library staff, counselors, teachers he didn't even have that semester, etc. His grades were so-so, as he would always start out the semester with lower grades, not turning in assignments he had completed, and then say "I'll get my grade up, don't worry." True to his word, he'd ace the final and make the honor roll every semester. Upon leaving that night; however, I realized grades were important, but the kind of person Matt meant even more and I was so proud of him. This year was the first year Bill and I didn't have to nag him about grades or assignments because he was committed to his college courses and was hoping for a scholarship.

PT plans to try standing Matt at the bedside today and I'm so excited I can hardly wait. Tomorrow he moves to inpatient rehab and I know we'll see leaps and bounds there too. He'll have a tough time psychologically as he realizes what he cannot physically or cognitively do initially. I tell Matt we love him and he's getting better every day, several times each day and I know he understands this completely. With God's love and healing, we will get through this, one day at a time.

Matt's Hope to be Home for Christmas

—◊◊—

Dec. 1, 2013

I had to write to share Matt's evening. He had PT this afternoon and with two PT's, Bill, and myself standing on the bed to help with his head support, he stood up without a lot of help as he has been bending and straightening his right knee all day in preparation. Matt tolerated standing for about five minutes! I've never been happier in my life. The nurse and respiratory therapist were so happy they were crying. She told me, "I even snorted." How cool is that? Mike, the PT, said "Should we try walking?" and although the rest of us were encouraged by his enthusiasm, we looked at him like "Are you crazy?" Instead, we worked on side stepping some and by the time we were finished Matt's heart rate was in the 160's. He was exhausted, but it was wonderful.

Matt got his trach changed to the fenestrated trach tonight without any difficulty—the nurses said he even gave them a "thumbs up" when they were finished. He hasn't attempted to talk yet, even though he should be able to make some sound. I encouraged him several times to no avail, then simply told him "maybe tomorrow" as I can't have everything in one day.

It reminds me of when Matthew was little and Bill and I were waiting for him to talk. He was about two and a half years old and said very few words, much to Grandma's dismay. I was working at a subacute nursing home and told my elderly patient about this. She told me about her son who wouldn't talk, even at the age of four or five. She said, years ago you didn't take your child to the doctor for not talking, only if they were sick, but finally she did as she was very concerned. Her doctor asked how her son communicated his needs

105

and she said, "Oh he points and makes an 'Aah' sound." The doctor said not to give him anything he wanted until he attempted to verbalize. She went home and he pointed at the bread on the counter and said "Aah". She said, "I don't know what you want, you have to tell me" even though she knew exactly what he wanted. His first words spoken were: "I want a peanut butter and jelly sandwich." Bill and I have joked about this for many years whenever any of the kids weren't talking. Bill would look at me and say "I want a peanut butter and jelly sandwich." I have a feeling Matthew will be like this when he talks again. I never thought I'd be waiting for him to talk again, but it will be extra special when he does.

Tonight Father Popp visited us again. I had Matt show him, "peace," "ok," "thumbs up," a wave, and even the hand gesture for "I love you" for the first time. Fr. Popp was astonished and I of course was jubilant. I told Fr. Popp in conversation not directed at Matt that Brooke tried to get him to hit the drum today and said it's all she wants for Christmas. Fr. Popp said, "Well, hopefully by Christmas, he'll be doing that" to which I replied "I'm hoping by Christmas he'll be home, cross your fingers." Matt raised his right hand and crossed his index and middle fingers! He was listening to our conversation and definitely heard everything and wanted me to know he was crossing his fingers to be home too. Needless to say I am very teary now, and every time I think of it. Even if he can be home for the day, I'll be thankful, but at the rate we're going, nothing is impossible with God.

I know God is hearing our prayers. The past few nights I wake up between two and three am several times to find myself praying the Our Father without being fully awake. Prayer is so powerful. Even the kids have changed, as we've never prayed out loud at a restaurant before, and now we do without a care in the world if anyone notices or comments. It feels great.

Being on the "Other Side"

—ɯ—

Dec 2, 2013

I have worked on the inpatient rehab unit on-call and then causal two Saturdays a month since 1999. I kept thinking I should quit, but I loved my therapy days of neurological patients and enjoyed seeing the awesome therapists I work with here at the hospital too. I remember Laura asking if I had to work Saturdays a couple years ago and I told her "no, but we might not go on vacation as often, or to Disney World again as soon if I quit" and her response was "Can you work Sundays too?" Absolutely not! Bill has every Saturday and Sunday off so is home with the kids and is better at getting them to clean than I am, but often they sleep until noon or busy with sports practices.

As we moved to inpatient rehab today and I think of all the cards and support I've received from the therapy and medical staff here at the hospital (in addition to Country Manor,) I know why I kept working here—it was all part of God's plan. I would often see family members staying with patients, or wearing the Gorecki House badge that I now wear. I now can appreciate to the fullest extent how it was for all these families after a life-changing event. I never pretended to say "I know just how you feel" to any patient and would tell them I had no idea how they felt. I would offer encouragement based on years of experience working with patients and provide new ideas for how to make things easier (for dressing, adaptive equipment, homemaking tasks, visual adaptations, etc.) Maybe part of the good that will come out of this tragedy, is that I will have more patience and understanding for even the most difficult family member. I know how difficult it is for families not to "over help" as the Mom in me doesn't want Matt to struggle. I recall countless times stopping a family member and asking them to give the patient a chance so he or she was one step closer to home.

Matt only had PT today with Bill and I helping to stand him bedside and even take a couple steps with help, bringing the bed behind. We trialed the Miami neck collar to give Matt head support as it's impossible to reach and hold his head as he walks. I think Bill has a new appreciation for the therapy world too. He was a bit nervous as the collar was covering his trach and he didn't think Matt was breathing. I loosened it and we continued, but Matt was so exhausted afterwards he took about an hour nap.

I've been asking Matt to try to talk with his new trach, only to find out from Dr. Anderson that they put in the wrong one and this one still has a cuff which prevents any air from going in/out of his mouth and nose. Now I feel like an idiot for asking Matt to talk and telling him "we'll try again tomorrow" as he kept pointing to the trach–probably thinking "yeah right, would if I could." Dr. Anderson plans to change the trach again tomorrow to the correct one.

Matt's new room in rehab is awesome. It's big enough for the school poster, all his pictures, accessories, and has room to walk around the bed, even with the extender making it a 9 foot bed. It has a great view of the river and when I asked Matt if he wanted to go out of the room, he definitely didn't. I was trying to find a channel on the TV he would like and after seeing he was definitely looking at the TV, I gave him the remote and showed him with his thumb where to press. He changed the channel several times, never officially "selecting" a show, but it was very heart-warming to see him doing this. He has helped me out with the remote at home so many times. One night we were watching a movie in Swedish, all closed caption, and Matt comes down and says, "Did you want to watch it in English?" Really? Like we even knew it was an option? Within seconds, Matthew had it changed to English.

Matt continues to listen to everything he hears. I told Bill this morning about the nurse and PT thinking basketball shoes would be helpful for ankle support. Before the accident, Matt had said he needed new ones as his were getting too small. I looked over and Matt was giving us the "thumbs up." Bill, being Bill of course, says, "What's that Matt, you want a new pair of dancing shoes?" Matt immediately dropped to a "thumbs down" position.

It's like he's floating below the surface of ice on a lake, trying to find that open hole to escape, or waiting for the sun to melt it. He's so close to the surface.

Tomorrow Matt will be evaluated by inpatient PT/OT/ST and get into a "real" wheelchair versus the Biodyne chair. I told Dr. Anderson about Matt crossing his fingers to be home by Christmas and he thought it was a bit too soon, but we'll see. I asked about a day pass; however, it will depend on our insurance coverage if he's gone for part of a day. Dr. Anderson said, "You can bring things in and celebrate in the family lounge"—not my goal for Christmas, but one day at a time. I've been thinking about our bathing set up, the stairs to get in, Matt's room being on the lower level and having a smaller doorway in the upstairs bedroom that Kami and Brooke have. I've also been thinking about whether we would need to add onto the house if Matt's does come home in a wheelchair, and then I TELL MYSELF TO STOP, STOP, STOP. It's too early for any of these thoughts and I truly believe Matt will come home walking without a wheelchair at the rate we are going. I need to take a step back and put it all in God's hands and know it'll be ok and we can figure out any physical barriers we need to. It'll all work out—we have had so many signs of this already.

Matt with Ella

Rehab

—〜〜—

Dec. 3, 2013

I was up at two am until four-thirty am this morning, almost calling the hospital to see how Matt was, but knew they had my number if needed. I came into Matt's room and saw blood around his trach and the dome that covers it. The nurse said "Oh, Matt pulled out his trach last night." Immediately I thought "Why did I leave him alone his first night in a new room?" After calming down, I knew as fast as Matt is with his right hand, he could have done this even if I had been in the room. Dr. Anderson was going to change his trach today, however due to swelling that may have occurred with Matt pulling out his trach with the cuff inflated, he decided to wait another day. Matt did trial the trach closed today with speech therapy for two minute intervals, and Matt's oxygen saturation stayed good; however, he was anxious, as anyone would be of course, breathing quickly. He also tried swallowing flavored ice and a couple of ice chips, but this was a bit delayed—possibly trying to savor a taste in his mouth after so long. Matt did follow five commands for her such as touching his shoulder, taking off his glasses, waving, etc., much to her surprise as she said, "You are so in there."

In OT, Matt got a wrist support for his right hand as he keeps his wrist flexed/bent most of the day and I've been worried about this. His OT is very patient with him as she worked on exercising his left arm and getting him dressed. I've known her for years and know Matt will do wonderful with her.

In PT Matt got in a real wheelchair rather than the Biodyne chair. It took him minutes to adapt his chair height and cut foam for a lateral support to keep his left knee and hip positioned correctly. Matt transferred from his bed and the mat in therapy with a ceiling lift today versus being slid over lying down. He was able to sit on the mat with only his PT helping him. What a difference from three or four of us on the edge of the bed in ICU. Matt had a mirror in front of him and even held his head up without support for a few seconds. It's amazing how everything is such a challenge, and at the same time a gift–it's difficult to put into words.

Matt was pretty restless tonight when two of his friends arrived with the poetry book they put together as a group project in comp class. I left to give them "guy time" and my heart melted seeing them read him the book and talking as if they were anywhere but the hospital, and as though Matt were just as before. I continue to tell everyone that Matt understands everything and is listening. By the time they left, Matt had relaxed and fallen asleep. Matthew has therapy three times a day for forty-five minutes each, so is finished by one thirty or two pm. The afternoon and evening get a bit long, so the company was good for him. We did bring him to the family lounge for a while too. Matt checked out the fish tank and had Ella the therapy dog visit with Matt even petting her today. It's amazing how the volunteers and the prayer team all are so supportive, ecstatic with Matt's progress and continue to pray for him every day.

Matt's youth group leader texted me about a dream she had last night, where she asked Matt if he was ok, and he said "Of course I am ok. Did you ever doubt me?" It made me think I too should not doubt Matt's capabilities or God's healing power. This brought her and myself peace. I've had two dreams about Matt so far–one he was in another accident, and in the other he was running and happy. Maybe tomorrow I'll wake up completely at peace too.

My mom brought me a booklet from church today that had a reading she thought was as if God was talking to our family. I wanted to share this with you.

Believe he is a good God. Trust that he will take care of you. Surrender your needs and the needs of your loved ones to him. Know that when you say this prayer, he has already responded. Be sure to remember his response may not look exactly like the response you're looking for. Neither will it always come according to the exact timing that you expect. But IT WILL COME, and that's what you need to base your faith on. Simply proclaim, Lord, I know you have heard my prayer. I know you love me. I know you love the person I am praying for. Now I'm leaving it in your hands. I trust you will do what you know is best for all of us.

It also said you will know the Lord is working when you have a growing sense of peace as you continue to pray–an inner confidence that God is in control of the situation. Keep declaring your faith and watch to see how God's marvels unfold.

The doctor who first took care of Matt, went to New York recently—to the top of the Empire State building. He said "I was as high as I could get, and it was there I said a prayer for Matt." Isn't that amazing? It brings tears to my eyes that he continues to pray for Matt–even with all he knows medically, he also knows it takes God's healing for Matt's future. This totally reaffirms my faith again and again. Keep the faith in God and Matt.

Surprise

—⚬—

Dec 5, 2013

I went to get my hair cut and colored yesterday morning as my sister made an appointment and then texted me to tell me what day it was and to remind me to go. It was a two hour appointment and when I got back to see Matt, I noticed he had a bandage where his trach used to be. They got rid of it versus changing to a new one. I was SO happy. I would have done a cartwheel if I physically could. Matt wasn't able to talk yet, but would moan some. When coughing, his bandage still goes in/out, so I was told I could put light pressure over it to make him more comfortable. His oxygen saturations have been great on room air even without the trach or any oxygen. This was such a big step for Matt. Once the trach was removed his anxiety decreased about two hundred percent and his respirations by fifty percent. What a huge gift for all of us. Now I can sleep better knowing he won't be trying to pull out his trach or snap the humidity dome on his neck. I did catch him attempting to pull on his peg tube, but I can't have everything I want in a day (or he'd be home and back on the court already.)

Yesterday in OT Matt worked on grooming and putting on his shirt. He was in the wheelchair, and before too long he was arching and sliding forward on the seat with his legs straight out. It was impossible to keep him in the wheelchair as well as to work on another task. When Matt was up later afternoon, we had the same problem, even with a wedge cushion in the wheelchair. It was wonderful to have friends visit who helped me reposition him multiple times.

Today, he worked on brushing his teeth and washing his face in OT and gosh–he sure doesn't want to bend his elbow to wash his face. It's hard to watch, but I know it wasn't his top priority at home either–so I will continue to pick my battles and so will his occupational therapist I'm afraid.

In PT Matthew worked on sitting balance and was much better at following one step commands. I think it was bonding time with his PT as they practiced hand gestures and Matt learned a few new ones. Today, Matt used the standing frame in PT to work on weight bearing, his ankle range of motion, and standing balance. His PT needed to stand on a foot stool to help with his head control. He made several adaptations to Matt's wheelchair to help him from sliding forward and to give him a higher head support. I struggle with helping, versus staying out of the way, never quite sure which he'd prefer.

In Speech, Matt trialed flavored ice and ice chips, doing well with this, but didn't do so good with pudding–which surprised me as it's thicker. They tried to have Matt make sounds or verbalize, but not YET. It'll come in time though I'm reassured. Today, Matt worked on swallowing again and verbalizing, and due to the way he holds his head and the way his tongue is positioned, Matt appears to be snoring even when he's wide awake, until his head is repositioned. The speech therapist explained it as when someone changes their position in bed, or if they are more relaxed after having a few beers, one will tend to snore, or snore louder due to the positioning of their tongue and air flow through the mouth and nose. I told her with Bill, one good elbow and a flip usually fixes his louder snoring, so I understood exactly.

She also trialed a communication board and had Matt try to copy pictures. He did ok with a circle which was encouraging, but the other symbols were tougher as he fatigues quickly and the motor planning needed takes a lot of effort. He wasn't as consistent with the cards of yes and no as he is with thumbs up and thumbs down, but we'll practice again tomorrow I'm sure.

Today when Matt was up in the wheelchair I told him he was doing such a good job and soon I was going to get my hug. Matt took his hand off the armrest of the wheelchair and put it around me—and yes I cried tears of happiness again. It seems to be 50/50 lately with tears of sadness versus happiness, but that's a huge improvement.

Last night, I talked to the girls on the phone and got a glimpse that all wasn't "good" for Laura and Kami as they tend to tell me. I've thought of them all day and continue to remind myself that "this is temporary" and we will be together as a family when the time is right. It's tough for both of them as their friends don't know what to say, say nothing about Matt and Abby at all, or have quit talking to them—more than likely because they aren't the "happy friend" they used to be. Kami was told by a classmate "At least my family isn't so terrible that they have to go whining to other people" and one of Laura's friends literally told her that she "was jealous of all the attention she is getting." If Laura could take back the accident and never be noticed again, she would do this in a heartbeat. Sometimes, without meaning to, kids say things that cause so much pain. Thankfully, the principals at both schools are very supportive and won't allow other students to make things more difficult for Laura and Kami at this time.

Laura and Kami are having a tough time playing basketball, feeling so guilty because Matt isn't playing. Kami still goes to practice when she's not at the hospital or piano lessons, and Laura has gone to basketball off and on, depending on how much she "can take on" in a day. She then feels bad not going and letting the team down, or thinking they are mad at her. Both are worried about baking and decorating for Christmas too. It seems nothing is easy for them these days, but I continue to tell them "It'll get better" to which of course they agree, but I'm not sure if it's heartfelt. I know emotionally it's more difficult for them than Matt and Abby at this time.

Overall, Matt has made huge gains in just four days in rehab. His PT wants to look at Botox for his tight heel cords/calf muscles and baclofen for his strong extensor tone to allow Matt to be able to strengthen and use his muscles functionally versus "fighting" the tone. Everyone wants what is best for him and it'll just take time to put all the pieces of the puzzle together as he recovers with God giving us the direction.

It seems the minute I'm down, or excited about something new Matt has done, my coworkers from therapy here at the hospital and/or Country Manor stop in to visit on a break, friends/family and even people I don't know have sent cards, posted, texted me, etc., and someone is always there for me. It is so amazingly overwhelming that I feel all these people are a gift to us, and certainly are keeping me strong (versus institutionalized)—just kidding, but not completely, so thank you.

Emotions Galore

—∞—

Dec 6, 2013

As I was getting ready this morning, I was teary thinking of how everyone has been so kind and overwhelmingly wonderful to our family—so much that I can't put it into words. Let me give you some examples: I went to the bathroom yesterday afternoon and when I came back, Matt had a card in his hand. Bill said, "Okay Matt, now you can give it to Mom" and he released the card immediately. It was a card from Kristy (one of his physical therapists) and from Matt. It had a gift certificate for a massage with a note to use this to relieve some stress, and twenty dollars too with Kristy saying she was praying that Matt would be home by Christmas and she'd like to pay for the gas for the trip. How can you just not cry? We went to dinner last night and a nurse I used to work with at Country Manor came over teary-eyed, saying she just found out about the accident and thinks of us all the time and prays for Matt often, even when she's on her walks. We had just done a health fair together and talked about our sons going off to college and how much we were going to miss them. One of the RN's I worked with on the rehab unit came in and asked how I was doing and gave me a card. I often receive a hug from one of Matt's therapist's (my friends and co-workers) before and/or after Matt's therapy session—all day long I have angels helping me to stay strong and positive and to feel loved.

As I was walking over from the Gorecki House this morning, I said a prayer that Matt would have a good day and give me a sign that he's getting better—just a word—anything. When I got to Matt's room, the nurse said "Matt was calling for you last night, he said 'Mom, Momma' and they heard him at the desk." My prayers were answered. I immediately felt sad I wasn't here when he was calling for me, but also was so happy he actually said a word. It was going to be a great day.

In OT Matt didn't resist washing his face today, but allowed hand over hand assistance. He helped to brush his teeth and even put his deodorant in his left hand, opening and closing his fingers to put it under his right arm. Matt was able to assist with his left arm during range of motion over his head, and also rolled his basketball on his thighs with both hands. His left arm tightness was better today–I immediately knew it was from all the prayers being said for his left arm and leg.

In PT Matt was able to sit on the mat with the help of just one person, demonstrating increased trunk and head control, even letting go of the mat with his right hand to reach for items and to put his faithful basketball in the hoop. That will motivate him any time for sure. Matt propelled his wheelchair short distances in the clinic with his right hand, but couldn't coordinate to use his right hand and foot together. He didn't push and arch to slide out of the wheelchair though and that's a huge step.

In Speech, Matthew was able to bring the spoon up to his mouth with just a little bit of assistance to raise his shoulder. He opened his mouth and put his lips on the spoon and took it out again. This was so exciting for him to be able to do this. He was given two cards of answers to questions and was able to pick the correct answers three out of four times. The speech therapist said "Every time I see him, he's making more progress."

Matthew tends to pick the times he wants to open his eyes. When the TV is on, his eyes are more open than ever. Today, Rick Grammond (the radio announcer for the Pierz sports games) came to visit and read Matt a Sport's Illustrated magazine, and he was very focused and listening to every word. Rick came to update Matt on the Pioneer sports and to set up the computer for tonight's boys basketball game for Matt and I to listen to. How nice is that? The St. Cloud Times called today too and want to do a story about Matt and Abby before Christmas, wanting to share our story and add a photo if I agreed.

Matt is getting his first shower tonight in a wheelchair and I'm sure he'll be exhausted afterwards, but happy to listen to the boys basketball game

Thought I'd share a story again about Matt and his 2087 international texts. Last summer Matt's phone was suspended due to charges. This was really odd as everyone else's phone in our family worked and we were all on the same plan. I called AT & T, and found out Matthew had 2087 international texts to Canada at twenty-five cents each. I found this funny as I knew some day we'd laugh about it, and at least he wasn't doing drugs, suicidal, etc. Bill on the other hand was very upset initially as the representative said "Uh-oh, I hear Dad in the background. Tell him to give Matt a five second head start." Bill said "I can't believe you are laughing" and I couldn't explain it other than "if that's the worst thing Matt does, someday we'll laugh about it." By the completion of the phone call, he changed our fee from over five hundred dollars to a fifty dollar one time courtesy fee. Whew.! Matt kept alternating between "I'm sorry Mom, or sorry Dad" and I knew how grateful he was that I found this humorous instead of being angry. By the time the phone call was finished, Bill wasn't upset any more either.

Brooke has been asking to add something to my journal from her so here it is: "I hope Matt gets better and gets out of the hospital because I LOVE Matt." I have to say there are a lot of people who would definitely agree with her.

My REAL hug

—ⅶ—

Dec. 7, 2013

They were unable to give Matt a shower last night, but had it finished before I arrived this morning. He didn't push and slide out of the shower chair, but totally relaxed and gave the nurses a "thumbs up." She told him to put his thumb down if he didn't like anything or was uncomfortable, and he kept it up the entire time.

In OT, Matt was up in the wheelchair the entire time and even went into the bathroom to the sink to brush his teeth. He still needs help with brushing his teeth, combing his hair, and getting his shirt on, but tries to help with each step of the task. He even took his glasses off himself today.

In PT, Matt was able to sit on the mat with only his PT helping; however, tends to sit slumped on his tailbone. We trialed a higher tray table to see if he'd rest his elbows on it and lean forward from his hips, but he decided to use the leverage to stand at a diagonal angle. I then asked Matt to come forward and give me a hug. We put his hands on my shoulders, then he reached his right arm completely around me to the opposite shoulder with his cheek next to mine for a good minute. My friend took pictures and it was one of my very best moments ever. I think everyone in the room was teary.

In Speech, Matt only took a few bites of flavored ice today. He was given pictures for yes/no responses of different objects and needed to give a "thumbs up" or down if what she labeled was correct. He was able to complete this with one hundred percent accuracy with pictures on the iPad; however, with regular picture cards after a while didn't give the right answer—possibly due to being tired, or bored. Part of me thinks he may be having fun tricking us at times—especially when he coughs and scares everyone who is near him in the room.

The nurse said Matt said "Mom" again today, and so did his OT when I went to get a basin for him to spit in after brushing his teeth. He will not say it to me, or with me in the room. It's like a challenge for him to have me wait—but I can wait. I'm so excited for him to actually start talking again like all those trips home from basketball games for years. Brooke stayed with me last night and kept busy picking up the balls Matt puts in the hoop he has next to his bed from therapy. We finally got smart and placed it so the balls would land on the bed versus crawling under the bed constantly. She says, "That's just the way it is with Matt." She crawled into bed with him and snuggled, with Matt putting his arm around her. I took a picture—it was so special.

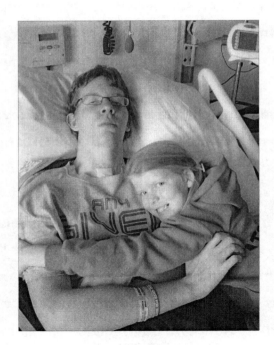

Matt and Brooke snuggling

I moved out of the Gorecki House today which was a big step for me, but I think it's time. I will still come to the hospital every day/evening but it's time to begin making meals for the girls again and to talk to them in person every day. They went to get a Christmas tree today with Bill and plan to put up the decorations this weekend and I know it's so important to give them some "normalcy" even though I really don't care if we have anything up this year. There will be many more family Christmas gatherings in the future, this is just one—next year will be completely different.

The Lollipop

—ɯɯ—

Dec. 8, 2013

Yesterday, as I left Gorecki House, an elderly man asked me if "my person" was leaving the hospital since I was packing up. I told him "No, we'd be here for a while, but it was time to go home." He asked what happened, told me his name, and gave me a big hug. He had said the person he was at the Gorecki House for was also in a car accident. As I went to put my room badge in the drop box, another lady who was with him, followed me and said in an angry, accusing voice; "You should be thankful. The person we had in the intensive care died on Monday and we had his memorial yesterday." I told her I was so very thankful the kids were ok, but she was so grief-stricken and upset, I don't think she listened or cared. I thought about this encounter all day yesterday and today. I know there are a lot of people suffering or have someone who died, which is tough especially around the holidays. I pray for this lady at the Gorecki House, and their loved ones hoping they are being shown as much kindness and understanding as we have.

One of Bill's coworkers and his wife visited this morning with a "Hi" from the head basketball coach at St. John's University for Matt (from the game last evening as Matt and Bill had toured St. John's and Matt has gone to summer basketball camps there.) He was teary-eyed watching Matt participate in speech and ended the visit with "Get better soon Matt, I don't know how much more my knees can take." At first I thought it was standing in the room that made his knees sore, then I realized he was praying that intently for Matthew. It made me realize it's been a long time since I've knelt to pray other than in church. I will begin to do so.

Matt had showered again before I arrived this morning. He had OT and was able to trial a long-handled comb and work on getting his shirt on again. Matt also tried electrical stimulation to extend his left wrist and open his fingers. He was able to extend his wrist and thumb with the e-stim, but not his fingers—yet. Matt did help me move his left shoulder when lying in bed this morning and straightened his elbow several times. He is trying so hard and it'll just take time and lots of therapy.

Yesterday a PT from Country Manor where I work, stopped in with a chocolate bar for me and two lollipops, for Brooke "or whoever." He said "Matt probably can't have one" and I thought of course not. Last night as I was looking at the lollipop, I thought about Matt working on sticking his tongue out for speech–to help with swallowing, breathing, and speech, and thought I'd try to get him to do so by trying the cherry lollipop. Matt really liked it. I figured flavored ice was runny when it melted, and this was flavored raspberry, so why not try? We did get caught by the nurse, but not scolded. Today in speech, I told her about the lollipop and she thought this was a great idea and tried this again with Matt who opened his mouth wider than normal. The speech therapist took it away to work on other cards and words. Matt began moaning and we both agreed he was mad about having the lollipop taken away–but at least we were able to work on vocalization. Matt worked on identifying our family member's names on cards and did fairly well and also identifying objects on iPad with sixty-seven percent accuracy. I'm so thankful he is able to identify words and pictures as this was an area of the brain that was affected.

In PT we again worked on sitting balance and head control. Matt hardly needed any help with head control today the majority of the session. We again had him come forward to work on good posture without a curved low back (lumbar flexion.) When I had Matt put his arms on my shoulders with help, he began giving me a massage. Okay, I think this was more emotional than the hug. Matt would always come downstairs after having a snack at night or checking the fantasy football results, etc., and would come behind me as I sat on the sofa, massage my neck/shoulder's for about a minute and often gave me a kiss on the cheek goodnight. I was not expecting this at all today–another gift.

Matt is moving more, removing pillows I've carefully placed, or taking his shoes off three times after I've put them on for therapy. I think back to when I just hoped he could move his toes and I'm so happy he is able to these things–even if it's not my plan at the time. He even propelled his wheelchair a short distance in the clinic with a bit of encouragement on Friday. It's all falling into place and rather than be upset with the change in seasons as I've been dreading for the past month, for some reason the fresh snow gives me hope.

First Steps

—☡—

Dec 9, 2013

Matthew had a good day today. In OT, he was able to brush his teeth more, turning the toothbrush several times without cues. He trialed e-stim again and was able to have full left wrist extension, thumb and the first joints of all his fingers (MCP extension for those of you in the medical field) better than yesterday, and he tolerated it well. In PT, Matt transferred in/out of the wheelchair, to standing, and on/off the mat in the clinic with only his PT helping. He needed help initially to get his head up when standing in the parallel bars, but then was able to keep his head up without help and to put weight through both hands on the bar for support, standing for about a minute. I helped him move his feet forward, two steps with each foot and he was able to move his right hand on the bar–which was huge, as he wasn't so dependent on his strong right arm or fearful to do so. I WAS SO HAPPY—AGAIN.

Matt isn't talking or swallowing yet, but does try to vocalize sounds, so it's just a matter of time. I read the speech therapist's note tonight and it said "he has overt signs and is at high risk for aspiration." My heart sank. It said he needed five to six swallows per bite of flavored ice and isn't using his tongue effectively. He has a difficult time swallowing his saliva. I need to remember less than a week ago he had a trach and was coughing much more than now. I'm thankful that his lungs are clear now, so just need to keep the faith that God will continue to heal him. Matt did answer questions of yes/no with one hundred percent accuracy and is working on identifying pictures and their function. I am very thankful he is understanding so much, his eyes are evenly opened now and he has begun to track visually much better to the left and right.

Matt started an antibiotic for a urinary tract infection today. He gets a heart medication, anti-seizure medication, a neuro-stimulator medication, Ritalin for alertness, and Tylenol or morphine for pain as needed. He's never taken more than multivitamins (preferably gummy ones) before, but I also know this is temporary and soon he'll decrease the meds he takes.

Matt continues to play basketball with the hoop by his bed and even tried to put a small ball in his left hand today. Tonight he tried to open his left hand with his right hand and couldn't, but I'm sure the e-stim and prayers will make this happen in time.

I took out my *This Too Shall Pass* book this morning with a heavy heart and opened it to a random page that lifted my spirits immediately, so thought I'd share it today.

Sometimes through our gloom, a gleam of faith comes flashing through the mind, and although it shortly fades away, it leaves a brighter world behind, fairer by that remembered ray. To believe in something enough that it cannot help but manifest is to know the power of faith. Just to imagine is not enough. You must back your imaginings with every ounce of courage, love, and conviction your heart can muster. That is when you will truly find faith.

I know that everyone who reads this and is praying for Matthew has faith. With so many people having faith in God's healing, Matthew will get better, finish high school, go to college, and be on the court again someday in some capacity.

Attitude and a smile

—⁓—

Dec. 11, 2013

Matthew has "copped" an attitude and it is FABULOUS. He never gave me much attitude before, often beginning to argue a word or two, and then say "Yes, Mom" as Bill repeatedly taught him. He'd say, "Mom, I know you're right, because if Dad's taught me anything, the women is always right." Seeing some spunk made me want to jump for joy proving he's thinking better and getting sick of his limitations, even though he continues to make small gains daily.

Example #1: Matt was given an alphabet board as a communication board in speech yesterday and decided to "toss it" rather than use it, per his therapist. I imagine him thinking "Really? Do you know what my IQ was at before the accident? I'll wait until I can talk to tell you what I'm thinking—and Mom reads my mind anyway."

Example #2: I was helping Matt with the remote control using his right hand. He was flipping channels, or rather holding down the channel button to go through them in warp speed, and then decided to hold the volume button until it was at level eighty. Yikes. I turned it down, and then he kept pushing the mute button versus the channel button which I could see was visually upsetting him. I'd move his thumb, or cue him to move his thumb up or down, which he did until finding the button eight. He alternated between channel eight and eighty-eight, (both static at this high volume.) When I tried to move his thumb, he pulled his hand back away from me with the remote in it, as if to say "Yeah right. You know nothing about remotes. How many times have I come to your rescue?"

Example #3 Matt's nurse moved his IV pole (stand) with his feeding next to him while he was up watching TV in the wheelchair. He apparently had his view blocked and decided to kick the stand out of his way. She said she saw it coming and was excited to see this "fight" in him. We found the MN Timberwolves game rerun and I asked Matt if this would upset him, or motivate him to get better and play again, and he immediately gave me a "thumbs up" to watch the game.

I brought in our electronic keyboard for music therapy which is recommended highly with head injured patients. I cannot tell you how proud and emotional I was to hear him "play" versus only banging on the keys. He even did scales and crossing over with his fingers. I told his psychiatrist who was in the hallway at the time, he should look at Matt. He said "Oh I will he's on my list of patients today." I said, "No, I meant now for a minute— he's playing the piano." Dr. Derr went in and when he came out, told his nurse "You have got to see this." I said to him–"Wasn't that cool?" and he replied "Way cool." The nurses hear him playing at the desk and come in to see him play and honestly, I believe he likes the performances. I remember one concert for school in which Matt switched from three different instruments in one song. Not like being 6'8" didn't already make you noticeable. He played the drums, piano and bells, reaching over a girl's shoulder to reach the bells for his cue time. I was never so proud.

Matt has had the therapy dog, Ella visit one or two times per week since the accident. I know I've mentioned this before, but yesterday was incredible. Matt went from having help to lift his shoulder to pet Ella last week, to him completely petting Ella bedside with her paws on a chair and the bed. Ella began with licking his lips and chin, which was rather entertaining for me to watch his reaction of puckered lips/startle. She then went up on her front paws fairly high as I watched Matt raise his right arm over his head–worried he was going to clobber her; however, his hand landed right on Ella's head and he began petting her like he had all day. The volunteer with Ella, as well as the Chaplain and prayer team are amazed at Matt's progress. The Chaplain said today— "I remember early on, your faith saying 'HE's IN THERE' like only a mother would know."

Matt has made progress in therapy yesterday and today. He tends to sit on his tailbone, all curved in the wheelchair, therefore Matt's therapist decided to try having Matt prone (or on his stomach) with a pillow under his stomach due to the tube. We needed three therapist's to get him in this position, weight-bearing through his elbows yesterday; however, today, after help to get into this position, he was able to hold it without assist and to bring his head up some too. This promotes being able to sit erect, improve balance, posture in standing and walking too. In speech, she believes Matt is getting more tongue control with the ability to "stick his tongue out" and now we need to work on also moving his tongue laterally too. Yesterday a high school friend came to visit. Matt waved to him and then fell asleep. He woke up with a cough and waved to him two more times. He also did a mouth-open smile for his friend for the first time. Of course, being the proud Mom, I tried to have him show this to the speech therapist, which didn't happen. He told me "Well, it's because he's trying to motor plan the smile when you ask him to do it, but when it's natural or reflexive, he can do it." Duh—that makes sense, I just didn't think about it that way. I continue to learn too.

The reporter from the *St Cloud Times* interviewed Bill and I yesterday. I have to share this because anyone who knows Bill, will think it's very funny. She asked him "How has the accident affected your life?" His response was: "There's been a little chaos and mayhem." I said "A LITTLE? REALLY, THAT'S HOW YOU WOULD SUM IT ALL UP?" Unbelievable to me, but Bill doesn't want anyone to feel sorry for us or say things are tough. I said, "Don't you mean it flipped our life completely upside down?" Guess I get the drama award during the interview, despite also not wanting any sympathy as things are getting better.

Abby is back in school over half of the day and plans to increase to a full day by the end of next week hopefully. She is much better with returning to her old self—always wanting to help everyone. Abby is going to watch the dance team in Aitkin tonight and is so excited to go—she absolutely loves her dancing. She said her bruises around her ribs have gone away and she can even do a little jump without it hurting. She wants to go back to dance practice and only do the stretches initially. It is wonderful to see her happy and looking forward to getting back to a normal routine. She still has outpatient OT/PT/ST, but only one time per week or every other week for some. Bill keeps track of her schedule and bringing her to the appointments, so I forget the exact changes in frequency.

My inspiration for the day: No matter how much we suffer or how bleak the world around us appears, the next moment is alive and pulsating with the possibility of healing and renewal. The future carries the promise of happiness restored if we hold on tight and ride out the storm. Hope is the vehicle that delivers us from the depths of despair up to the light again, where we can see ourselves and our lives from a whole new perspective. With hope in our hearts, we rise to greet that new day, stronger and wiser than before.

Prayers Answered in Warp Speed

—ᴍ—

Dec 12, 2013

Today was a huge day for Matt and me. Matthew was able to tolerate bringing his left arm over his head when sitting in the wheelchair without resisting the range of motion. He continues to increase his neck and head control, therefore needs less head support in his wheelchair. Matt was in his wheelchair for three hours this morning after having a shower, so I'd say his activity tolerance is improving tons too.

Matt walked with two physical therapists today, with AFO's (ankle/foot supports) and sliders (placed over his shoes so that his toes don't catch with walking) for approximately ten feet. Matt did try to initiate stepping with his right leg, and one time only on the left leg. I initially tried to keep his head up, but the PT said not to worry about it because he probably needs to look at his feet for visual feedback. He again worked on mat activities to increase his trunk control and balance. Matt was able to bridge (lift his bottom off the mat) several times with increased ease and movement today—with his therapist saying "It's better." He began doing this even before asked at times—it's like he had extra drive today. Matt chose chocolate pudding today for speech therapy and didn't cough at all. Last week his speech therapist said he was aspirating into his lungs and "it probably was a bit soon to try it." What an improvement. The speech therapist had Matt read a word and match it to an object such as a plate or whistle and he did this correctly every time. He asked Matt to put up his fingers on his right hand to answer simple math problems such as 1+4, 1 + 2, and 4-3, and he immediately answered without any hesitation. I don't have to tell you I was teary-eyed and thanked God for another gift.

Let me further explain the cranial nerve changes. Matt was "wrinkling" his nose last night, mostly on the right side and I wasn't sure why—not an itch as he can reach, possibly a muscle twitch, or Bill's idea that someone stunk. Anyway, today he was able to do this with both sides of his nose. The right was more predominant, but he did do both. Every time I told someone he was doing this, he immediately began to do so again—it was so entertaining and good therapy so I decided to just go with it. Also, for the first time ever, Matt was able to raise his eyebrows—both of them. Matt has been scratching his face, wiping his mouth, and taking his glasses off, but today he did another thing, letting me know he'll be ok in time—HE BIT HIS FINGERNAILS! Anyone who has been at a basketball game knows Matt spent all his time on the bench biting his fingernails, and also when watching TV, until we looked at him. This was so normal for him to do and also works on his oral motor skills (being able to open/close his mouth, move his tongue, etc.) Matt had friends visit tonight and I was of course "asking him to perform" with his new facial movements and mentioned he soon would be able to wink, AND HE DID. I am now on cloud nine. I've never known why this cloud is more special than any other, but I'm positive it is cloud nine, and none other.

This afternoon I asked Matt if he wanted to watch TV, or listen to music and he said no to both with a thumbs down so I asked him if he wanted to play the piano, and he did. It was amazing to see the difference in just one day. Even though he's only able to play with his right hand, he was crossing his fingers over to reach keys and even did a "chord" playing two notes at the same time with his index and ring finger. It was amazing Matt had the coordination to do this, keeping his middle finger off the keys. I put on a Beach Boys CD then and gave Matt first the maraca, then the hand bells and noticed he was actually keeping the beat. I switched him to the drum stick (from a band member at school—signed by all the percussionists, which must have really inspired him) and he would hit the drum/ cymbal combination I was holding rapidly keeping the beat again—it was unbelievable. I thought about having him try to hold the drum in his left hand, but was afraid he'd hit his hand and that he wouldn't be able to see it on the lower left quadrant. In time he'll be able to do more two-handed tasks.

Matt had a couple of friends visit tonight and I just have to tell you how his improve-ments have affected his friend, Andrew. The first time he visited, he cried so hard seeing

Matt on the ventilator, and I couldn't say anything to cheer him or to have him believe that it would be ok. The next visit was "sober," a bit teary-eyed, but not a smile to be found. The next visit he smiled at Matt's improvements, but was quiet and didn't smile at all after leaving the room even with me trying to be funny—imagine that? He did visit on Thanksgiving Day and brought the basketball and poster from school and I wasn't there that day. Last time he visited with his Mom and was pretty upbeat with Matt being more alert and showing his new hand gestures. Today, I saw him coming down the hall with a smile before he even got to the room. It is something difficult for me to put into words—how Matt's improvements have had such an impact on him. What a friend!

The support continues to be tremendous. I had a visit from the parent of one of the boys Matt played AAU basketball with today. She was so wonderful telling me how her, and her son, pray for Matt every day and both of them wrote this in a card too. When teenage kids are praying for Matt it is so special. I know each prayer said by anyone is helping Matt's recovery without any doubt; however, part of the good coming out of our tragedy is teenage children turning to God with faith. I received a text from Rick Grammond, the announcer for Pioneer sports yesterday, letting Matt know the score of the game, telling him hi, and that the entire BBE (Belgrade-Burton-Elrosa) basketball team wore green shoelaces to support Matt at the game. HOW COOL IS THAT?

I'm sure I don't need to add any more inspiration to this journal. I may be on Cloud 99999999999, if it exists, with my happiness so multiplied today.

Every Day is a Gift

—⚬—

Dec. 14, 2013

As I was driving to the hospital this morning to get to Matt's OT session at 9:15 am, I realized how much more anticipation of Matt's progress I have each day. When he was in the pediatric intensive care unit, I'd find myself stalling the beginning of another day–still with hope of an improvement, whereas now it's the joy of anticipation knowing I'll see changes every day. My faith has changed a hundred fold since Matt and Abby's accident. I now KNOW God will heal Matt every day–whether I can see the change (which I do ninety-nine percent of the time) or whether it's not visible such as improvement in his mucus/lung status, less swelling in his brain or further blood absorption. I know without a doubt healing is happening. What a gift faith is.

I thought of other things we anxiously wait for: a baby's first word or first step, walking out to the garden to see if any seeds have come up, how many apples the tree will have, our cat having kittens, getting to the top of the roller coaster at Valley Fair, waiting for that first nibble when fishing, etc. The longer we wait, the more appreciative I believe we are when an event finally happens. I believe Matt's thirty-two days in intensive care is the reason every accomplishment I see in rehab is even more awesome and appreciated. I know time heals; however, the number of people praying has also multiplied—which is the reason for the rate of his recovery.

Yesterday, Matt put his right arm and leg in his clothes without any help (he dresses his lower body lying down, able to bridge, or bring his hips off the bed, with very little help. Matt seems to be decreasing some of the tone (muscle tightness often related to brain or neurological injury) in his left arm. He is able to obtain full shoulder motion in the wheelchair and in bed now with less time needed to relax. The doctors still don't know if he needs a medication, baclofen, to decrease his "tone," but some tone is good for movement and function. It's a matter of being able to get strong enough to perform the opposite motion to prevent contractures. I'm still on the fence, we'll need to wait to see if Matt's tone or strength increases.

In PT, Matt trialed the light gait system—-a machine that helps you to stand, harnessed in for support. Matt "walked" the distance of the gym, turned around and went back two times without resting. He needed two therapists, myself, (mostly for moral support and to get in the way, but assisting his upper body and head to stay in the middle,) and another person to advance the light gait system as he walked. I'd guess Matt went approximately seventy-five to one hundred feet altogether, both slowly and with increased speed to make it an automatic, or subcortical function you don't have to learn. Today, Matt walked with his PT, myself, and Matt's uncle assisting in the parallel bars–approximately five to seven feet two times. His standing balance was better and he didn't have any salvia, even looking down the first trial. Matt held his head up for at least one to two minutes without any support at all. He advanced his right leg without any assistance, often before being asked, and advanced his right hand on the rail without any verbal cues. Matt needed a little assist to pick up his left foot, and to keep it out to the side, BUT HE'S INITIATING IT. Matt needs bilateral foot/ankle supports and slides to help his shoe slide on the floor to walk.

In speech therapy, Matt continues to surprise everyone. Yesterday he was able to look at a picture on a card, choose the word to describe it, out of two choices, without any errors. Today he did this on the iPad; however, with three choices, with seventy-five percent accuracy. He was able to identify a sentence spoken by the therapist, in writing on the iPad screen, given seven choices, with only one error in five or six trials. In other words, HE'S READING–something the neurologist said he may not be able to understand with his specific brain trauma. Go Matthew! It's difficult to know if Matt has difficulty with depth perception (knowing how far away objects are) or motor planning (moving your arm/leg, or tongue, in Matt's case, the way you want –getting the message from your brain to the correct muscle.) I believe it's motor planning versus vision and know this will get better. Matt coughed more today than yesterday on the famous flavored ice;

however, every speech therapist states he is getting better control of his tongue and swallowing–especially if it's been a few days since he or she has worked with Matt. Last night, my friend was offering a Resse's peanut butter cup to her son and you should have seen the glare Matt gave her for not sharing. She felt so bad, she didn't have one herself. This morning, I got that glare eating breakfast in Matt's room. I told him he'd be eating soon, but needs to work his tongue. Matt then worked on sticking his tongue out and side to side which he did for the first time, I know of, with his mouth open. Nothing like watching someone eat in front of you for motivation. I have a difficult time knowing if this is warranted to motive Matt or just plain cruel. Either way, it's tough love, because he's working on it.

Matt's personality is shining through. My first gift of the day was when I woke Matt up for therapy this morning, he opened his eyes and raised his eyebrows way more–and symmetrically. He is able to wrinkle his nose a lot more on the left side and definitely has that wink down. His smile is only on the right side, but often it looks like the cutest smirk ever. Matt was watching the basketball game this evening with his aunt when a nurse came in and asked how the football game was going. She said "Matt smiled and I laughed as the nurse said ('I'll blame it on being blond') he caught on right away." Matt is beginning to tell me "no" when I ask him to play the keyboard, or give a high five, etc., with a "thumbs down" or a look that says it all. Tonight, he didn't want to play his keyboard; however, when Bill asked him to play, he gave an immediate "thumbs up"–knowing better than to tell Dad "no" I guess–some things never change. My friend brought Abby to the hospital after watching the dance competition all day in Albany and she asked Matt to play "Hot Cross Buns" a beginner piano song. Matthew did, finding the right keys. We were all awestruck. He is amazing and it's fabulous what music can do. Of course, I had him drum to the Beach Boys CD and he banged his drumstick so hard, you'd think it would go right through. He hit my finger twice, and let me tell you, his right arm is strong as he drums with vigor. He also nonchalantly began twirling the drum stick around in his hand like a baton.

I fell asleep on the sofa with my feet up on a chair yesterday afternoon, and completely intentional without a doubt, I woke up to a pillow being dropped, or rather swung at my legs. Matt had taken a pillow off his bed and decided to wake me since he couldn't nap after just having his Ritalin medication for alertness. Guess that's fair as I know he was exhausted from walking and probably wished he would sleep for a little bit.

Another tremendous improvement is that Matt is letting me know when he needs to go to the bathroom for the past two days. It's such a gigantic step after a brain injury to figure this piece out, even though he would be embarrassed I included this, I felt I needed to as all your prayers are being answered. I find my prayers are about forty percent asking for specific improvements such as talking, eating, walking, left arm strength and function, and about sixty percent being prayers of "thank you." Remember to include thank you's in your prayers too. There is SO much to be thankful for.

The page I randomly opened my book to today is this: "God, give me strength to get through this day. Give me hope to arise anew tomorrow with the courage to go forth and do what needs to be done. Give me a little joy here and there to remind me that the situation is not as bad as it seems. Give me laughter when my heart is heavy. Give me understanding when my mind is filled with confusion. But most of all, give me one more day to get it right. Thank you, God."

I think this prayer was written for me. Keep the faith and prayers for Matt's full recovery. We can do it together.

Crazy Cats

—〰—

Dec. 16, 2013

Thought I'd share some memories again since it's been a while. One day Matt told me he had gone for a run (to keep in shape for basketball) and he said "Mom, it was so embarrassing. Like five of the cats followed me and ran down the highway with me. I didn't go as far as I would of, because I didn't want any cars to see me." (Also he was probably afraid some would get hit by a car.) I wish I could have witnessed this–it probably could have made *America's Funniest Home Videos.*

Another memory I've been thinking about is my time with Matt in the garden–one of my favorite things to do. We have a rule that "What's said in the garden, stays in the garden." It's amazing what the kids will tell me in the garden–I highly recommend it. One day this summer, Brooke decided to bring all six baby kittens to the garden, much to Breezy –our mother cat's dismay. She would bring two or three kittens to the garden, some would run and hide in the tomato plants, others followed Brooke in the grass, and inevitably all going separate directions. Breezy would carry one, or meow to call her kittens, and one or two would follow her part way back to the garage, and either they would run back to the garden on their own, or have assist from Brooke. Breezy was frantic, trying to keep track of all of them, meowing loudly in a frenzy. Matthew starts laughing and says "Mom, is this how you felt when we were all little?" I told him, it's how I feel every day. (Remember, anything can be said in the garden.) I felt this way when the kids were at separate hospitals, Kami and Brooke at my brother's house, and Laura staying at home–if

I could have meowed and brought them all back home I sure would have—but Breezy and I know it often doesn't work that way.

Matt continues to improve with his facial expressions, raising him eyebrows, winking or smiling at me, and what's cool is that it's spontaneous—not because I've asked him to. After six weeks of having a flat affect (not showing any facial expressions), I can't begin to tell you how seeing him smile on his own, even going through what he is, brings tears to my eyes every time. Matt is now able to stick his tongue out farther and even made circles around his mouth and licked his lips this weekend. The speech and swallowing has to be coming soon. He was able to swallow several bites of chocolate pudding yesterday and SPIT for the first time today after brushing his teeth. The therapists continually tell Matt "If you can spit, then you'll talk." I motivate him with a future of pizza, spaghetti, chips, bacon, etc.

In speech therapy, Matt was able to find specific words or sentences she asked him to choose. He has a difficult time touching the word or phrase he wants, with his right arm/hand jerking due to lack of motor control/planning. I think to myself "we should try a wrist weight"—-then I decided to just be quiet for a change. It'll happen. Matt uses a stylist to touch the correct place on the screen (which is like a pen with an eraser.) Yesterday, he began twirling it like one of his drumsticks. How funny is that? I'm thinking about getting him an iPad for Christmas, but don't think I've convinced Bill yet. Today, the speech therapist trialed the alphabet communication board again, but with a different technique, having Matt put up fingers for the row the letter is in and then again for the column. This seemed to work better, but he'll need some practice (guess it was better than him tossing it like last time.) I feel once we have him using a communication device, he'll start to talk fluently. It's like couples that finally apply for adoption and then are expecting. I just know it and I'm ok with that. Matt trialed eating applesauce and strawberry yogurt today and did wonderful. He ate about eight to ten bites each and didn't cough hardly at all, so he may soon switch to a pureed (ground food) and thickened liquids diet. I know it's not what he has in mind by any means, but it'll be an excellent start.

Today, we trialed having Matt propel his wheelchair with only his right leg. It is so difficult to watch him learn to get around in a wheelchair, but he did well and I need to remember that this isn't the long-term plan. He also trialed being in the wheelchair without a head support. This went "so-so" with periodic assist for neck flexion or verbal cues. Matt tried to stand pulling up on a bar, however, threw his upper back and head backwards, making this difficult. The nurses will do this with him to go to the bathroom when he is able to stand and keep his posture controlled.

The issue of "tone" continues to be an ongoing concern. Yesterday, after posting about Matt's tone, it was SO much better. I could get full wrist and finger extension (like a wave) and all shoulder motions—even external rotation (or as if you were putting your hand behind your head or holding up a stop sign as in *Frosty The Snowman*.) We discussed this again today and Dr. Derr wanted to trial the lowest therapeutic dose of Baclofen which is ten mg three times per day. He said we can also discontinue it if it isn't helping.

In OT, Matt has worked on getting ready in the morning and is able to wash his face with an open hand. This is a huge improvement from resisting bending his elbow, to washing with the washcloth in a ball, to being automatic. Matt will reach up to wash his eyes, forehead, etc., where before he was only able to reach to his chin or mouth. He's doing well with working on putting his shirt on, is able to put his right leg into his shorts and almost get his shoe on.

Today when Matt was in the wheelchair, I was leaning over in front of him to correct his hip alignment, as I'm almost obsessive-compulsive about this. He reached his right hand over me and gave me a hug, then began to massage my shoulder, and then when he was finished, tugged on the drawstring of my jacket hood. I was so happy—it was all unexpected without me asking him to do it (for a change) and my heart melted.

Speaking of which, I came home today to groceries delivered, our driveway plowed by someone we never asked to do so, and my sister cleaning the house. Already being emotional, I went to the Christmas band-choir concert tonight and as each group sang their beautiful music, I could see the sadness in Laura's eyes across the gym from me as I wished I could take that away from her. I could feel the tears coming—burning my eyes in anticipation of the senior high school band performance. By the time they finished their warm-up, I couldn't stop the tears, and of course didn't bring a tissue. I had reminded myself to remember to bring tissues, if not 10, then 20 times today. I was doing "ok" then looked over and saw Laura wiping her eyes and then get up and walk out. I was blocked in the bleachers and didn't want to make a scene, which I may have anyway. The emotions were so mixed. I'm SO sad not to see him joke with the percussionists standing next to him before a song and seeing him stand out in the back row at 6'8". I so wish I was like all the other parents watching their boys perform, however I'm happy that Matt is playing music for me at the hospital that has never sounded better to my ears (including any concert over many years).

I was overwhelmed looking at all the "community of people" in the gym and thinking of the cards, food, calls, texts, letters, etc., that all these people have done, and are planning for the benefits. Now I want to sob as I hold my breath not to. It's ok as I was so overdue for a good cry and I guess tonight's the night. I do know tomorrow I will pull it altogether and be very grateful for all Matt has already accomplished and will accomplish in the future and quit my pity party. There's so much hope and I'll refocus on this—tomorrow. Laura came out of the locker room to me sobbing and I felt terrible knowing I started her sadness when she saw me, but she said we were both destined to cry anyway, with or without seeing each other. A parent came over to me after the concert and said, "You don't know me, but I saw you struggling. Can I give you a hug?" She went on to tell me her name and that she reads my journal every day. Now I know why Laura cannot play basketball when the boys are playing in the gym and why I've been avoiding the boys basketball games to some extent to be with Matthew even though friends and family have offered to be with him. I keep telling myself that he still may be in college band or basketball and I need to keep the faith. I reserved the family lounge on the unit at the hospital for Christmas day as we will not be able to take Matt home even for a few hours—this may have also contributed to my "struggle" tonight. TOMORROW WILL BE BETTER, so look forward to an uplifting post.

As Promised

—∿—

Dec. 17, 2013

I woke up this morning knowing it'd be a better day. I thanked God for everything Matt has been able to do so far and for what the day would bring. On my way to work, I came across a car accident. The SUV was already on the tow truck, completely demolished for the most part, they were sweeping the glass of the highway, and picking up the clothing and personal belongings from the road. This is the second accident I've seen in the past six weeks, and I wonder what the reason is. I know it cannot be for me to realize we are "lucky"—I thank God that Matt and Abby survived the accident every day. After pondering this all day, I came to believe that it helps me be aware of how much healing God does for millions of people every day and how powerful he is. With God all things are possible–Matt's healing is a testimony of this.

Matthew saw me this morning, smiled without me asking, then gave me a wink. How much better could he have lifted my spirits? He had a really good day in all therapies. Matt was able to eat applesauce and flavored ice in speech–so well that today he will have a video swallow test to see if he can begin to eat a pureed (soft) diet. Matt has difficulty feeding himself due to his right arm being shaky from decreased coordination/motor planning and only being able to use his right arm to eat. He likes to flip the spoon over as this is what he did in the pediatric ICU, so now it's challenging to change to eating with the spoon correctly oriented and positioned. He'll get it in a few days–I'm sure of it. He still hasn't spoken a word yet which is frustrating for all of us—especially Matt, but it'll happen.

In OT today, Matt tolerated left arm and hand exercises and trialed electrical simulation to strengthen and get pain free range of motion. Matt was able to straighten his wrist and then his fingers with his wrist in neutral. Matt also tolerated passive motion for every motion of the left upper extremity with less tightness today. I try to encourage him so he can play the piano and bells with both hands and to hold a basketball. He does seem to try harder, or tolerate more discomfort when thinking of the outcome. I brought the bells today for Matt to trial but didn't have the right "bell mallets" in the case (Can you tell how musically inclined I am?) Matt tried to play it with the drum stick but had a difficult time hitting the bells sitting in his wheelchair. When Matt plays the piano, he can keep his hand or a finger in contact the entire time, versus having to lift his arm to coordinate the movement. I know it's tough now, but it's "the next step" and will help Matt progress with other tasks, such as feeding himself, dressing, writing, etc.

In PT, Matt was able to wheel his wheelchair with his right arm and leg for a few feet today for first time. Matt worked on lying on his stomach with his head up, tall kneeling and being on his hands and knees. When resting on the mat, Matt reached up and began to massage my left shoulder, and then again in sitting when working on his balance reaching forward. Matt did not use the head support all the time he was in the wheelchair today until this evening when he was more tired.

Kami commented last night "You sure don't mention Dad at all in your writings." Bill said "I think everyone assumes or knows that I'm keeping things going at home." Bill gets everyone up in the morning, makes me breakfast, keeps up on the permission forms, mail/paying bills, bringing the kids to/from school, dance/piano/sports, all Abby's appointments, (in St Cloud and Brainerd) and in his spare time, does all the laundry and majority of the dishes. Bill has been coming to the hospital a couple nights a week so I can go home and make or have dinner with the girls and go to some of their activities. Every time Bill sees Matt, he says "Hi Bud. You just take your time and get better. Mom and Dad will be here for you." It touches my heart every time, thinking how much Bill has pushed Matt with grades, staying in shape, etc. and now he tells Matt every day to just take his time. (Oh yah, Bill somehow manages to work as much as he can every day and comes to visit Matt every day.) We are so fortunate that his work is flexible and understanding with our situation.

I need to decide when and how much to return to work too. I spoke with my boss about coming back part-time for a few hours per day to have my sick time last longer and she told me I could come back as much as I wanted, whatever hours or days I wanted. I am so lucky to have this flexibility, understanding and wonderful bosses and coworkers who continually tell me I am missed at work. I loved my job and I'm torn between being with Matt and returning to work, so this will be a great option to be able to do both and extend my leave longer by coming back part-time. God is looking over our family and will provide for us everything we need—-physically, emotionally, and spiritually. It'll all be ok.

My inspiration today: "Lead me gently today, Lord, through the moments when I may fail to trust that you are beside me. Remind me that no path is too twisted for you to straighten, no heart is too sore for you to heal and no problem is too big for you to solve. Give me an extra measure of faith today so I can glimpse the bright beauty at the end of this road, and give me an extra measure of courage for the journey. Thank you for walking with me every step of the way."

"Have no fear for what tomorrow may bring. The same loving God who cares for you today will take care of you tomorrow and every day. God will either shield you from suffering or give you unfailing strength to bear it. Be at peace then, and put aside all anxious thoughts and imaginations."

Chocolate Milk!

—∞—

Dec. 18, 2013

Matt had already finished his swallow study when I arrived this morning, therefore I was greeted with great news. Matt will have honey thick liquids and a pureed diet starting tomorrow. This will include eggs, mashed potatoes and gravy, and other blended foods—but it's real food. What a huge step. We have gotten rid of the trach, the external catheter, and hopefully soon the PEG tube. Matt knows what his body's goals are. His speech therapist today said Matt could even have a few bites of cake on his birthday. I'm hoping his diet will be advanced before that since it's almost two weeks away yet—December thirty-first. Time and prayers will determine what Matt will be able to eat for his birthday. Matt needs his liquids thickened and taken from a spoon at this time with extra time to swallow. He had thickened chocolate milk this morning and both of us were so happy. Matt would drink about sixteen to twenty ounces with a meal at home and often refill his glass. He gave us a "thumbs up" that he really liked this.

The personal care attendant said "I'd like to get rid of the ceiling lift." Matt stands without a lot of help if his feet are positioned well; however, getting him to sit–bending and relaxing his knees is more difficult–probably fearful of whether he'll "land" safely. We stood Matt at the bed rail to change the wheelchair for a commode and he was able to stand and pivot to get into bed without needing the lift today. It'll be good to transfer and stand throughout the day with nursing staff, versus only in PT—-helping him to progress more quickly. It's everything in me not to transfer Matt myself, but there are rules and the best I get right now is to be one of the helpers.

Today, I tried having Matt wear his contacts. He so wanted to try them and it went really well. Dr. Derr said "I don't even recognize Matt without his glasses." I told him "and his friends don't recognize him with them." It beats having his glasses bumped, or falling off when he looks down in PT (as I need to get them tightened for him). His PT, Mike, and another PT, Eric, (who states "he used to be 6'7") walked Matt about 10 feet with one on each side. Afterwards Eric said, "I think in my entire career, you're the only the second patient I've worked with who was taller than me." Their height advantage is very beneficial, not to mention their skills and caring personality. Matt was taking steps with his right foot and almost able to step with his left. As his uncle watched, he kept saying quietly "Come on Matt, you can do it"—he's just that close. Uncle Kenny suggested we take Matt outside after therapy and I hadn't even thought of this—weird, I know. We went out on the patio attached to the dining room on the unit, plowed through a snowdrift and came back in about 5 minutes. I think Kenny and I were more excited about our venture then Matt was. When we came in with snow on the wheels, I took a bit of it and Matt threw the "snowball" at Kenny while the nurses watched with a smile. It was so automatic for him to throw this, like the basketball in his room—it was wonderful and he did hit him once.

Everyone who visits, or staff that work part-time and see Matt after a few days, say "He looks so much better." He has his eyes completely open and tracks people who are in the room without being asked a lot of the time. He is able to completely lift his head off his pillow. I fell asleep for a few minutes on the sofa today and when I opened my eyes he had his head off the pillow, and turned to look at me. It scared me at first, then it was just precious. Matt is nodding or shaking his head more often for answering yes/no questions and his eyebrows are able to rise higher each day. Every time I encourage Matt or tell him I love him and we'll get through this, he winks at me. Laura says "He always was a Momma's boy" and of course she's right. I brought a basketball photo of Matt I found in his room at home this morning and put it on the closet opposite his bed. I saw Matt look at it and smile a few times today and it brings mixed happy and sad emotions. A classmate visited tonight and when I asked him what his plans for college were and that I hoped Matt could go on the senior class trip in March, he said, "Matt has a tear going down his face" (he was turned toward him—I can't imagine what Matt was thinking about college, the trip, etc. nor do I want to at this time as the tear is tough enough.) I've told Matt all day he'll be eating tomorrow, has started walking, and soon he'll be talking and using his left arm. I think the use of his arm worries me the most right now. When the prayer group came in tonight, they always ask what I'd like to pray for and I answered to have Matt talk and use his left arm. What a big order, huh? It used to be "for a smile and a hug" which was huge and also already answered. The power of prayer is amazing.

My friends, family and the community continue to be amazing! I came home to a large basket of Christmas goodies last night and received a card from one of my former patients that said how much I affected his life and how much I would affect Matt and Abby's (The card described me as a oak tree with unfailing roots—well, let me tell you the whole tree was swaying Monday night at the concert, but is stable again!) My closet friends text or call every day which is a huge support for me. My friend, Carla, called, bummed that Matt couldn't go home for Christmas. Carla said, "As soon as I read it, I planned on bringing you Christmas dinner." I told her not to worry about it and we'd order or pick something up; however she adamantly stated "I'm not doing it because you asked, I'm doing it because I want to". Friendship is an amazing thing. If you've put off calling, writing, or texting a friend for a while, as I had before the accident, get in touch with them and you'll both feel good. That's what life is about—caring and being good to others. My family has really learned this lesson first hand and I know it'll change all of us for the better for the rest of our lives. My Mom's favorite teaching is the meaning of the word JOY as Brooke tells me almost every day. "Grandma's favorite word is JOY—Jesus, Others, then Yourself." I somehow believe she totally comprehends this at age seven, especially because it came from Grandma.

Well, Matt and I had a long day without much of a lull in therapy, cares, visitors, prayer group, pet therapy visit, etc. He was so tired tonight he could hardly keep his eyes open. As I type away deep in thought, Bill's snoring continually gets louder and I'm twice as tired as before he started, so I'm going to call it a night. Matt has and will continue to recover with strides—I have no doubt.

Wake Up Mom

—w—

Dec. 19, 2013

I walked into Matt's room and he gave me the hand gesture for "I love you" immediately. What a way to start my day–I knew today was going to be awesome. Matt had scrambled eggs for breakfast, but they were on the dry side, so he did cough once. We mashed them and added butter and more salt and pepper, then he didn't like them. Dr. Anderson is back and changed his tube feedings to be continuous at night only so Matt has enough time to eat meals and do his therapy during the day. For lunch Matt ate ALL of his mashed potatoes, ground turkey, and gravy as well as a "magic cup" of high calorie frozen thicker chocolate ice cream. I fed him some, then let him take the spoon and guided him to avoid having him flip the spoon over as he likes to do. When I scooped again, he grabbed my wrist and rather than take the spoon, guided my hand to his mouth. How is that for problem solving? The dietician came in and said she will count the calories Matt consumes during the day and adjust his tube feedings accordingly–meaning if he eats a lot, he won't need the tube feedings, but will get extra water flushes. His diet will advance to different foods as he manages this better. I was so happy! While he was eating he cleared his throat and I KNOW he said "mom" clearly. Only once, but I'll take it!! Of course I had tears of happiness as it'll be seven weeks tomorrow since I've heard him talk.

In OT, Matt continues to obtain more left wrist and finger extension using electrical stimulation. He continually gave a "thumbs up" that it was ok, even with more intensity, and when asked if he liked the stretch. Matt was able to straighten his left elbow today when I placed his arm over the top of his head. His biceps are so tight and strong, it's difficult to do this with his arm at his side. Overhead, this was the best I've seen him able to do yet and SO encouraging that strength is returning to his arm. I had Matt brush his teeth today and he spit three times—getting more tongue and facial muscle control every day.

In PT, Matt was able to sit on the edge of the bed, with his hands under his knees for support, for at least fifteen to twenty seconds without any help. Sitting on the edge of the mat in the clinic, he was able to keep his balance without help for a few seconds for the first time today. He worked on trunk strength and rotation lying on the mat, lifting his hips off the mat and holding his legs on the mat with his knees bent without dropping his left leg out to the side. Matt was able to bring his leg up that was off the mat, bringing his hip up (flexed) for the first time today, versus only straightening his knee to try to do this. I keep thinking I'll have a day with nothing to report, but God and Matt continue to amaze me every day. One of the PT staff asked Matt again today if he still wanted to be a PT, thinking he maybe would change his mind, since this was his original plan before the accident. Matt not only gave her a "thumbs down," but tucked his entire hand under his left arm immediately. It makes me very sad he no longer wants to do this, but of course I know this may change. When Matt recovers more, he may be more determined than ever to be a PT and help others like he has been helped. It makes me think God has altered his path for a good reason and he'll find something he loves even more and will affect many people in his future.

Today I had Matt in the wheelchair next to me while I was lying on the sofa in his room. I fell asleep briefly and Matt reached over and shook my knee to wake me up. This happened at least three times in about five minutes. He was really watching me and obviously did not want me to sleep if he was sitting up. I thought about this and figured it was completely fair as I tried waking him up for weeks and he was far more gentle than I was initially after the accident—stretching his tight hamstring muscles to have him give me any kind of response that he'd be ok.

Faith is believing what you do not see; the reward of this faith is to see what you believe.

Faith is the strongest foundation upon which to build a dream. It is the only foundation that can withstand the forces of nature and the fears of the intellect. Faith stands up against all tests, all challenges, all trials by fire. Faith is backed by God, and there is no greater power. With faith, we are able to endure what we never thought we could. With faith, we are surefooted as we make our way through life. With faith comes knowing that we are always grounded in a solid and unmoving foundation of truth, love, and divine guidance.

WORDS

—⁓—

Dec. 21, 2013

I forgot to mention that Matt had his first bite of the Eucharist on Thursday night. Matt gave an immediate "thumbs up" when asked if he wanted the Eucharist. The chaplain said, "God has been on your left, on your right, above you, below you, and now he is within you." We prayed the Our Father and Matt tried to make the sign of the cross, but it was difficult with his right arm tremors and impaired coordination. I helped him finish the sign of the cross, but it was amazing that Matt initiated it himself without anyone asking him to do so. I believe this was the reason he began to talk yesterday.

Oh my gosh, yesterday I was on top of the world. Matthew transferred into bed with the two nursing assistants (Bill and I were both in the room) and I asked Matt to say thank you to the girls as he was so tired and relieved to lie down. Thinking he would gesture sign language for "thank you", Matt totally surprised us all by saying "THANK YOU" loud and clear for everyone to hear. It's just like Matt to have that be the first words he'd say. I love him so much. Bill asked him to say Mom, and did fairly quietly, but we heard him. Later at dinner time, I gave Matt a scoop of green beans and scooped another bite, asking him if he wanted more–he very clearly said "NO!" I almost jumped out of my skin–he scared me with that deep voice. I know he then thought it was funny.

After Matt had his PT session this morning, I asked him if he could tell his therapist, Brian, "Thank you." Brian said "Tell me anything, Happy Holidays." Matt then whispered audibly "Happy Holidays." The speech therapist had just walked in and instantly was teary eyed. Matt said the numbers one through ten and the days of the week from a list, one by one after the speech therapist said them. The therapist asked him if the therapy dog had been here, as she knows the volunteer who brings Ella, the therapy dog in. I asked Matt what our dog's name is and he said "Saddie." He also said our cat's name "Breezy." He will not have expressive aphasia—difficulty being understood. I'm beyond happy. He also named all four of his sisters. Matt named most of the animals on the iPad, however thought the picture of a steak, was a seashell. In his defense, it did look like a shell. He also followed several two-step motor commands (actions) correctly. HE'S BACK!

In PT, Matt worked on his sitting balance in the room (the electricity was out for four hours for a drill so the gym was dark.) Matt has a difficult time bending forward from his hips and tends to keep his low back flexed and sit on his tailbone. He pushes when he's fearful and because the extensor muscles are stronger. We had Matt work on bending forward and hitting the balloons in his room overhead on his right with his drum stick—as this motivates him. It's difficult to keep his left hand in weight bearing on the bed as this is tight. The therapist hadn't seen him seen in a week, so he was just so surprised Matt could keep his head supported on his own. He has come so far in the past week.

Matt ate seventy-five to one hundred percent of every meal today. Good thing he likes mashed potatoes and gravy as this will be the most abundant food for him at this time. At breakfast, and with an ice cream cup for snack today, Matt coughed pretty hard, but then got rid of mucus, so it wasn't food/diet related—whew. I'm thinking that might be part of the reason he was able to then talk—getting rid of all that in his throat.

Matt's personality is coming back. The activities aid came in and asked if he wanted to play bingo, I told her no, that Matt was exhausted. I asked Matt if he wanted to play after she left and he gave me a "thumbs up," I said, "Do you really want to go play?" and he gave me a thumbs down. I try to clarify the answer I get is correct by asking both a yes and no question to be certain, and Matt continued to alternate thumbs up and thumbs down—then began to smile as if to say "Hey, this is kind of fun—I'm going to enjoy teasing Mom." When I was helping Matt with dinner, he began resting his left elbow on my shoulder. Dean, Matt's assistant basketball coach, says Matt does the same thing to him in the hallways in school.

Dr. Anderson is back and discussed Matt's discharge date of January 3rd, stating "he is making good progress, so we plan to keep him as long as insurance approves until hopefully he can come home and just have outpatient therapy like Abby. This would be so wonderful. I thank God for their discussion to keep Matt longer than the average stay, because he is "still in the pediatric world." Thank you all for the prayers that Matt would talk. Thank you, Thank you, Thank you.

Friends smiling

—◆—

Dec 23, 2013

I had thought Saturday was going to be such a sad day—with Bill's family Christmas (realizing Christmas is here and Matt will be in the hospital despite our hope of having him home, or at least on a day pass) and having the basketball alumni fundraiser. Instead it was a joyous day. I was so happy about Matt talking and eating, instead of being teary-eyed, I was excited to share the news. I did have teary moments when the winner of the "split the pot" drawing declined his prize and put the money into the benefit fund, and when Coach Dahmen gave me a super large poster of three hundred teachers and students who were wearing Matt's t-shirt. It was beyond heart-warming. Again, to acknowledge all the support and love our family is receiving–as much as I write and talk, I can't find the words to express this and know that unless you were in our situation, it wouldn't be something you could possibly understand. I had at least six people tell me throughout the afternoon and evening that they cry with every post they read. It's so hard to comprehend that "our story" has this effect on our family, friends, the community and even strangers. Someone told me "I read your post every morning and it puts me in the right place for the day." It is wonderful to know that my posts are helping anyone to appreciate their family and all the small things in life we take for granted. Do know that I didn't appreciate the small things either before the accident, unless I worked with a patient and their family who had a life-changing event, but this was for a short time only–not like now, thinking of this all day long, every day and being so thankful for the gift of healing and each accomplishment Matt and Abby has already achieved. I keep thinking of the saying that "before you finish saying a prayer, God has already responded. Prayer is the telephone call to the Great Physician, putting in motion the divine love that will bring about healing." I know it'll all be ok with prayers in time.

Today was a very busy day. Matt was up in the wheelchair from the time I arrived this morning until three-thirty pm. We had visitors all day and I could see Matt's spirits lift (as he was a bit down yesterday.) Three of Matt's classmates visited and brought him a basketball quilt from the senior class with everyone's name on it. It is priceless and he did not want to let go of it. It was devastating for me to see him open the package with only one hand, then I think about how wonderful it is that he's awake and KNOWING he's opening a gift from them. I also know that I will help Matt regain his left arm function every day for as long as I need to help him get his strength and coordination back. With God's healing through the many prayers being said on Matt's behalf, his arm will get better. Mike, the PT, came in and asked Matt who his friends were and he said all of their names in a whisper, but loud enough to be understood. I told the guys I had asked Matt to count in Spanish, but couldn't help him after the number six, so his friends helped him and he was able to count from one to ten, repeating a few numbers they said, but understanding it was Spanish. They smiled many times during their visit and it was wonderful to see their true friendship and how much they want Matt back too. I told them I'm hoping to reserve the family lounge on New Year's Eve for Matt's 18th birthday (yeah, I'm not going to even think about this right now–still focused on Christmas for him) but didn't know if any of his friends would be coming to visit. Before I left the hospital tonight, one of his friends had already texted Matt that he wanted to see him on his birthday. How cool is that?

Matt had more friends arrive, recognized, and whispered their names. We went to the therapy clinic with a fan club cheering him on. It was wonderful to see Matt look up (to increase neck/head control) and see the smile his friend Cole had waiting, and seeing Matt trying so hard for him. Even though Matt was exhausted, he worked very hard on sitting balance, tall kneeling (giving me a hug) and weight bearing on his hands and knees. I bought Matt knee pads which are in his room, but have yet to remember them for a PT session on the mat. It's amazing I muddle through an entire day. Sometimes I feel like the chant "send in the clowns" is more than appropriate as I look for things in the room, forget the rest of my sentence with visitors, etc. Funny thing is, I know Matt loves me just the way I am. I asked him yesterday if he knew I loved him and he whispered loudly, without hesitation, "I know." It felt so good after weeks of telling him this—that he knows without a doubt.

Last evening when the nurse asked Matt how dinner was, he rocked his right hand in the air, indicating the "so-so" gesture. We all laughed, knowing he meant it. As much as Matt does like mashed potatoes and gravy, twice a day, every day, is a bit much. The speech therapist came in saying Dr. Anderson had said in rounds that Matt's not a big fan of his diet, so they would try some soft foods with him today. The speech therapist, Shawn, brought in pineapple chunks and saltine crackers to try. Matt coughed quite a bit with the pineapple, but it may have been due to the thin juice it's in. He ate a piece of the cracker uneventfully. I asked Shawn if he could try a peanut butter cup as this is soft and Matt has glared at everyone who has had one in the room. He said Matt certainly could, and after a few bites requested that Matt verbalize to ask for more, which he faithfully did with each bite—eating a Christmas tree and regular peanut butter cup. Needless to say he didn't eat much for lunch and we were both okay with this. Matt had a peanut butter cup and he didn't cough. Yay!–another gift. Shawn said Matt can now have soft chocolate treats. Good thing for Matt, I know every option available as this is one of my basic food groups.

In OT, Matt worked on his left arm motion and strength, looking in the mirror for visual feedback, and using e-stim to help his wrist and fingers straighten. Matt tolerated this well and gave a "thumbs up" every time we asked if the intensity was okay, or if it could be increased. Matt wants his left arm to work again and I know he understands this will help him. I've told him this multiple times (it's what I do and have said to my patients for 25 years now.)

Dr Anderson came in this evening and said that they officially moved Matt's goal discharge date to January 15th (from January 3rd)–pending insurance authorization of course. It's a relief the date has been moved many days ahead of time. Matt's medical team feels he is making good progress and want him to continue to have rehab at the hospital until he can hopefully return home with outpatient therapies.

Looking through my now favorite inspirational book, this had a great impact on me tonight. I think it was written specifically for our family. "God does not cause your misery, he eases it. He sends you his messages of love; hands to help you, ears to listen, and hearts to share your deepest burdens." I believe everyone reading this is a message of God's love to us.

Christmas at the SCH -Abby, Lynn, Matt and Bill.

Christmas Day

—〰—

Dec. 25, 2013

Bill woke me up this morning to make spaghetti for Matthew. I went to the kitchen and noticed a new golf bag and clubs under the tree with a tag that read To: Mom, From: Dad. I instantly was teary as we agreed we weren't getting each other anything. I also had an overwhelming feeling there would be a light at the end of the tunnel where we would enjoy golfing again. It brought so much hope to me—it's difficult to explain. Matt was on the varsity golf team and would often golf with Bill and me. His golf coach had written a letter about a month ago, describing all the trips to tournaments—how Matt always rode shotgun and ordered a huge fast food meal. Coach Dobis was also one of Abby's tennis coaches and he wrote about Abby and how happy she was when he invited her to practice with the varsity team this summer and how she always gave it her all. It's amazing how well he knew both of them. I know they will both return to golf and tennis in the future. I always looked forward to having Matt golf with us when he came home from college on the weekends in years to come—and still do.

We went to church at the hospital chapel this morning; however, needed to leave before mass started because Matt was pushing on the pew and when I asked him what was wrong, he said "bathroom." We left and came back during the sermon. Matt wanted to go to church today without a doubt when I asked him last night and again this morning. He watched them play the bells, held onto mine, Brooke and Laura's hand during the mass, shook hands at the sign of peace, and I even saw him make the full sign of the cross. Yes, the tears came, especially when they sang "*Silent Night.*" I don't know why. Kami asked if they were happy or sad tears and I told her I didn't know—"I think both." I was sad we were at the hospital and how our life has changed, yet so happy Matt was able to be in church, winking at me during the mass, holding my hand and making the sign of the cross. We have so much to thank God for. We went back to Matthew's room and Bill helped him into bed using the floor to ceiling pole. Matt nearly stood on his own, surprising Bill as he immediately went to the left. Matt has a more difficult time straightening his left knee which affects his balance and transfers. I immediately thought "Yes, he will be walking" as I see his trunk and head strength continue to improve.

I was again overwhelmed by all the cards we received yesterday and all the texts from coworkers and friends. It's unbelievable to me that people are thinking and praying for Matt even on Christmas Day. I can't explain the emotions I feel. My friend, Carla, who made Christmas dinner for us, had strep throat and texted she was cooking dinner while wearing a mask. I told her she was a goof and shouldn't have—we could have ordered pizza. Her response was "that's just how I roll." My friends are so caring, understanding and giving—I think that was part of my happy tears in church today—all of you. One of Bill's co-workers who visited recently said, "You need to know that all the things the community and students are doing for Matt, is also a reflection of the type of person Matt is." Wow—I've thought of this many times, especially when I look at the poster of teachers and students on Matt's hospital door, you can feel the love.

Matt enjoyed all of our family who visited today—"high fives," many smiles, hand-shakes and hugs using his right arm. He had spaghetti for lunch and loved this, eating 1/2 a plate full of ground texture. The nurses told me he coughed so much with breakfast they had to take it away. He coughed on everything from eggs to honey-thick apple juice and hasn't done this all week. Matt did just fine with lunch, to my relief, and I brought extras for leftovers. Matt would eat spaghetti for several days straight at home and loved it, so it wouldn't be any different now. He opened his gifts, loving the new basketball shoes he had wanted—that will give him more ankle support in therapy, and the iPad—to work on vision and cognitive skills. Matt smiled for many pictures, and then Bill transferred him to a recliner in the lounge where he enjoyed putting his feet up and waving to Grandma several times across the room.

Matt did better today with initiating his speech, although still whispers, I only helped him start to open his mouth about half the time, versus all the time as before. I think he's working so hard on forming the words to say, he doesn't automatically open his lips to talk. It'll come in time, as will the volume. Brooke crawled in bed with Matt today and he tickled her, much to her delight–it was heart-warming for me. She is forever saying, "Matt give me a thumbs up if. . . . ., Matt can you smile? With your teeth?" (Wonder where she gets that from? In my defense, I did ask Matt a couple days ago if he was getting sick of me to which he said "No" louder than usual.) Brooke came back to Matt's room this afternoon from the lounge and said "I'm mad at Matt." When I asked why, she said "I'm trying to play the DS game with him and he's not paying attention." Matt was so tired, as he had been up for early for his shower at six-thirty this morning and was still going at three thirty this afternoon. I tried to explain this to her. How lucky we are he's awake, can push the buttons with his right hand, and how he's trying his very best.

One of my coworkers sent me a card yesterday with an encouraging verse for Matt. I thought I'd add a few for him, knowing someday he'll be reading my "tell-all story" just like he referred to my yearly Christmas letter. "For I know the plans I have for you, declares the Lord; plans to prosper you and not to harm you, plans to give you hope and a future." Jeremiah 29:11.

I found another inspirational verse this evening for Matthew: "Let me feel the glory of your redemption and renewal, God, as I embark on this new life. Today, I will walk with you to guide me, to direct my every step, knowing that with your love and wisdom, I shall not be misled. Today, I will have hope, faith, and courage as I have never had before, knowing you are always there to give me the strength I need."

Memories

—⌇—

Dec 26, 2013

Hi, this is Laura—there are a few memories I would like to share about Matt. When I was about 6, and he was 8, we were out biking together. I had pulled into the garage first and gotten off my bike. He pulled in after me, going really slow because I refused to move out of his way to let him park his bike. He told me to move, or he'd run me over. Of course, I took it as a challenge, and refused to move. He ended up scratching my knee a little with his bike tire, and I immediately found leverage over him. I threatened to tell Mom and Dad, to which he begged me not to. I ended up holding that over him for years after the incident. I made him do silly little things for me, like bringing me ice cream or feeding the cats for me. Eventually, he said, "Go tell them, I don't care." That put an end to that.

About a week or so before the accident, another scenario happened. He was working concessions at varsity football game. The game had ended, and I wanted to go to the car to warm up. He was still cleaning and everyone working concessions found it funny, watching me trying to get the keys and Matt not letting me have them. Eventually I got so mad, I stormed off. He threw the keys after me. He would always give in if he saw one of us girls cry or be mad. The whole ride home I refused to talk to him. I had been so embarrassed. I went without talking to him the following day too, and he finally caught on. After school, he came to my locker and asked if I was mad at him. Getting no response, he hugged me. We both ended up apologizing, to which he said, "Don't ever be mad at me, I love you." Every school day when I'd see him in the hallways, I would shout, "I LOVE

YOU MATT!" at the top of my lungs. He had never said it back, only smiled at his 'embarrassing' little sister. But that day was the first time he had said he loved me in public. I will always cherish that day, and I think about it all of the time. Matt has always been so caring, especially to his four little sisters. He would never fight or lay a hand on us, even when we threatened to tell Mom and Dad about him giving us a scratch with his bike.

I miss him beyond words. I never thought I could miss someone this much. It is hard remembering how he was, and looking at how he is now. But I have faith in God, and know he will be back to his old self again, it will just take time. He has been improving beyond expectations. Every day he amazes us, and makes us thankful for the other parts of our lives we often take for granted. He is my tall angel, and will be back shooting hoops again in no time. Please pray for the motion on his left side, too. I'm sure Mom and Dad would love to see him throwing things with his left hand. All of your prayers have been helping, and thank you so much for them.

My scare and faith renewed

—⁓—

Dec. 27, 2013

Yesterday, was very exhausting and scary for me. Matt started a new medication for tremors, (used with Parkinson patients I believe) taking his first dose at 8 am. I was helping him eat lunch–spaghetti left over, milk, juice, etc. and he began putting his head down. I helped him fix his positioning two times, telling him to hold his head up, then realized he had beads of sweat pooling at the side of his neck. He wasn't looking or responding to me and was turning grayish/yellow. I was more scared than I had been seeing him in ICU, sure he was having a seizure or cardiac arrest. I could see the house-keeper at the desk and asked her to get a nurse right away. She asked if I was ok and I said "NO!" The nurses were there within two minutes and said we needed to get him back to bed. I knew he couldn't stand, or use the slide board she suggested, so I reclined his wheelchair and the four of us lifted him into bed. His entire shirt was soaked in sweat and he was near fainting. The nurses put oxygen on him and took his blood pressure, which was low, a side effect of the new medication. His vitals were okay overall, so all his medications were held the rest of the day and the new memedimedication discontinued. I left the room to find five of the therapists (my coworkers and friends) standing outside Matt's room next to the crash cart (which has an AED in case Matthew did have a cardiac arrest.) I was touched they all cared so much, waiting outside Matt's room to make sure he was okay on their lunch break. I called Bill an hour later and the moment he heard my voice, he said "What's wrong?" Guess that's what being married for almost twenty years does. Matt had another near fainting episode later in the afternoon in PT after standing for three minutes, dropping his head, buckling his knees, therefore they checked out his heart with an EEG, which turned out just fine. I cancelled the team coming to visit because Matt was exhausted. By the end of the day, even without company, he was putting his blanket over his head. Not-so-subtle hint, huh?

Matt continues to let me know his thinking is going to be great. Yesterday, he told the speech therapist what he had received for Christmas, remembering an Xbox game, basketball shoes, and with a hint, his iPad. This shows me his short-term memory is pretty good, not only long term like remembering friends and family. Today, his cousin asked him who his favorite player for the Lakers is, and Matt said "Gasol." I was amazed again he had identified a current player, without hesitation.

Matt tried thinner liquids today and also honey thickened from a cup without coughing. Dr. Anderson said if he keeps eating so well, we'll get rid of the feeding tube. Wouldn't that be wonderful? Matt is talking a bit louder now, but mostly whispers. When I asked him what he wanted to do in PT today—"Work on sitting balance, standing, walking?" He replied "Sleeping." I asked him two more times and yes, he consistently said "Sleeping" without a smile. I honestly think he meant it. He worked on trunk control, sitting balance, and standing in PT. He's able to stand with Mike, his PT, without a lot of help for two to three minutes before getting tired. Bill and I are able to get him in and out of bed ourselves, and Matt is able to hold his head up the majority of the day without any help. We have a long road to go yet, but he is making gains every week.

Matt is beginning to be more aware of his left arm and hand, which is SO wonderful. He often is straightening his thumb or fingers as much as he can, and when I lift his arm over his head, he helps with the right hand without me asking him to. Dr. Anderson was very pleased about his awareness and that he was holding his left thumb up today when he visited. He was very encouraging saying "He'll get function back in that arm." It was just what I needed.

The team came tonight and brought Matt a Pierz Pioneer banner for his room. It is super cool. It was wonderful to have Matt say a few words for them and to see him looking so much better. I know it's been tough on the whole team, but you can see their hope too.

Yesterday and last night, I was feeling overwhelmed and defeated, not sure I could keep the positive spirit for both of us. After a decent night's sleep, seeing Matt feed himself a good portion of breakfast, as well as putting on his pants, socks and shoes sitting up in the wheelchair for the first time today, I regained my hope and could feel my faith being renewed. It was a very good day and we will get Matt home and someday running again. I know the key is having so many people praying for Matt. As a result, Matt is beginning to have changes in strength, sensation and awareness.

Angels everywhere

—⚊—

Dec. 28, 2013

Today, was a much better day. Matt was talking a bit louder, especially when asked to say something again–he is finding his voice which still seems to surprise me and bring such emotions of thankfulness. He is trying hard all day long and was exhausted tonight, coughing more with dinner and asleep the minute I tucked him into bed before seven pm. Matt was able to drink from a cup in speech today for the first time without coughing. He has difficulty managing the hand to mouth motion due to tremors, but did several times and was able to even put the cup back on the table. I told the speech therapist about a cup I use at my work and she was going to order it with a two-day shipping special herself and get "reimbursed later." That is how all the therapists are who work with Matthew, going above and beyond to have him succeed. I asked her about Matt possibly having homemade pizza for his birthday on Tuesday and she said they would try toast next week. I didn't want to order pizza for his friends and have him watch them eat his favorite food on his birthday—so I'm hoping he'll do awesome.

In OT today, Matt tolerated the e-stim for his left wrist and finger extension and even the Bioness unit (like an electronic splint that opens the hand and extends the wrist.) He totally hated it the last time we tried it, so this was encouraging. I was able to use an extra e-stim unit tonight in Matt's room to work on increasing his wrist and finger extension and he did amazing—tolerating it wonderfully as he watched college basketball. Matt tried the arm bike in OT today, able to keep his grasp on the handle without any difficulty, and able to actively bend and straighten his elbow to make the circular motion. His wrist relaxed with repetition of the motion and I was super excited to see him use his hand "semi-functionally." It'll help him to push his arm into a shirt sleeve or reach for that hoop someday.

When Mike came in for Matt's PT session, I was sound asleep on the sofa in his room. I didn't sleep well last night, having leg cramps–(probably need to drink some water this week versus coffee and Diet Pepsi), thinking about changes to the house, ideas for therapy sessions, etc., and couldn't turn my mind off. With Bill's help, we got Matt onto a floor mat. Matthew was able to side-sit with his right arm supporting him without any help for at least one to two minutes. It was wonderful to see him on the "floor" like he always was when he played Xbox. Matt worked on walking in tall kneeling with his arms on my shoulders as I walked backwards on my knees and Mike helped to keep his trunk tall and weight shift to advance alternating knees. Matt wants to walk and move so much, but still needs the trunk control for this to be possible. I remember his pediatrician saying "Matt's going to take longer to sit, stand, and walk due to his long trunk/torso" and I know this definitely is the case now too. He worked on crawling on hands and knees with his left hand fisted for the most part, and was able to lie on his stomach and hold himself up on his elbows without any help after positioned. Matt worked on standing with Mike, leaning to each side and backwards, however, did correct himself and "line up" with Bill making faces at him to find midline behind Mike. I'm not sure who is more exhausted after a session–Matt or Mike, but I know they are both giving it their all. I'm so thankful for the caring way Matt's therapists help him and how much thought goes into each treatment to make it "the best." Mike described it as "a village of ideas" as all the therapists think of new activities to help Matt progress as quickly as possible. It totally is beyond overwhelming to know how much everyone cares for him. It's like angels sent from heaven, disguised as therapists, nurses, doctors, personal care assistants, and all of you. Bill totally quit "tweaking" my posts, saying "you write from the heart and are doing just fine."

Bill said tonight that I have no idea how it is to be in Pierz, since I spend most of my time at the hospital. He said "everywhere I go, people tell me how they are praying for Matt and Abby and it is so overwhelming." We know we'll never be able to thank everyone enough for all their prayers and gifts in this lifetime. How humbling is that? I do know that my entire family will "pay it forward" from this experience. (If you haven't seen this movie, I highly recommend it.)

Abby continues to struggle with a cold and "what to do about dance." She decided that since dance is only until February fourth, she won't rejoin the team this year. She said "I don't know if I'll be able to keep my balance for the spins" which I also worry about. Abby texted her coach and said she'll certainly go out for dance next year, which I thought was wonderful insight on her part. I continue to tell Abby and Laura, that dance and basketball will be there next year too and they need to do what it right for them, not what anyone else wants them to do. Abby had OT/PT/ST therapy sessions yesterday and still hasn't "graduated" from therapy yet. She is doing awesome overall, but becomes frustrated easily which is not her norm. I'm very confident in time she'll be herself completely—especially with all the cards and prayers that are not only being said daily for Matt, but for her as well.

I opened my favorite inspirational book to this quote and revised it just a bit: "Father, help me remember to praise you and thank you for the moments of my days that lighten my spirit: the first glass of fresh orange juice (or in my case, texts from my best friends), the people who greet me, a happy song on the radio, an email that makes me smile, a friend who stops by. If I counted the good moments and the bad, the good would win— EVERY day. I need to take time to thank you for the moments that make me appreciate my life today despite the trials I may encounter. Set me alight with a powerful faith, a faith in you, dear Lord, to move the mountains of my life. I am putting my complete trust and faith in you, God, where it belongs."

Heart Strings Jerked

—⚹—

Dec 30, 2013

Yesterday on my way to the hospital, it seemed like my thousandth trip and I asked for more strength to get through the days that seem slower and more trying. Matt had coughed so much at dinner the night before and when I arrived, the nurses said breakfast "did not go well at all either–he coughed on everything." Matt's Baclofen had been increased and since this relaxes muscles, I thought he needed the dose decreased. They talked to Dr. Anderson and obtained the order, however, at lunch (before decreasing the dose, Matt didn't cough at all). Matt was ready for the day when I arrived, just finishing with his OT session. After OT, I helped Matt back to bed to rest for forty-five minutes before speech therapy. I told him to close his eyes and rest as I sat on the sofa in his room, looking at my Kindle. Matt said "Mom" loudly, as clear as can be. I went to him and asked him what he wanted, and he said "You have no idea." I asked him what about and he said "how bad. . ." and then I couldn't understand the rest of the sentence. I had tears running down my cheeks (which I try very much try not to do) as I told Matt I had no idea how it was for him, but that he's getting better—can breathe on his own, doesn't have the trach anymore, the catheter anymore, is eating, talking, etc., etc. I told him he would continue to get better because we have more than a thousand people I believe praying him every day and God will listen to so many people. I told him he was a miracle in what he is able to do already. Today I asked him if he remembered telling me yesterday "that I had no idea," and Matt immediately nodded. I asked him to finish the sentence and he said "how bad I want to get better." I had asked him yesterday if he was down in the dumps and he nodded yes. I told Matthew his determination and positive attitude is what had been and continues to get him better. He totally understood and agreed.

Matt has made really good progress in PT the past few days. Yesterday, he walked in the LiteGait system (the harness gait assist) for one hundred feet with two PT's—one to guide the system and Mike helping him walk, mostly to weight shift to be able to step with his left leg. They increased his speed and Matthew was able to advance his left on his own. Oh my goodness. It was completely amazing. Today he walked in the parallel bars with Mike about seven feet three times. I initially tried to keep Matt's left hand on the bar for support, but he was too fast for me to be able to open and close his hand to advance it. Being 6'8", Matt takes big steps and was trying to step around Mike, who was standing in front of him. Wow-he really wanted to move. We have the most difficulty getting Matt to bend at the hips to sit down as he brings his trunk backwards instead, but his trunk is definitely getting stronger.

In Speech, Matt had TOAST with grape jelly on it today. He is able to bring his tongue into the side of his left cheek, an exercise he couldn't do at all three or four days ago. Matt will only have one can of formula/feeding tonight and if his calorie count is good, he won't need any tube feedings after tonight, just water flushes until the tube is taken out. I'm so excited for this and I know Matt is too, eating just a bit more every time I remind him of this. We had cupcakes with the team tonight for Matt's birthday and before I could spoon some with frosting, mixed with his MAGIC CUP to help swallow, Matt picked up the cupcake and took a bite. I told him I was going to be in so much trouble if he began coughing, but he took a bite, licked his lips and fingers, and didn't cough at all. This was a special moment for us both. His smile is still mostly on the right side, but he's able to open his mouth much better on the left to eat. It's all these little things I think about when I post that makes me appreciate "baby steps" and lets everyone praying know we are making changes daily. Yesterday, Matt was able to say the number, color and suite of cards in speech loud enough for his therapist to hear, with one hundred percent accuracy. There definitely are things that are difficult for Matt to remember, but it's getting better every day too.

One of the nurses commented that he doesn't realize how tall Matt is until he's out of bed. I said, "Matt, what is your favorite joke when people ask you how tall you are and if you play basketball? You say, why yes, do you play. . ." and Matt loudly and clearly said "minature golf." He remembered his joke. His speech therapist is surprised that Matt's words are so articulate (clear) even with his left facial weakness—that no words are slurred. How frustrating it would be to work so hard to say a word loud enough to be heard, then not to be understood? I am so thankful to hear Matt's voice and to be able to listen to someone other than myself all day long when we are alone. Matt's Uncle Kenny visited yesterday (he was with us at the hospitals the night of the accident, daily, and frequently now.) When he said hi to Matt yesterday, Matt said "Hi Kenny" loud enough to be heard and Kenny was teary-eyed, saying how long he's been waiting to hear Matt's voice too. During lunch Matt was looking at Kenny, and so he asked him if he wanted to say something to him, to which Matt replied "something." Matt had his right eye closed (his winking eye) and I asked him if he was seeing double to which he replied "No." When I asked him why he was closing his eye, he replied "because I just did." It's fun to see Matt's personality come back, now I can't wait to hear him laugh again soon.

I had a phone conversation with the Social Security office regarding disability qualifications. Everything in me wanted to hang up, knowing this is going to be short-term, but I answered all the required questions. Dr. Anderson then informed me since Matt is eighteen years old tomorrow, Bill and I need to file for guardianship. It may be for only three or four months, and we may need to go to court to do this. These are things I never thought about, even being in the medical field for many years. We are fortunate others are able and willing to guide our way.

Give your family an extra hug tonight.

A Great Birthday Despite Altered Plans

—∿—

Dec. 31, 2013

Matthew and I had talked about what he would do on his eighteenth birthday, but never had officially decided. Today was tough initially, knowing his birthday "sucked," but by the end of the day I decided it was a great day with family, friends and even strangers who cared and wished him a happy birthday. When I arrived in the morning after making homemade pizza for Matt, one of his basketball coaches, Dean, was already visiting. Coach Dahman told me that when he asked Matt how he was, he replied "I've been better." Matt is gaining insight and talking in longer sentences every day. He does get teary, but that's a good sign, despite how tough it is for me to see, and he's so determined to get better–that's his "ace in the hole."

Matt walked with a railing on his right side with only Mike, his PT, and me nervously following behind with the wheelchair. He walked eight to ten feet, three times, with Dean standing in front of him, encouraging him to look up. We all agreed this was great progress, and although Matt did need help to complete his step with his left leg, he did initiate the step. After resting, Mike (with Dean helping on Matt's right side to hold his hand and give him support) walked Matt across the clinic, turned around and walked back. Mike asked someone to stand in front of Matt to have him look up. Laura was very willing and the perfect inspiration for Matt–versus looking at me all the time. I'm not sure who was more tired by the end of the walk, but I knew this PT session had changed Matt's spirits.

Matt had OT and speech before I arrived this morning to allow Matt to have a rest before his birthday party at three pm. I asked Matt if he wanted his lunch, or to have homemade pizza twice today and he clearly said "pizza." Matt ate three and a half slices cut very small and didn't cough at all. I know he thoroughly enjoyed it. It had minimal cheese on it, very, very small pieces of pepperoni, pork, and Polish sausage, and doubled the sauce. Watching Matt have pizza and loving it, was wonderful for me. I think I'll be making pizza often now and I'm totally ok with that.

Matt received a basketball decorated basket of chocolate candy and balloons from the Father Pierz School of Religion today. He set the basket on the floor next to his wheelchair in the lounge after pulling on the balloons some when it was on his lap. He then punched the large balloon and it sang, "Happy Birthday," much to our shock. Then Laura said, "Mom, it says tap to sing on the bottom of the balloon." I'm about ninety-eight percent sure Matt read this, so put the basket down to be able to punch the balloon and hear the music.

Matt had the girls visiting today (of course needing to tickle and hug Brooke and follow every command she asked of him) then his friends came for his birthday party. His friends were all in the lounge where the girls were playing Connect Four. Matt watched the game intently and when I asked if he wanted to play, he nodded his head yes. Someone asked him who he wanted to play against and Matt said "Mike." They played three games and I had to leave the room teary eyed. Oh my goodness–he was really playing and understanding the game. He lost the first game, I think Mike let him win the second game per Abby's report and Matt completely won the third game without help. I was so happy Matt's right hand tremors weren't as much as usual reaching to place the checkers, so he could functionally do this without help. He was so tired by four pm (not resting since his six-thirty am shower this morning) that Bill transferred him into a recliner in the lounge. Matt didn't want pizza with his friends, but did say yes to a very large piece of cake with tons of frosting and a honey-thickened glass of chocolate milk. Matt didn't seem to mind me feeding him in the recliner, and I told his friends about our agreement that he would someday feed me when I'm old in return– to which Matt nodded and continued to thoroughly enjoy the cake as if "I'm enjoying my moment now." By four forty-five pm, Matthew clearly told me "I want to go to bed."

I spoke with the dietician and Matt will not get a night time tube feeding tonight. He'll get water through the tube yet until it's taken out, but it shouldn't be long. What a huge hurdle he jumped with the help of all his angels. Walking better, having pizza, and not needing a tube feeding tonight, I'd say was a wonderful birthday. God is listening to our prayers and he's already doing things that were "questionable" from the MRI. God's healing goes far beyond any medical test–Matt is definitely showing us this. I know the prayers are also keeping Matt's spirits way brighter than I ever would be in his shoes. I asked Matt if he wished I'd shut up and that he should tell me "Shut up Mom," as he hears my stories repeated all day long. Matt whispered, "Shut up Mom," without a smile and it made me think of how many times I'd say "Matt, that was funny, you're not even going to smile?" to which he'd reply "I'm laughing on the inside. Show no emotion." I believe Matt is laughing on the inside, and soon he'll be able to laugh again as his breath volume improves. I can't wait. Matt had two chipped teeth from being intubated (one front tooth on top and also on the bottom.) Every time I see his chipped tooth smile, I think of Matthew when we were talking about Kami needing braces only one to two weeks before the accident. He was in the kitchen and came over and gave me a hug, saying "Mom, thanks for all you've done for my teeth," I was surprised and touched as Matt has had his braces off for years already, and I don't think he ever said it before, but appreciated everything. We will get him teeth fixed as soon as we can, but right now it reminds me of the wonderful person Matt is. All things happen for a reason.

2014 in God's Hands

—◊—

Jan. 2, 2014

When I was thinking of what my New Year's resolution would be, I decided it would be to stay in contact with all my friends, no matter how busy life can be. It's amazing how a ten second text, letting someone cares know you care, brings a "lift" to the day. I also decided I would acknowledge every day I have with all my children, as a true gift, no matter what the day brings/has brought. I now know I am so very lucky for all the kids; however, didn't think about this before the accident—especially if I or they weren't in the best of moods. I will thank God every day for the rest of my life that Matt and Abby survived the accident and will appreciate my family beyond what I can describe. Knowing this brings me a warm peace like I've never experienced before.

Matthew has been able to talk much louder over the past few days, without being told to "find his voice" as often. He doesn't "reply" to a question, or hello, spontaneously very often, thus this is a new therapy goal. I've made Matt leftover pizza for the past three days and he has enjoyed every bite and would eat it every day. He coughed with a very small bite when my sister-in-law gave it to him, but with bigger bites, didn't cough at all. I told Matt's speech therapist she would think I was crazy, but he seems to swallow better with larger bites. This is against the cardinal rule typical for eating an upgraded diet. She said she didn't think I was crazy and maybe Matt has more sensory input with an increased amount of food in his mouth. I bought a mixer/chopper/dicer combo to "ground" chicken dumpling soup, hotdish, and anything else Matt might like. I knew it would be a while before I'd have the time or energy to make the soup, so called Grandma. I gave the phone to Matt and he said "Grandma, I want chicken dumpling soup." It was only a whisper that she couldn't hear, but with repetition, he did eventually say it loud enough to hear. Grandma had the chicken out of the freezer before hanging up the phone and called today saying it was ready. I knew talking to Matt brought tears to Grandma and without a doubt, knew Matt would have soup very soon. He is eating very well and a lot, much to my delight. For example, Matt had a regular peanut butter cup, three mini-cups and an apple juice before dinner. At dinner he had larger portions of mashed potatoes, roast beef, gravy, green beans (I think), chocolate milk, orange juice, a cupcake, and a magic protein ice cream cup. I'm hoping he'll gain back his thirty pounds quickly, even if the two hundred and ninety calorie MAGIC CUPS and peanut butter cups are the key.

Matt was able to repeat up to five digits in speech therapy today and worked on counting coins. We still aren't sure if he sees double at all, identifying three pennies instead of two placed in front of him. He added some coins okay; however, did need help with some trials too. He knows all the coins and their value, so I have no doubt it'll come back to him soon. We downloaded a game for Matt on the iPad, but ran out of day today to try it as Matt does need to rest too and is asking to sleep or go to bed several times during the day.

Matt has begun to figure out moving in the wheelchair using his right leg only. It's very difficult to coordinate with his right hand and foot together and stir, so he does it all with only his leg. I don't worry about it at all as the wheelchair will be short term. Matt continues to work on looking and attending to his left arm and hand. In bed, or the wheelchair, he'll hold his hand for an hour or more especially if he falls asleep; however, in therapy there are so many other things he'd rather look at. Tonight in his room, with e-stim, Matt was able to extend all his fingers and even bring his wrist up a bit simultaneously. When I brought his arm over his head and rested his hand on his forehead, with a cue to look and straighten his elbow, he was able to do this actively several times. I also saw him straighten his ring and pinky finger some when beginning to straighten his elbow—this is a first—my hope renewed. With his left hand close to his chest, Matt gave a "thumbs up" fairly quickly today too. It's something he hasn't done much since ICU, before the "tone" made his hand tighter. Matt was only able to hold his arm over his head for one to two seconds, but this is encouraging for me as it shows he is activating shoulder muscles too. PLEASE continue to pray for functional use of his hand—I keep telling him we need to work on it so he can play piano, hold a basketball—especially the left hook shot that's his favorite—and to play the Xbox again. I have been worried as it'll be nine weeks tomorrow since the accident. That's a long time not to see muscle return; however, I keep reminding myself that the first four to five weeks, he wasn't even able to wake up and know to try to move his arm. In that theory, it's really only been four to five weeks and Matt's brain is continuing to heal—the neurons regenerate one millimeter every three to four days, thus every day I hope it's that day so I see something new. Sometimes I think it's every day as he progresses in other areas of thinking, memory, talking, swallowing, moving his left leg, and improving his trunk control. Isn't it exhausting to think of all the areas that he's putting effort into? Not to mention my continuous nagging all day long about talking louder, looking to the left, making choices to give him some control at this time, etc., etc.

Dr. Moore (Matt's pediatric intensivist) came to see him on rehab yesterday, holding a form. She was pleased with how good Matt looked and that he said a few words to her. She lives in Colorado and said about a month ago, on her flight back, she was thinking about Matt and our family, and wondering if she could set something up with the Timberwolves since Matt loves basketball. She said, "Anyway, I began to talk to the lady next to me on the plane and asked her what she did for a living and she told me 'I work for the Timberwolves.'" It gave me shivers down to my toes. Dr. Moore said the lady knew everyone of course and after she told her about Matthew, she gave her a business card and asked her to send more medical information about Matt's situation. The form was a release of information which was all filled out but the signature. Dr. Moore said "Maybe nothing will become of it, but maybe something will. I have no idea, but it wasn't just a coincidence we ended up sitting next to each other on the plane." Matt seems to touch so many people—to have Dr. Moore go out of her way like this, Dr. Joey saying a prayer on the top of the Empire State Building, as well as all the care shown to us by Dr. Johnson and Dr. Derr. They really have wonderful doctors, nurses, and therapists (of course) here, but somehow I feel the "extra TLC" is due to all the prayers for Matt to get better—angels everywhere.

I've been thinking non-stop about the future, waking up multiple times every night. I'm going back to work on Monday four hours a day and maybe more if Bill goes to the hospital over lunch, and only have three more weeks of my twelve week FMLA where my position is held. I have no idea what the future holds for our family. Will Matt be able to stay for another month at the hospital, will he then transition to subacute rehab at Country Manor, or will he be able to go home with continued outpatient therapy? Will he need twenty-four hour supervision in addition to his therapy? If so, how will I manage work, or would he be mobile enough to have friends and family stay with him part of day? Will I be able to work full-time, or some from home? Will I need another leave of absence when he does go home? Should I just work weekends at the hospital or on-call at both jobs? ETC., ETC., ETC. . . I decided on my way to the hospital this morning that working four to six hours now while Matt is at the hospital is a good transition and I really do love my job and all my coworkers. I've really missed this part of my life, but being with Matt was like needing air to breathe over the past two months. I have a strong feeling that I need to let go of this constant worry and will know what I need to do as we continue to see God's healing for Matthew. The future is in God's hands and whatever path I need to take, will be for a reason—even if I may not understand it. It'll all fall into place I'm sure of it.

Matt did get a sign for his birthday that a bus driver made for him: "PRAYER— World's greatest wireless connection." How cool is that?

PB & J and Soda

—∿—

Jan. 4, 2014

Yesterday was an unbelievably awesome day. I came in thinking this was my last full week day, and was on a mission. I asked the PCA's if we could try having Matt go on the "real toilet" versus a commode or urinal. He transferred very well with the grab bar and went immediately. He hasn't had any difficulty going or letting us know he has to use the restroom, after surprising Aunt Pam by saying, "I have to piss" this afternoon. Well, he is a teenager you know.

Matt had speech therapy, and since he has been doing so great swallowing bigger bites of homemade pizza, including the bread, I asked if he could try a PB & J sandwich. The speech therapist, Shawn, made a sandwich and Matt ate the entire sandwich without coughing, as well as two cartons of chocolate milk upgraded to nectar thickened (from honey thickened.) His diet was updated to nectar liquids with the okay for PB & J sandwiches. They will assess soft foods versus pureed on Monday, but didn't want to change everything on a Friday without his primary therapists being here over the weekend. Matt filled out a football pool sheet with in speech to see who would win, him or Shawn, the speech therapist. He verbalized his choices loud enough to hear and didn't hesitate with his picks. When I asked him later if he remembered what he did with Shawn, he replied "fantasy football." They worked on simple money and math skills, as well as time problems, such as "What's a half hour before ten o'clock?" Matt knew it was thirty minutes prior, but couldn't answer nine thirty without extra cues. It was difficult to see Matt have difficulty with this, but I'm sure in a few days, this will all be super easy at the rate he's improving. I immediately thought I'll bring in our math and time flashcards which will help bring this knowledge back for him.

Matt walked eighty to one hundred feet with two PTs in the hallway and with cues to keep his head up, he stood as tall as I've ever since him yet with his upper body. His PT, Mike, said, "He is improving so much—I see changes every day. It's rewarding for me." Gosh, did that touch my heart, knowing Mike is so vested in Matt's recovery and as much work as it is for Mike physically, he finds Matt's progress rewarding. Matt was able to keep his balance sitting on the edge of the mat, holding onto his right sock, reaching forward. Over the past few days, Matthew is bringing his right foot under him to push up to stand. This is wonderful as he always sneaks his right foot forward and pushes his knee straight to stand which requires more help. It shows that Matt is not as fearful to lean forward and is finding his sense of balance as well as problem solving. It's all going to come together for him.

One of my friends suggested acupuncture for Matt (and Abby) as it can help with increased blood flow and getting nerve innervation to his muscles to strengthen them. I asked Dr. Derr about this yesterday, to help with getting Matt's left arm working better and relaxing his low back tightness, and he immediately put in a consultation for acupuncture. I asked him about the PEG tube, (stomach tube) and if Matt's intake of food, as well as liquids, are good over the weekend, it'll be taken out "early next week." Another amazing gift—our last tube.

Laura got her driver's license on December nineteenth and doesn't have a vehicle to drive since the van was "totaled." I'm petrified to have her driving, but know I can't stop her from growing up due to my fear and this will certainly help Bill and I out without needing rides for the girls to and from school and to dance class if we are still in St. Cloud. After completing a few errands, I went back to see Matt and found a letter from a former physical therapy student that was at County Manor previously and goes to Augsburg College. She had seen the article in the St. Cloud Times and knowing Matthew had toured and wanted to also possibly go to Augsburg, she had talked to the basketball coach there and told him about Matt's story. She left a signed basketball of all the players and coaches, saying they are all praying for him. It was incredible. When I asked Matt who was here, before seeing her letter, he loudly said "She goes to Augsburg." Matt's voice is way louder and his memory (especially short-term) continues to improve daily.

Oh, I almost forgot my soda story. I was in the dining room for dinner last evening and left Matt to go get the Nesquick for Matt's milk. When I returned, the PCA was by Matt, which surprised me as I was only gone a minute, and Matt was leaning very far over to the right, trying to grab the Diet Pepsi I had left on the table. I asked Matt if he wanted some, and he immediately nodded yes. I thickened it for him and he drank it, very much enjoying it and nodding yes that it was good. I can't imagine not having soda for nine weeks—another gift. I brought him Mountain Dew tonight which he also very much enjoyed.

FAITH

"They say if you have steadfast faith, the size of one mere mustard seed.
That you can move a mountain high and place it where you see the need.
They say having faith is the way to manifest the dreams you dare.
But faith is far, far more than that—It's knowing you're already there."

I think this was written just for me. You have shared your strength with me, God. Through your testing, you have shown me how to withstand some of the painful experiences of life. Enable me to share this knowledge, offering honest counsel and reasons for hope to others. Do not let me pass by someone in need of your strength because I am too busy. You have never been too busy to help me.

Matthew's first basket

—∿—

Jan. 5, 2014

Matt was in bed when I arrived this morning–taking a break between OT and ST. I noticed his left hand was more open and he was trying to straighten his fingers. I brought his arm up over his head and he kept his elbow straight, and in the process was able to actively open his fingers even more. worked on reaching forward with shoulder and elbow motion and could do this too. I am beyond happy. I have no doubt his arm will eventually be at one hundred percent, but seeing him increase strength is SO wonderful as this has been my greatest worry.

In speech, Matt worked on short-term memory and categorizing fruit, furniture, transportation items. He couldn't recall any of them, but since he immediately told me nine times five was forty-five today and couldn't yesterday, I know it will come back too as he heals. Matt also worked on describing pictures with longer sentences and it still surprises me to hear his deep voice. Kami came with me to the hospital this morning and Matt reached for her and pulled her down for a hug without saying a word when she was standing next to his bed. My heart melted–that is so like Matthew.

In PT, Matt "moon-walked" for the first time, walking backwards in the parallel bars. He needed help to move his left hand on the bar, but was able to put weight through it to help keep his balance and to stand taller. We have been working on having Matt lean forward to stand, continuously for the past five weeks. I previously needed another person to reposition him in the wheelchair, then could reposition him myself, and yesterday and today, Matt is holding onto the armrest and scooting himself backwards without any help.

This is such great progress—Matt even leaned forward and grabbed the pole in his room today without any help for the first time.

I arrived after OT, so don't have anything to report, but know Matt is getting better at his self cares. He rinses and spits after brushing his teeth (I remember when we were so happy to even get the toothbrush above his tongue.) Matt doesn't like his socks on and is now able to take the right sock off in bed without any help. He wheeled backwards in the family lounge today and when I asked him what he wanted, he said "I'm cold." How cool is that? I went to get his sweatshirt jacket and realized I need to bring other warmer clothes as he's been in shorts and t-shirts for the past month. Matt has begun to use his call light too. Instead of squeezing his soft call light, he pushes the nurses light on the bed rail with his elbow. The PCA told me he had put on his light, but she didn't know what he wanted as she hadn't ever worked with Matt before. I went in and asked Matt what he wanted, and he pointed to me. My heart was totally bursting at this.

Matt wanted to go to the family lounge and get up, so I brought him down just as visitors arrived (someone who played basketball with him last year.) We brought the over the door hoop, given by his basketball team for his birthday, to the lounge. Matthew threw the ball from about four feet away, let go, and made a basket–just as Bill arrived to see it. It couldn't have been better timing. I brought chocolate chip cookies from Subway for Matt and he loved them, taking bites and not coughing at all. I gave him a Mountain Dew and a blue Gatorade thickened to nectar consistency and he loved both. I asked him if he wanted a chocolate caramel candy, or a cookie and he replied "BOTH."

Matt surprised the night staff saying "I want a Reese's" (peanut butter cup) in the middle of the night. (Matt has gained five pounds, I am so excited–he's eating close to 3500-4000 calories a day which may be why.) He has twenty five to thirty pounds to gain back yet–thus I just finished making him more homemade pizza. One of the PCA's said "He is just rocking" after taking him to the bathroom himself. He thought Matt was throwing the basketball at him, then realized he was aiming for the hoop over his closet door. Matt doesn't smile a whole lot, but you can see a smirk often when something funny happens, and he still hasn't laughed–but it'll come as his breathing and voice continues to improve.

I told Matt I was going back to work tomorrow, but would be there for lunch, or right after, as the girls can stay with him with no school today. Matt nodded he understood and this was okay. It reminds me of the first day I went back to work after having Matthew. My brother Russ was living with us and didn't work, so watched him that day so Matt didn't even have to go to daycare. When I arrived at work, PT I worked with asked me how Matt was doing, and I burst into sobs—saying "he won't know why I'm not there." When I told Russ about my outburst, he said "Well Lynn, he was with me—why would you cry?" Matt has always been so special to me, as the girls are too. I love them all so much, but it's just different with the first child as you all know.

Every week is a blessing for us as God's healing continues through your prayers. It is so amazing to see and now I'm in the "Thank you Jesus" mind frame more than the "asking" stage with Matt's needs as I know he's going to continue to improve and I'm beyond thankful for all he's accomplished and what he WILL accomplish in the future without any doubt. God knows what Matt needs without my asking, as he knows every-one's needs—just trust in him.

Back to Work

—◊◊◊—

Jan. 6, 2014

Today was a long day—getting home at nine forty-five pm from the hospital. Abby stayed with Matt all day, therefore I was able to stay at work for our Monday rehabilitation services meeting I had forgotten all about. It was nice to see all my coworkers and friends and to get several hugs from people even in different departments. My job has changed some due to changes in procedures, so I felt like it was "a first day" learning new systems. I am so lucky to have the support I have from everyone at Country Manor. Bill's work has been super flexible and understanding, allowing him the time needed to run to appointments with the kids and to visit Matt at the hospital. Bill has been at Trim Pac for fifteen years and I have now been at Country Manor for eleven years and the St. Cloud hospital for fifteen years causal. I thank God we haven't changed jobs, unable to imagine how it would be without all the wonderful support we have both received. When Matthew is better, we'll "give it all we have" to try to repay the caring support we have received and continue to receive during this time.

When I arrived at the hospital, Coach Dahman and his family were visiting. His four year old son had been snuggling with Matt, who gave him a big hug. I asked Matt if he missed me and he said "yes," which was the correct answer in case you were wondering. The PCA said he asked her "where's Mom?" when I was gone and of course this did make me feel guilty—but I do need to work and it was good to get in an altered routine today.

When asked if he wanted to walk today, Matt shook his head "no" for the first time. I'm not sure why, but he started with working on sitting balance on the mat, walked, and then went back to the mat as he still had time left in his session. Matt did walk about eighty feet two times, walking with less effort and increased speed, although definitely needs two people to assist him. If Matt wasn't 6'8" he probably wouldn't need an extra person. Mike has his technique down to a science, even using his head to keep Matt's upper body tall. As Matt was walking, he was reading the student's name tag, looking in patient rooms, and watching people in the hallway–especially Dean. It reminds me of AAU basketball when Matt was with the team on a timeout, while listening to his coach, he would be watching the game on the next court. His first year with the Comets, his coach asked him what he had said, and of course Matt repeated it word for word. His coach said "How do you know, when you aren't even looking at me? You look at me when I'm talking or I'll make you run until you puke." Matt did look at his coach from that day on.

Dr. Derr came and talked to us and said Dr. Romanowski did not feel he had anything to offer in terms of acupuncture at this time. It was a bit disheartening but it must have not been meant to be. He said he could give Matt another medication to reduce tone; however, I do not feel he needs it, as some tone is good to depend on for stability with mobility. He asked about Botox for Matt's left hand, but I really don't think we need it at this time. Matt is tolerating the e-stim well with me. Today when I arrived, I brought Matt's arm over his head and he opened his hand more than I have ever seen—with his wrist bent, but it's a wonderful start. I'm not sure if it's the right decision, but we can provide this in the future if needed. Dr. Derr, then asked, if we wanted the PEG tube taken out–OF COURSE WE DO. It's amazing. One good yank and it came right out with a sponge-like tip and Matt shaking his head "no" that it didn't hurt. Matt was down about two and a half pounds from two days ago, therefore I gave him four large peanut butter cups tonight and three dove peanut butter chocolates. I brought more homemade pizza tonight and Matt was upgraded to a mechanical soft diet today so even had lasagna on his tray–but wanted pizza instead. I went to the cafeteria about four-thirty pm as I hadn't eaten since six-thirty am and was super hungry. Matt watched me have a roll and as I began eating breaded shrimp, picked his head up off the pillow and really looked at what I was eating. I asked him if he was hungry and he nodded "yes." Abby then said, "Mom you know it's his favorite. That's mean." Needless to say, I may or may not have gone against his diet and given him a small bite, which turned into him eating half of my shrimp order.

However, in my defense, he chewed very well and never coughed. I know he'll soon be eating everything.

Matt was crying a bit tonight which always breaks Bill and my heart. I asked him if it was because he was in the hospital and he said "yes." I reminded him of how wonderful he's doing and that he couldn't even open his eyes for a month, and he seemed to understand. I asked him if he knew he was doing amazing and he nodded "yes," but it still is tough for him when he wants to be able to use both arm and hands and to be back in school. Dr. Derr asked me about Matt's mood and to let him know if I thought we needed an anti-depressant, so I'll continue to encourage Matt and to monitor how he's feeling. The chaplain is coming to see Matt every day to offer spiritual guidance to help him deal with his grief and loss and to lean on God for support, so hopefully Matt won't need anything. Please pray for Matt's spirits and know that every visit cheers him up.

My inspiration for tonight: "You discover your own worth when you give yourself away in the service of those who need you. All praise to Him who now hath turned my fears to joys, my sighs to song, my tears to smiles, my sad to glad." I definitely feel that this has happened to me; however, now I pray that Matt will have this also.

McDonald's Fries Lift Matt's Spirits

—◊◊◊—

Jan. 7, 2014

At work today two of my former patients gave me a hug and told me how much I had done for them and how sorry they were about the accident, knowing how much I love the kids. It was emotional for me, to "get love and caring" from patients who I've treated more than once in the past several years. I know it was heart felt, as is everything these days it seems.

I thought about what I could surprise Matt with today after work. I left at two pm because Matt had a busy morning and Bill was with him at lunch. I decided to get him McDonald's French fries, a large Diet Coke (his favorite despite my addiction to Diet Pepsi) and chocolate cookies from Subway. When I arrived at the hospital, Matt was wide awake in bed. I asked him how he was doing and he replied "I've been better," clearly and loudly. I asked him if fries, a Diet Coke, and cookies would make him feel better and he immediately shook his head yes. Needless to say he ate every last fry I handed him. I've been rather spoiling him, because he first opened his mouth for me to feed him until I told him several times to take the fry I gave him. He loved it. I asked him if he felt better and he said "yes," and was in good spirits the rest of the night. I spoke with Bill and he said the speech therapist wants to try a hamburger with Matt tomorrow. His PEG tube was removed yesterday and tomorrow he'll be eating a hamburger–how amazing is that for God's healing?

Matt had OT before I arrived of course, but has what he did in a memory log. Kelly, his OT, worked on his left arm using vibration to have Matt work on increasing his active strength with elbow flexion and extension (bending and straightening) and it went well. I brought Matt's hand up and he was able to open his fingers some without any e-stim. He even tried to put a basketball in his left hand today to hold without me even suggesting this–or nagging him–can you believe it? It's a smaller ball, slightly larger than a softball. It will take time, therapy, and prayers, but his left arm is getting better.

In PT, Matt worked on his sitting balance and core strength. He was able to hold his balance without support for a full minute today, for the first time, without reaching down to his feet. Matt was able to hold his left leg, with his knee bent, lying on the mat without having his leg fall to the side. He brought his knee up in a bent position for the first time, off the mat too. Mike talked to him about different sports teams, players, etc., and was amazed at Matt's speech. He's excited as Matt is talking more to give him feedback regarding what he's feeling (pain, sensation, etc.) which will help his progress. I can tell Matt has a special place in all the therapists, doctors, and nurses hearts. It's wonderful.

I spoke with the social worker this afternoon who had contacted the district attorney's office in Little Falls about guardianship. He "highly recommended" we hire an attorney to do all the paperwork. It involves getting doctor's information, many forms, looking at any financial aspects, and meeting with the judge. Since this is an emergency guardianship, they may grant guardianship without Bill or I needing to go to court, for three to six months until a hearing where Matt can be interviewed to determine the future. She said guardianship may then be granted for another six to twelve months, or "permanently" (WHICH WON'T HAPPEN) or deemed Matt can make his own decisions. It was tough not to be sad during the conversation, but it will only be temporary. I then spoke with the RN who obtains insurance authorization. She said weekly updates are sent, and our insurance hasn't made any indication that coverage wouldn't be continuing for some time yet. They both said "there hasn't been any talk about discharge yet, but they are extending the date 2-3 weeks at a time." This is a relief for me as Matt may be able to stay for another one to two months with the rate he's progressing. I'm hoping we can then discharge home with outpatient therapy, but that will be in God's hands.

The chaplain visited and Matt wanted two prayers said today. He brought a letter he had written for all the CentraCare employees. "It's a letter from the Chaplain" he said, wanting me to read it because the letter was entirely about me. I read the letter and it talked about a mother's love after a changing event, which is similar to having a new child being born. I didn't think anyone would know he was referring to me and told him it sounded good–no big deal, right? He told me how much Matt's recovery and being with our family has impacted his personal and spiritual life. He said "Seeing the love you had in your eyes for Matthew (especially that very first day) is as close as I'll ever be to seeing God's love on earth." Oh my goodness. Now we were both teary-eyed as you may have guessed. To think a chaplain, of all people, to be so influenced by our family is beyond my comprehension.

As I was writing this, Matt looked at me and said, "I wonder when I'll be healthy." I told him to give himself another month. I again told him about how much he's progressed with eating, talking, going to the bathroom, moving his left arm and leg some, and walking in just four weeks. He understood completely and was okay with my timeframe, agreeing with me that he would be play basketball again someday.

Believe It or Not

—ᴟ—

I was angry yesterday. An emotion I don't believe I've experienced since the accident. I've been sad, lonely, upset, afraid, happy, worried, etc., etc., but not angry. Let me tell you why. . . . I was coming to see Matt after work about noon to see him finally have a hamburger for lunch with Shawn, the speech therapist. I had a lighter step in anticipation and was excited to spend time with Matt. As I was walking in, another family was behind me and I heard "Oh the kid next door?" and the other replied "Yeah, he's really messed up." to which the response was "You know he was in a car accident." I was immediately hurt, then angry, making sure I looked back at them, making eye contact before walking into Matt's room. I so wanted to turn around and say "Really? He's not messed up! He's my son and I love him SO much. It's not his fault that he's not at school and captain of the basketball team! How dare you!" I wonder how many individuals with disabilities such as Autism, Down syndrome, etc., or their families hear comments from people that really hurt, make them sad, or angry? I bet it's countless. I have always tried to teach the kids to smile, not stare, and look away or offer help if needed (such as to open a door) and not to talk about an individual. If they have questions, they need to ask later. I then spoke with the doctor about Botox for Matt's left hand so it isn't so tight and he can use it functionally. The big debate was whether it was a possibility as an inpatient or to wait until it can be provided on an outpatient basis. He then said "We'll have to look at how much therapy Matt gets here at the hospital, since his progress is slowing down." I again became argumentative and immediately to his shock, I said "I completely disagree. He

190

kept his balance on the mat for a minute yesterday, he's talking, he had a hamburger for lunch, and he's walking better. He is not slowing down one bit." Needless to say, he didn't pick this battle with me. I proceeded to write about 20 things Matt is able to do now over the past week, that he couldn't before, for his progress report this morning. I want Matt to get to the point where a shorter therapist is comfortable walking and working with him so he can continue to progress in strides. Don't get me wrong, the doctors have all been wonderful and at times need to play the "bad guy" to bring up the "what if's," however if I hadn't already been so angry, I probably would have begun crying. It was really bad timing for him.

Anyway, about that hamburger—-Matt ate a bacon hamburger with lots of ketchup for lunch. He puts as much into his mouth as he can at one time, and did fabulous. Matt even ate a raw carrot, even though he doesn't like them, chewing and swallowing just fine. He was officially upgraded to a regular diet. A nurse came into the dining room after he had finished. I told Matt to tell her what he had just eaten. Matt looked at me and said "I don't know." I said, "What did you have with lots of ketchup?" Matt again said, "I don't know." It was within minutes of finishing it, but thank goodness he did believe me that he had eaten a hamburger. It even had bacon on it, so with the reminder of "What did you have with bacon on it?" He then remembered—it'll just take time.

Yesterday my friend asked Matt if he was ready to walk before Mike came and he said, "No." I asked Matt if he wanted to stay in a wheelchair and he said "yeah." I think he meant at the moment in hindsight, but I asked him if he wanted to play basketball, golf, and run again–to which he of course said "yeah." I told him "the first step is to get out of the wheelchair and work on walking in therapy." When Mike came and asked Matt if he was ready to walk, he replied "Yes" much to my delight. So Mike and my friend, a PT from Country Manor, walked Matt using a hemi-walker (like half of a walker to use with his right arm only.) He walked about eighty feet with the two of them, and also with the walker, doing amazing–even taking two steps with his left leg without any help. Matt really doesn't have a chance of not doing amazing with so many of my friends being therapists or RNs.

Today Mike and I walked Matt with a rolling quad cane (like a four pronged cane with two wheels.) I was surprised how little Matt was using the cane for support; however, did have a "death grip" on his transfer belt. It's much easier to have a hand on Matt, to have some control, versus standing back and trusting others, although it continues to improve for me. Matt walked about eighty feet, turned around, and walked back—amazing.

Mike was quizzing Matt about different states, basketball, hockey, football teams, their names, players, logos and colors and he did amazingly well. I told Mike that he was in knowledge bowl and loved trivial questions. Mike asked him what the tallest mountain was, the second tallest, and in which country. Matt immediately answered all the questions and I still haven't checked if they were accurate. Mike then said "Now Matt, it's your turn to ask me a question." Matt replied "What is the elevation of China? I repeated it, to make sure we had heard him correctly and he nodded "yes." I asked Matt if he meant the elevation above sea level, and again he replied "yes." We asked him if he knew the answer and he replied "no," therefore I asked him if he was just teasing Mike and he said "yes." This is the REAL Matt—(Gosh I miss him.) It was awesome, even if he didn't even smile about it. It reminded me of our family vacation to Walt Disney World when Matt was ten years old. We went to a dueling piano restaurant where they asked people to request songs. Matt raised his hand immediately and asked for a song from a different language—something like "The Ballad of . . . . by Pierre Van . . . . . ." The pianists looked at each other and one said "It's all yours," while everyone roared in laughter as he proceeded to play a made up a song I'm sure. I asked Matt how he knew that song, and he said, "We read about in history class and I wanted to know what it sounded like."

One of the main concerns right now is Matt's memory. The therapists continually ask Matt what he had for breakfast, lunch and dinner, and Matt does not remember. When I came back on Friday afternoon, a PCA who works with Matt said she was stacking linens in the room, and heard something. "I turned around, and here Matt was throwing his socks at me." I went in the room and asked Matt if he remembered throwing his socks at Judy, and he immediately nodded his head "yes." I really think he remembers what he deems important at this time. Not to say we shouldn't be working on him remembering everything from his day, but it gives me hope he will someday if he does remember some things already. I thought only two of his friends were with him last night during Matt and Abby's Benefit, however Matt named three. I thought he was wrong, but then his nurse told me "Oh no, there were three guys here with him." Thus, again he deemed this important, but he spent more time with them too– hours, versus the time he spends eating for a meal.

When I arrived today, the PCAs were so excited with Matt's progress in actually putting on his light and asking for water, his contacts, and to go to the bathroom. They tell me the things he's saying and one PCA today said, "He's a sweetie." Last night, Matt asked my sister to call me on her phone. He unzipped her jacket and began looking in the pocket he knows where she keeps her phone. I answered the phone and was pretty emotional to hear his low voice say "Hi Mom." He did repeat "I miss you, I love you." and it melted my heart. Gosh, I've missed hearing him on the phone. See every day turns out good.

The Benefit

Matt & Abby Athman Benefit

L to R: Kami, Laura, Matthew, Abby, & Brooke Athman

Date:
Saturday, January 11
Time:
4:00 pm to 10:00 pm
Location:
Pierz Ballroom (133 Main St)
Spaghetti Dinner:
4:00-7:00 pm (Free Will Offering)
Events:
*Silent Auction
*Live Auction @ 7:30 pm
*Bake Sale & more! (Call for details)

Matthew & Abby Athman were involved in a car accident on Nov. 1, 2013. Both were airlifted to separate hospitals & sustained closed head injuries. Abby is at home & currently participating in outpatient physical, occupational, & speech therapies. Matt is currently in Intensive Care at the St. Cloud Hospital, requiring a ventilator to breathe & tube feedings. Matt will need extensive medical care & therapy for months to obtain the best possible outcome.

Your gifts will help off-set the cost of medical bills, traveling, and Bill & Lynn being off work to care for their children.

Hope to see you there!

Please support. Your help is greatly needed & appreciated!

Monetary gifts may be sent to:
Farmers & Merchants State Bank
Matt & Abby Athman Benefit
80 Main St N
Pierz, MN 56364

To donate auction items,
please contact:
JR Brausen 320-468-6076
Dean Dahmen 320-232-5120
Contact JR Brausen for general questions.

Jan. 12, 2014

As a mother, my greatest fear always has been for my child's photo to be on a milk carton, Walmart bag, or a benefit flyer. As it turned out, the benefit was amazing. The love and support was overwhelming. There were so many people who donated to the silent and live auction, and yet, still came and bought items. The entire Ballroom was packed and they served six hundred and fifty people I believe. I thought I'd be crying all night (prepped with tissue in my purse); however, everyone was very positive, asking how Matt was doing, or saying how happy they were for his progress. It was like a celebration of Abby and Matt's progress, versus feeling everyone was feeling sorry for us. Everyone was instead giving us the feeling of abundant support and love. It was so overwhelmingly humbling to see the committee who volunteered work hard all night for us, many of them my high school classmates. We are very lucky to have such a wonderful community, willing to take away our financial stress at this time so we can solely focus on our family. I told many people, when I was asked "How can you be so strong?" this was the reason why— all this support to lean on. It gets you through it, day by day. We haven't had any lapse in support for ten weeks. God's love is being sent to us every day by our community, family, friends, and coworkers every day. Even some of my ex-patients were at the benefit. That made me teary the most–having them "give caring back to me." I will spend the rest of my life "trying to pay it forward."

Last night during the benefit, we were skyping with Matt, stopped for him to eat, then tried to connect again. His friend texted "They took Matt for a test." Laura told me this and my response was, "Oh no they didn't!" He texted again and said Matt wasn't there and he didn't know what kind of test he went to. I went outside and called the hospital immediately to find out. Matt was complaining of left leg pain and Tylenol wasn't taking it away, so she called the MD for something stronger, and they ordered an ultrasound to make she he didn't have a deep vein thrombosis (DVT or blood clot) in either leg. His nurse called back later and said the tests were negative for any DVTs and she wasn't going to call until after she knew the results because she knew we were busy and didn't want to worry us for no reason. Today, when I crossed Matt's left leg over his right in bed, Matt was able to uncross it quickly and easily like I've never seen before. He also began bending his left knee up on his own when lying in bed, which I haven't seen either. Matt was able to straighten his knee quicker than usual too, with his hip flexed. When I helped to get him out of bed, I barely had to help his left leg–it was way stronger today. When I told the nurse about this, she said, "maybe the pain he was having last night was because of getting more nerve connections to those muscles for movement–it can happen just like that." I believe it did aa a result of all the prayers and support shown last evening. With so many people gathered in one place caring for Abby and Matt, I believe they each received a boost of healing.

My sister-in-law asked me the other day if I "always had been this spiritual." The answer is simple–"No." I believed I was going to be a nun in the third grade when I had Sister Rachel for my teacher, and that was probably the most spiritual I had ever been. But, I also wanted children so I was torn at age nine. (The husband part really wasn't a concern at that time.) I began to literally feel God's healing about three years ago when I took "Healing Touch" classes for a total of sixty hours. It's so clear when pain goes away from someone during healing touch that God is the reason, and it is so powerful. Before the accident, yes, we said prayers before meals and bedtime with the girls, and I'd often fall asleep saying an Our Father in bed at the end of the day. I told her when something tragic like this happens, medicine and therapy (believe it or not) can only do so much. God is ALL you have. If any of you had seen the MRI with the severe brain stem damage between the cerebral hemispheres (two sides of the brain) with shearing of the nerves from the brain to the spinal cord, knowing all Matt is able to do already that he most likely shouldn't be able to, there isn't ANY doubt of a much higher power (God) who is shining his blessing upon our family.

One word frees us of all the weight and pain of life. That word is love. There will be times when we are asked to be more than we ever thought we could be, to do more than we ever thought we could do, and to give more than we ever thought we could give. Faith is knowing that we can and will rise to meet every challenge. I turn to you Lord with complete faith in your strength and your dedication to Matthew's happiness and healing. Thank you, Lord.

"Matthew the Awesome"

—ᴍ—

Jan. 14, 2014

This is Matt's name on our main log in screen for home computer—-true in every sense of the title. Matthew has improved so much since Saturday night during the benefit when he was experiencing left leg pain—it is surreal to me. On Sunday Matt could keep his knee in a bent position, straighten his knee and bend it six to eight inches up from the bed. Since yesterday he is now able to use his right hand just a bit and cross his left ankle over his right knee in bed (with an expression like he's just relaxing–no big deal.) It is a huge deal to me. Matt was able to bend and straighten his left ankle, wiggle his toes, and bring his left leg off the bed today. He walked a lot in PT both days and is now able to advance his left leg about fifty percent of the time, depending on how tired he is and the speed he is walking. Before Saturday night Matt would maybe not need any help for two or three steps of an entire walk. Today Matt went up and down four steps, two times, with Mike and me. Of course, I was a nervous wreck, despite my complete trust in Mike. Going up went well, with Matt even lifting his left leg onto a step without help. Going down wasn't so "pretty," with Matt trying to step too quick with the right leg, and even trying to skip over a step vs placing it on the same step as his left foot. After resting, Matt began pulling up on the railing to go again, so Mike asked him if he wanted to go again, and he nodded yes. He was more determined to do steps than anything yet–I think it's because he wants his room back downstairs and knows Laura is using it now. Whatever the motivation is, I'll take it. I know this increase in left leg strength and function is due to all the thoughts and prayers at the benefit. My mom said "Wherever two or more are gathered, God is in their midst and answers all our prayers." Well, with the number of people at the Benefit, the prayers were answered like an explosion going off. It gives me the goose bumps every time I think of it.

Matt had two friends visit with Laura last night, and when they asked him how he was doing, he surprised us all by saying "Shitty." A friend called Laura's phone to talk to Matt, and when they asked him how the hospital was, he replied "It Sucks." It's good that he's aware to say this with some insight; however, I still worry about his mood, knowing he is grieving his losses too of playing basketball and being with his senior class. My remedy of course is food, snacks, pop and Gatorade to cheer him, which has been quite successful.

Dr. Derr said we could have a four hour pass as long as it didn't interfere with Matt's therapies. I asked Matt where he wanted to go and he immediately said "Little Falls." I asked him what he wanted in Little Falls, Walmart? Matt shook his head "yes." When asked what he wanted to do there, he said "shop." I can't imagine what he wants to shop for, after just having Christmas and birthday presents. I told Matt we could go out to eat and asked him where he'd like to go. He replied "Dominos." I told him I could bring Dominos to him or order it—-what about Mongo's Grill, Red Lobster, Applebee's, or Olive Garden? He's sticking with Walmart and Dominos, every time I ask. I'm so happy he is making requests and this is a possibility, if it's Walmart and Dominos, so be it. We will be practicing car transfers tomorrow in PT and possibly go out for a bit on Sunday. Today was like sliding down a rainbow with the pot of gold at the end in sight, despite being tired physically and emotionally. It was a "good tired."

Matt continues to talk and remember more every day it seems. Mike asked Matt who was in the football playoffs and he named all the teams and who he thought would win without any hesitation. His proficiency with answering was more than likely due to the repetition of information, watching ESPN so much–but he retained the information. He even asked for a different channel today (other than ESPN) and after declining several channels, I gave him the remote and he selected: *Let's Make a Deal.*

In OT, Matt is able to put on his shirt with just minimal assistance, he has begun to propel his wheelchair more, and continues to make gradual progress with left arm strength. I was so hoping that Monday would show an increase in active movement with his left hand since having the Botox on Friday, but typically it takes seven to ten days. I put kinesiotape on his left fingers and wrist to help "kick in" the muscles that open his fingers and straighten his wrist. I'm not sure how much it helped, but Matt was able to obtain increased wrist and finger extension with the e-stim tonight. I asked Matt if he wanted the e-stim and he replied no, but was agreeable when I explained how much I wanted him to be able to use his left hand and how I pray every day it'll get better.

I brought the girls to dance pictures tonight and there was a JV boys basketball game in the elementary school. I spoke with Coach Dean and he asked if I was going over to the high school for the varsity game. I told him I was just too tired and I wanted to go home and make popcorn for Matt for tomorrow. Dean said the Howard Lake coach e-mailed him and asked if it was okay for their team to wear Matt's t-shirts during warm-ups before the game. I said I definitely wasn't going, or I'd be a mess of tears. All the high school teams have been so supportive for Matt, it's unbelievable. I think Matt's story has made so many of those boys appreciate the gift of being able to play basketball and compete, yet still have it be more than a game—if that makes sense.

"Ready to Listen" (from Matt's view) as he now prays the "Our Father" out loud, makes the sign of the cross, and closes his eyes if I do during prayer with the Chaplain or prayer group. Matt's faith has not withered at all.

What should I do, Father? I have placed my will, my faith, and my hope in your vision of perfection for my life. Thus, I will trust whatever action you give me to take. Your will for me is my desire, no matter where in life it leads me. I have faith that whatever comes my way, you will help me to conquer it. I believe you know what is best for me, and I am ready to listen.

"Blow This Joint"

—⁓—

Jan. 16, 2014

Matt's exact words when I asked him what we going to do on Sunday when we go on pass. He raised his arm up in the air and loudly said, "Blow This Joint." We practiced van transfers yesterday in the snow under the north entrance shelter of the hospital. Mike did the transfer first, and then Bill. After Bill got Matt in the van, I helped to scoot his hips over. Matt crossed his folded arms over his chest and did NOT want to get back out. I'm not sure who's heart shattered first, mine, his, or Bill's. We promised him to go out on Sunday and that we'd get him home as soon as we could.

We went back in and Matt walked about eighty feet (with Bill helping until I criticized his positioning of the rolling quad cane to help Matt on his right side) and Mike helping with Matt's left leg. His leg strength was even stronger yesterday than on Tuesday. He was able to bend his knee up towards his chest and lift his entire leg about six to ten inches off the bed with it straight. Matt is also beginning to increase his left arm strength, especially his shoulder, and how much he can open his fingers. When he works hard with his mobility, his left elbow, wrist and fingers flex though His fingers are much less tight, but still have a ways to go and I'm still praying the Botox continues to work. The optimal time is seven to ten days, and it's only been six days, so I need to again be patient and trust.

Matt's memory continues to improve. Fr. Popp visited today and asked Matt if he knew the name of the new Pope, to which Matt immediately replied "Pope Francis" to his delight. I asked Matt some multiplication questions he couldn't answer a few days ago and he got every answer correct. It's like my friend said, "he just needs a reminder to locate all that information he knew." I think she's so right. I asked Matt yesterday what he had for lunch and he replied, "Vals" because Bill had picked up double bacon hamburger and fries for him. He deemed it important and remembered. I think it's like before the accident when Matt didn't remember to replace the garbage liners after taking out the trash. He didn't deem it important. One time after telling him to do so for months, if not years, I had Matt scrub out the waste paper basket with soap and water, because no one looks before throwing garbage in it, or would think to put a liner in if it wasn't their official job. He remembered the garbage liners for at least a month afterwards and I felt very smart. It did wear off however, as it wasn't a priority for him. Today, I asked Matt what he had for lunch and again he said, "I don't remember." He did remember playing the iPad in speech therapy today, but when I asked him what specifically, he wisely responded "Rehab Games."

Matt was upgraded to regular liquids because he's doing so well with swallowing. Matt's room is like a grocery store. . .he has candy, chips, popcorn, Doritos, Gatorade, cookies, etc., etc. Not only are Bill and I continually encouraging him to eat, but the nurses and therapists are also enjoying giving him treats. I came in one day and Kelly, OT, was giving him Doritos. She said "Matt had his light one and was fidgety, so I asked him what he needed and he said, CHIPS." She didn't have him at that time, but was waiting for a patient to come back, so was helping Matt out.

I asked Matt if he wanted Abby or Kami to spend the day tomorrow because they didn't have school and he said "No." I asked him why and he said "Because they need to focus on school." I again told him they didn't have school and he continued to say "No" to company. It makes me worry about his mood, but then I think it might be improving. Matt always liked his alone time without anyone bugging him at home because it happened so seldom with four sisters.

I left the hospital to go home for dinner just as Bill arrived. It's like tag-teaming every day. The nurses comment on "what a great system we have." We make it work, because it has to and try not to ever have Matt alone in the evening as the day does get long for him. He continually asks to sleep or go to bed, but then doesn't sleep anyway. I can tell he's improving physically and cognitively. It'll still be a long road, but with all the support our family has, we'll get through it and become better people because of our journey.

What a Weekend

—w—

Jan. 19, 2014

The roller-coaster continues—-seems like months since my last entry, versus three exhausting days. Everyone has been asking how work is going. It is going well and my time goes so fast. Although I'm torn about not being with Matt all day long, it's good to be productive and to have this part of my life back. I'm working between four and six hours a day, then go to the hospital right after—having Matt be my reward, along with all the stories the therapists and nurses tell me about what he has done or said every day. On Friday Kami stayed with Matthew all day because they didn't have school. Bill and I met with an attorney about guardianship and tried to absorb the reasoning. Legally, at age eighteen, a parent does not have the right to medical records or decisions about care, surgeries, discharge plans, etc. unless the person gives permission. Although it's an expensive process we definitely agreed with her that we really didn't have the time, energy, or want to take the risk of not doing something we needed to with something this important.

I then went to the hospital and found out that our insurance is asking for "functional goals and a target discharge date" as they don't feel Matt is making enough progress. Really? I so plan to call the Health Partners case manager Monday morning. It's all in the documentation. Everyone who works with Matt after not seeing him for even a couple of days cannot believe how much better he's doing. Dr. Anderson is back and literally tapped on my shoe as I was asleep in Matt's room Friday night for a few minutes (while the girls were having pizza with Matt in the lounge) to discuss this. I explained to him how

Matt has only gotten left leg strength back since last Saturday night during the Benefit. He didn't know this, and said he was surprised at how much he has been moving his left leg when he assessed him. He assured me that he'd do a thorough review of all his notes and send an update to our insurance on Monday. Dr. Anderson said that our goal is for Matt to stay until he can transition home with outpatient therapies; however, we need an alternative plan in case the insurance denies coverage. My alternative plan is still for Matt to go to Country Manor, although he needs to be at a level where he can progress with a PT who isn't six feet tall like Mike. Dr. Anderson, doing his job of course, needs to offer other suggestions or alternative settings available. He suggested Courage Kenny Rehabilitation Institute—Golden Valley campus. I told him "No, that would tear our family apart." I would have to quit work and be in the cities, and it wouldn't be fair to the girls, or to Matt, who needs his friends for support right now. I want Matt to work with therapists I know and trust, who are one hundred ninety-nine percent vested in getting him better, to be able to have pool therapy (as Country Manor's pool floor is a treadmill) and to have consistent in-house therapy versus contracted therapists. I know he'd get a lot of therapy every day, and be able to be in the clinic with our outpatients—several who are high school aged knee surgery patients. As I thought about Matt's progress and the need to show the carryover with nursing staff for insurance authorization, yesterday I decided to ask for Matt to go on a regular therapy schedule. He now has OT/PT/ST each for forty-five minutes a day, seven days a week. With a regular schedule, he would have three hours of therapy a day during the week days, two forty-five minute sessions of PT, forty-five minutes each of OT and ST, and only thirty minutes of therapy Saturday and Sunday combined. This would help with carryover of mobility and balance skills and increase his independence with dressing, bed mobility, toilet transfers, etc. I'm hoping this will start tomorrow, and Bill and I will work with Matt on mobility and leg exercises, the new iPad games for speech (math, memory, money, problem solving, etc.) and I'll continue to work on Matt's left arm on the weekends.

I was a bit down yesterday, finally deciding on a vehicle, only to find out it had sold. I was upset we didn't have a new vehicle to take Matt on pass with, worried about insurance authorization, etc., etc. One of the PCA's noticed my mood and said they were worried about ME, oh my goodness. I told her they were so good to Matt and that's all I needed from them. I went home and had received a card from someone anomymous, post-marked in Minneapolis, no return address or name, saying they were praying for Matt's recovery every day, had enclosed money and a gas card, and signed it "someone who cares." At this moment, I knew everything would again work out okay, having a sense this card was sent from someone above to renew my faith. Not because of the generous gift, but that this person wanted no acknowledgement, wanted me to know Matt is in her prayers, and she cared. I can't describe it in a way to do justice for how it changed my view of the day and the future.

I arrived at the hospital today to have Matt's RN tell me "How he couldn't believe how much stronger Matt is since he last worked with him, saying that the two PCAs even walked him to the bathroom with the rolling cane this morning." I calmly told him, he must be talking about someone else, not Matt, in room fourteen, as they are still using two staff to transfer him. Another PCA came to the desk and confirmed Matt had walked to the bathroom. I was elated (after being relieved that it went so well.) They are taller and have watched Matt walk with Mike a few times and felt comfortable with this. Stacey said "We needed to progress him on the nursing side and he did great." Matt walked to the bathroom again this afternoon with them and did wonderful, despite my "mother-hen" nervousness making sure his left knee was straight before stepping with the right foot. Matt is picking up and positioning both legs to step, turn, and back up—it's incredible.

After being in the bathroom for about thiry minutes unsuccessfully before going out on pass, we decided to just go. The transfers in and out of the van went exceptionally well with the girls all wanting to help too and being worried Matt was cold, despite the wonderful day. We went to Walmart and Matt immediately said he needed to go to the bathroom. We found the family bathroom and after much time, again decided to wait until later to try. As it turned out, he didn't go to the bathroom from mid-morning until after we got back to the hospital around 5:30 pm. He has the bladder of an elephant, whereas I have the bladder of a squirrel–per the kids. Matt picked out a comedy movie, Gatorade, Code Red Mountain Dew, Sour Patch Kids candy, Skittles, Reese's peanut butter cups (of course,) gummy worms, etc., etc. Brooke was continually offering him everything and wanting to push him in the wheelchair, and at one point he literally pushed her away a few times. Several times yesterday and today he was tickling her, so I think he was just a bit overstimulated.

Brooke continually asks to feed Matt, even though he can do this himself. She will say "At least I can poke it with the fork." Abby and Brooke stayed with Matt when we went to Buffalo yesterday and as we left I heard Brooke say "Now Matthew, if you need to go to the bathroom, just tell me." When we got back Brooke said "Matt tricked me. He said he had to go to the bathroom and when I got the nurse he said no, he didn't have to go." Stacey said it was so funny because Brooke came running down the hall to tell her Matt had to go to the bathroom, and when she came in the room, he had this huge silly grin on his face. I can only imagine he wanted a break from Brooke asking him if he needed to go—how funny.

We went to Jimmy's Pour House to watch the football game and have dinner. Matt's knees and wheelchair armrests didn't fit under the tables, so he had to sit on the side of our table. He ordered a bacon hamburger, fries and Mountain Dew–no surprise there. He kept pushing his hips forward in the wheelchair, even more so after I told him not to. I asked him why he was doing this–"are you uncomfortable?" Matt then said "because I'm uncomfortable." I asked if he needed to stand and he said "yeah." I told Bill and he stood Matt in the middle of the Jimmy's in a hug for two or three minutes. It wasn't very busy, but we wouldn't have cared if it had been. Bill helped Matt sit down again and said "Any time you need to stand, Bud, just let me know." I was very touched and thankful to have Bill at my side every step of the way. Matt then sat without sliding at all until we left. He is starting to get a cold with a runny nose which makes him cough some. He showered Abby with Mountain Dew yesterday (face, clothes, iPad, etc.) and today at Jimmy's coughed so hard he didn't even get any on his clothes, missed Abby, and thankfully didn't look toward the table next to him. I reminded Abby of Laura being sprayed by Matt's trach, seems like a lifetime ago in ICU–so it was her turn and she should be thankful it was only soda.

My mom said she read a saying that was "just right for me":

"Dear God, I know that you never give me more than I can handle. I just wish you didn't trust me so much." I truly think that our shoulders were getting a bit heavy and God lightened the load this weekend through others.

Candy Crush

—◦◦◦—

Jan. 22, 2014

What is the object or purpose of this game? Matt loves playing it on his iPad and I've yet to figure it out. I asked him if I'd ever know what he was doing and he replied "No." Matt is so totally honest, with no emotion shown for the most part, unless I ask him to smile–it is so difficult not to see him laughing, joking, smiling, but in time it'll happen. I remember Matt always saying "show no emotion" when something was funny before the accident, and although he'd try to keep a straight face, he would burst out laughing. I miss this beyond words. I tried telling him of the story of our cat having a diarrhea outburst (over a six foot path that I had to clean up) when Saddie, our golden lab scared it about three weeks before the accident (as he laughed harder than I've ever heard him laugh) and he didn't remember or even smile. I tried tickling him too yesterday—bad idea as I was on his right side and that arm is very strong. Not so much as a smile. I smiled at Matt tonight and he did smile, mostly on the right side and although it wasn't automatic, he did so without me asking him to and I melted. There is so much hope for Matt emotionally, physically, cognitively. It's so wonderful, yet draining this week as I want it too much, have been fighting a cold and been super tired. I try to put it all into perspective, and have decided this is much easier when I'm rested and healthy. I feel like I don't have a lot to report now that I'm at work and not seeing all his therapies every day.

Matt's honesty is not always the most favorable for others. Example: Laura asked him who his favorite sister was and he looked at her and said "Abby." My parents and brother visited him yesterday and asked Matt if he was tired and he said "yeah," so they asked him if he wanted them to leave, and he replied, "yeah" so they did after only a thirty to forty minute visit. Laura asked Matt if Brooke was annoying and he replied "yeah" and after laughing, she asked Matt who else annoyed him. Without hesitation, Matt replied "Dad." Laura said, "But he loves you so much, right?" and he replied "yeah." So, just to let you know, now is not the time to ask Matt "Do I look fat in these jeans?"

Matt has continued to gain strength in his left leg. He can raise his leg up off the bed, almost get it into bed to lie down without help, bend his knee up to his chest, move his ankle up and down and wiggle his toes. Today he walked with Mike, his PT, about seventy-five feet without any help, or use of a cane or hemi-walker. As they walked, he even went further away from the wall which he was to lean on for support. It brought me so much hope again, knowing Matt will definitely walk on his own someday—now I just need my patience renewed. Mike was helping him advance his left leg, alternating between working on Matt's left leg strength and his balance. Matt is able to keep his sitting balance significantly better—even for several minutes, especially when resting his right elbow on his knee, and he is beginning to attempt to catch his balance when leaning—which is huge. The decision to have PT twice a day was a good decision as improving Matt's balance and mobility will affect all his self care skills.

I read in Matt's memory log he had played "blackjack" with Shawn, the speech therapist and "he took all Shawn's chips," so obviously his math and problem solving continues to improve. Matt is now talking more without prompting too. When I told him I think of him all day long tonight, Matt said "Really?" which was completely unexpected for me. I told him some guys quit the basketball team and Matt looked at me and said "Why?" How wonderful is that thought processing? Matthew is now using his nurse call light to ask for a drink, to go to the bathroom, etc. He even put his light on to ask to go to the bathroom at five am this morning. Many of the patients on the rehab unit have really "taken" to Matt and ask him how his day was, tell him how good he looks, etc. and Matt has begun to respond to them without any prompting.

Matt's left hand hasn't improved like I had hoped and prayed for. He is able to open it when I help him lift his arm over his head, but more in a movement pattern than voluntary. I use the e-stim with him every day to increase his strength to straighten his wrist and open his fingers, and I can get more movement, but the carryover functionally is tough yet. I keep thinking of when I worked on a stroke and neuro unit in the cities for five years. I told all my patients that the leg strength comes back sooner than the arm because we bear weight through it to transfer into bed, onto the toilet, etc., and the body gets that feedback and joint compression. If we were monkeys and walked on our hands and feet, our arm would come back just as quickly. I need to keep this in mind, because with therapy and prayers, Matt will get function back to his left arm and hand. His shoulder is definitely getting stronger, but this is usually easier as the muscles are larger and require less coordination than the hand. Matt tries to straighten his left thumb and fingers continuously, which is encouraging that he attends to it, yet tough to watch as he tries to open a pop bottle, or put something into his hand unsuccessfully. I know he'll be a stronger person because of going through what he is and appreciate all he is able to do from now on—just as I know Bill and I do.

Everyone asks about how long Matt can stay on the rehab unit. The answer is simple: I have no idea. All I know is staff need to update his case manager at the end of the week about his progress. As I watch Matt, I've come to the realization he'll need therapy on an inpatient basis for quite some time yet, beyond what they will approve for him at the hospital. If Matt were to come home, he would most likely have outpatient therapy only three times per week and intensive therapy, six to seven times per week is critical right now to get as much function back as possible. If I were to take Matt home now with twenty-four hour supervision, it would be selfish on my part and not in his best interest, as he needs more inpatient therapy, whether he can understand or agree at this time. Thus, I've been in a "funk" all week about this and need to let go and let God handle the future, as difficult as it is. One of the patients I saw in the therapy gym today at Country Manor, to my surprise asked me how Matt was doing. I have no idea how she knew who I was, but she said, "Ever since we read the story in the paper, a whole group of us in the apartments decided we would pray for him every day. He is getting so many prayers." It was what I needed today—to know people are still remembering and praying for Matt even though the newspaper articles and benefit are all completed. He still needs all of you.

I received a card with a wonderful saying on it I wanted to share tonight.

NO ocean can hold back

No river can overtake it

No army can defeat it, no law can stop it

No disease can cripple it

No force on earth is more powerful or effective than the power of PRAYER

Chocolate

—w—

Jan. 25, 2014

Today was a busy day again. I went into work in the morning to work on employee reviews, then to the hospital to see Matt, back to work to interview a prospective PT, and then back to the hospital until four pm. Kami's basketball tournament was in the afternoon and her and Brooke had a part in the Catholic School's week mass at four-thirty pm and I missed both of these, but Bill was able to watch a game and Grandma and Grandpa went to mass to watch the girls, so it all worked out as usual.

I continue to get reports of Matt's personality from the therapists and nursing staff immediately when I arrive–it's wonderful. Matt put his call light on after OT one morning, immediately after Kelly left his room. When the PCA asked him what he wanted, he replied, "more deodorant." He must have worked hard to work up a sweat. I asked Matt what he wanted to drink yesterday and today, and both times, he replied "surprise me." That's pretty cool and shows me his thinking continues to improve. He is spontaneously responding to staff more often too. When the chaplain told him it was good to see him again, Matt cleared his throat and said, "good to see you too" without me prompting him to reply.

Mike suggested we get Matt a different wheelchair. I called a vendor and as I figured, a wheelchair isn't covered by insurance while someone is in the hospital or a care center, until discharge as the facility needs to provide this. It doesn't matter that he needs a more specialized wheelchair being 6'8". He currently sits on his tailbone, sliding down unless restrained with a belt which he absolutely hates, or he's lying in bed, so he doesn't have good trunk positioning to carryover for upright posture in sitting, standing, or during walking. The vendor initially suggested Goodwill; however, I told him I didn't want Matt in a junker of a wheelchair as he will be at Senior night for the boys basketball game in February. He had a tilt-in-space red wheelchair we can rent reasonably and will bring it for Matt to try on Tuesday. The phone call was difficult to make, but as I told Matt, we'll rent it for a couple months and it won't be long-term—he'll be walking long-term. Matt nodded and completed agreed with the plan. In all honesty, Matt would agree with anything he felt Bill and I thought he needed or should do, but it made me feel tons better and now I'm excited for him to get it. If it's comfortable, Matt will sit better and do better in therapy with his balance and mobility.

In speech yesterday, Shawn said they "went on the Internet and Matt wanted to Goggle himself, which is actually a perfectly normal request." Shawn said he read Matt the article from the *Morrison County Record* on the night of the boys first basketball game. The article showed Matt's jersey on the bench and had comments about him from teammates and his coaches. Shawn's eyes became teary and he said "I think it was harder for me to read it, then for Matt to listen." My heart again melted as Matt has completely touched so many people.

Matt's discharge date is tentatively set for February third, although it's just an estimated date and may change based on progress. I left a message for his case manager from HealthPartners, but didn't get a call back yet. Mike said, "There should be an exclusion for patients as tall as Matt, like there is for obese patients who need specialized equipment and care." I completely agree and continue to push for Matt to be at a level where he can make strides with a shorter therapist in his continued rehab needs. Dr. Anderson wrote a detailed note regarding Matt's progress to continue his stay. Matthew was so tired on Friday, he even fell asleep while getting dressed with Kelly in OT. We are not sure why, but possibly a combination of having a busy day with our pass last Sunday, going to three hours per day therapy this week, and discontinuing his Ritalin on Thursday (which helps with alertness and attention, as it was a low dose and Matt doesn't seem to need it anymore.) Anyway, they let him sleep in until almost ten am this morning "like any teenager on the weekends" and he seemed to be a lot less tired today. Part of the problem with insurance is showing carryover of level of assistance with nursing documentation, as they at times document he needs three staff to transfer. I have never seen nursing use three staff; however, that's because I transfer him myself and only have help with getting him on the toilet, although I know I could do it all myself. We changed his transfers so the shorter PCAs who have difficulty when Matt stands tall for transfers, can just partially stand him while he holds onto the bedrail and have him turn and sit in the wheelchair or on the bed. I was on a mission on Friday during his PT session and since Matt had a different PT (as Mike is on vacation,) I asked if I could show the PCAs how to transfer him. I only need one arm to transfer him and use the ceiling pole to balance myself for leverage and it goes super easy–they were very surprised, so hopefully this will help to justify Matt's progress to stay longer on the rehab unit. I did talk to my boss's boss Friday briefly about Matt and his probable need for continued therapy as an inpatient at Country Manor after discharge from the rehab unit. I told her, "He's the perfect rehab candidate" and her exact response was, "We'd be honored to have him." The relief and sincerity of her words would have had me cry, had I not been focused on getting work done and tried not to reflect on this at that time. Now, however is another story. God will take care of Matt and our entire family through others we encounter–I have no doubt.

Matt continues to eat, and eat, and eat. I have a good feeling that by the time he gets home, he'll weigh more than he ever has. I asked him what he wanted to eat yesterday, and he replied "chocolate." Obviously, he's been spending too much time with me. They say people remember everything subconsciously while in a coma, and God knows I've lived on chocolate, coffee and Diet Pepsi for three months. He probably thinks he needs Dove chocolates, Hershey's, truffles, and Reese's peanut butter cups of course for survival. He had a ham sandwich, fries, watermelon, strawberries, chocolate protein ice cream and chocolate milk for dinner tonight. We brought him to the cafeteria for the first time with us while Bill, Abby and I had dinner and Matt ate a Snicker's ice cream bar, a double chocolate chunk cookie and then peanut butter cups when we got back to his room. I have no doubt he consumes four thousand calories a day. The funniest is when the dietary aids try to take his order, often with salads, soup, and vegetables. Now that Matt can talk and order his meals, after they give him each of the two options, he looks at them and says, "No." We then order the back up bacon hamburger and a double order of fries. This, as well as French toast and bacon for breakfast, never gets old for him.

Matt's left leg strength continues to improve, especially when he's in bed. He continually moves his leg and tries to straighten his left fingers. His hand has decreased tightness, not as much as I had hoped; however, it's easier for me to open his hand and he is able to open his fingers progressively more too. It will just take time, therapy, and prayers. Matt's memory continues to improve—especially short-term when I ask him who was visiting and events about the day. He watches basketball continuously and has less interest in his keyboard and bells—preferring TV or candy crush on the iPad. He is now able to scoop and feed himself his entire meal with us cueing him to eat with every bite. Watching his progress is totally a gift for me. I continue to wait for him to laugh again. Even coughing salvia into Bill's left eye tonight and burping about four inches from my face, didn't cause a flicker of a smile despite Abby and I laughing and me telling him "it was funny." Bill somehow didn't think so either, which made it even funnier for us. These moments get me through it all.

You are the rock to which we cling, Father. Let me be an example of your presence in the world to let others know you are there. Show me what I can do to bring your healing touch to the weak so they can smile again. God has invited us to call upon him and lean on him in times of trouble or sorrow. He has promised to help and comfort us, to rescue and revive us, and to do great things for us. God wants us to come to him—to let his strength be our strength and his hope be our hope. God continue to be my family's strength and hope. I have no doubt that all of your prayers for Matt, Abby and our family is the reason for our strength and never-ending hope for Matt's recovery.

Whack-a-Mole

—m—

Jan. 28, 2014

This was how I felt yesterday–with my head just above ground when the mallet struck. Let me explain. Sunday, Laura and I spent most of the day with Matt–Bill was on his way to the hospital with Abby, Kami and Brooke, but with the blinding snow needed to turn around and go home. The nurse came in and was doing an assessment of Matt's strength and he was able to bring his left leg over his right, lift it up toward the ceiling, bring his left hand to touch his chin and opened his hand completely two to three times. I took Matt to the bathroom by myself and he transferred with minimal assist, turning and stepping with both legs, and for the first time I left with a very, very strong sense that Matt would regain all the strength throughout his left side and would physically get back to himself.

Yesterday, I went to Matt's room and saw Bill's coat on the chair at two fifteen pm, much later than he ever stays after having lunch with him every day. Bill came down the hallway and said he was waiting for his car to be towed in the ramp because the power steering went out and it was a two to three hour wait. I told him I was going to see what our insurance had said because the updates were sent on Monday. They said, there was no news from them yet, but the social worker wanted to meet with us. We met her at Matt's room and she said, "How about we go to the family lounge because the doctor wants to meet with us too." She talked to us about how the guardianship was going, about funding through the traumatic brain injury organization, (for home modifications and home health care to take care of Matt in the home) and long-term Social Security Disability. I was so tired upon arriving at the hospital, discussing these topics were exhausting, but I knew also necessary. I was glad Bill was able to be with me for this spontaneous meeting–guess that's the reason his brakes went out–God looking out for me again.

The doctor came in and said Matt's discharge date was February 3rd. I asked if this was set, or could move out after further review. He said the date is their set discharge date and he is in agreement with it. "You are lucky HealthPartners approved nine weeks already. They wouldn't have if he was eighty-five years old." He said, my rationale that Matt needs a taller therapist, isn't warranted because he needs core strength (trunk strength and balance) and any therapist, regardless of height can work on this. "The mom in you feels good to see him walk, but the therapist in you should know it's not functional and he needs to be able to sit first to work on neuro-developmental skills. If you don't know this, I question your skills as a therapist." I told him we were working on both. Matt needs to work on standing and standing balance too so he can transfer to the toilet and keep his balance to manage clothing. I didn't tell him I took a three week course a long time ago and I'm actually certified in neuro-developmental techniques. I instead said "If you're trying to make me feel horrible, you've succeeded." He said, "I'm not trying to make you feel horrible. I'm giving you a reality check."

The Doctor said, Matt can't sit up, doesn't catch his balance when he loses it, (which I interrupted and said, "he does sometimes") his carryover of new learning is poor, his short-term memory is poor, he will not be able to walk functionally, therefore we needed to get our home ready for him to be in a wheelchair. I told him Matt is getting strength throughout his left leg and I disagree. He'll get there in time. Apparently, the doctor has no idea of the power of all your prayers and God's healing. For the record, I do a reality check, at least every other minute of every day, thinking about a ramp, railings, grab bars by the toilet, bathing equipment, what carpeting and living room arrangement we should do, etc., etc., etc., etc. I am now devastated and would have taken Matt out of the hospital right then and there.

Today, I went to visit with a heavy heart. Matt was in PT and wasn't doing as well walking because he seemed tired, didn't have his Ritalin, or just wasn't very motivated. Mike is on vacation until tomorrow. The vendor brought Matt's new wheelchair and he loved it, saying at least three or four times, "It's better!" He was able to propel it with only his right leg all the way to the dining room. It's not perfect but Matt was very happy and that's all that matters as this is just a rental wheelchair. When we were almost to the dining room, I received a phone call from the case manager at HealthPartners, who apologized for not being able to call me back last Friday and said yesterday was her day off. I told her I had been calling to talk about Matt's coverage and what it would be at Country Manor too, but I knew the February third date was "set in stone" so it was a mote point to discuss extending this. She then told me that "They did not give a discharge date at all. Matt still has coverage at the hospital, but the rehab team felt his needs could be met in a less intensive rehab setting. They have a medical director that reviews Matt's case monthly and they had not given any denial or discharge date." NOW I AM ANGRY. Not for the fact that Matt needs to discharge, but that I've been lied to. Probably shouldn't write this at all, but I AM ANGRY and hurt, to say the very least. The transition could have been such a positive one, saying how far Matthew has improved, but it's time for a change, etc., versus questioning my skills as a therapist and being lied to. I told Bill afterwards I couldn't believe he didn't say anything to the doctor. Bill's response was "I was waiting for you to lunge at him across the table. I did go talk to him after the meeting and told him he had no right to go after your skills as a therapist." I asked Bill what the doctor had replied, and he said "There were things Lynn needed to hear."

The good thing is that I am now so excited for Matt to go to Country Manor as a change will be good for him with new goals, ideas and positivism. The therapy pool will be incredible. For some strange reason, I believe Country Manor had the pool built (God's plan) just for Matt's recovery. He will be able to walk much easier with the bottom of the pool being a treadmill, and he won't want to push to the left, because he won't want to lose his balance in the water. Matt was at the level below a lifeguard when he finished swimming lessons so he won't be afraid of the water at all. When I asked Matt to tell his friends tonight what was going to happen this week, he said "I'm getting out of here." I said tell them where you are going, and he replied, "I'm going to Country Manor." Matt knows how much I love it there, and he's been there multiple times, so he's actually looking forward to it.

Matt typically asks to go back to bed the minute a meal is finished. Tonight in his new wheelchair, he didn't ask to at all and sat up for four hours. I asked him if his bottom hurt at all and he said "No." Hind sight is twenty-twenty, and I wish I had rented a wheelchair for him a month ago. It was Mike's suggestion so he could sit upright and work on his posture versus sliding and sitting on his tailbone or in bed. I just didn't think of it. Matt picked out the movie, *Dumb & Dumber* and watched it partially, had his classmates visit, and then watch a bit more of the movie, without asking to go to bed. It was wonderful for him to have classmates visit again as it's been a while. With sports, jobs, and the weather, I know it's difficult, so the visit was much appreciated and enjoyed by Matthew.

Everything happens for a reason. The fact that I was hired and work at Country Manor for 10 years is for a reason. Matt will have a lot of therapy (even more than at the hospital if he tolerates it) and have the pool therapy too. His friends asked if he could still have visitors, and Bill asked if he would have meals provided there. The answer is yes, and yes. Matt had wanted to get a job there this fall in activities, but with basketball and the drive, we told him we'd rather have him do well in his college classes and apply for scholarships. He was taking four college classes and just missed the A honor roll the day of the accident when the quarter ended. Matt is excited to move, knowing it's something positive.

I so appreciate what all the hospital rehab team—nurses, therapists, doctors, and especially, Mark, the chaplain (who even came and played floor hockey with Matt tonight in his new wheelchair) have done for Matthew. He has made gains beyond what was predicted when looking at the MRI. I have no bad feelings and think of them all as my friends and will be forever indebted to them. Thank you so much for how far Matt has come. It's now time for the next chapter in our journey; however, and with faith and your prayers, the story will have an amazing ending.

Tilt-a-Whirl

—⚡—

Feb. 1, 2014

Yesterday morning before getting ready for the day, Bill said "We're getting there, huh?" Yes we are. We finally found a new vehicle after rushing to Brainerd Thursday night. They had a used GMC Acadia crossover, which we had been trying to find for weeks. Laura was so frustrated with asking for rides from friends and their parents (forget riding the bus after having Matt drive her to school for a year.) I'm hoping by having my van now, it will brighten her mood. I know it'll make her feel much more independent which will be good for her. The vehicle is a 2011 and has remote start and heated seats. I have to make sure I go to the bathroom before driving it. It is wonderful, and yet, I feel guilty as we never would have bought it without the accident or Benefit. We needed a newer vehicle that still seated seven with Matt most likely staying home for another year, and I refused to buy a van. I've driven one for fourteen years and wanted four wheel drive, so this served both purposes. My sister-in-law made a very good point, saying that was what the Benefit was for and if it wasn't for the accident, we wouldn't have needed a vehicle. So again, I need to be humble and say thank you to everyone.

Matt has been so excited to move to Country Manor and it's all set now for Monday. Yesterday, he was a bit down and I know it was because he's going to miss all the PCAs, nurses, therapists, chaplains, etc. I asked him if that was why and if he was a little scared and he said, "yeah." Of course, my solution to everything these days to cheer him, is chocolate or ice cream, so we went to the cafeteria and got a Snicker's ice cream bar. I also brought Matt around the rehab unit and to the PICU and he gave everyone a bracelet of "I Wear Green for Matt." The nurses on PICU were so excited to see Matt and hear him talk, as he never spoke a word for the four weeks he was on the unit. It was heart-warming all over again to see the smiles on their faces, astonished he looked so good. I told them we were bringing treats on Monday before he left, and one nurse said "Are you bringing something good?" Matt replied, "Yeah" even though he has no idea what we'll pick up.

The chaplain called me yesterday and literally brought me to tears. He said the whole chaplain team went to see Matt in the morning and there wasn't a dry eye in the room. Each of them shared with Matt what they remember, or what stood out for them during Matt's entire stay at the hospital from day one of his journey. He left a series of books that Matt likes to listen to and also contacted the people who publish the books to see if they would visit Matt at Country Manor when they come to St. Cloud. He said, "I told Matt he couldn't get out of my prayers, even though he's leaving the hospital." He then THANKED me for being the person I am, for the great love he has witnessed with Matt and me, and my faith—even when the prognosis was poor." He said "They make movies about people like you." I had tear-brimmed eyes for about three hours.

One of the nurses asked Matt if he was having a Super Bowl party, and Matt looked at me and said, "No." I said, "But he's having a Valentine's Day party right?" Laura has told Matt several times the girls in his class are coming for Valentine's Day and he's very excited about this. I said "I bet they'll bring peanut butter cups" (I'll pick some up) and Matt said "I hope so." He is getting so spunky. When my mom visited today, she asked him if someone was pretty, and Matt replied "No comment." I told the PCA about this, and Matt says, "I knew she'd tell my response." His thinking is getting so much better. I asked him yesterday if he remembered running down the highway with the cats following him, about a month ago he hadn't, and he nodded yes immediately. I am absolutely over-joyed.

Brooke was visiting today, stating she hasn't seen Matt in two weeks. When did she get so smart? Matt and her rough-housed when she crawled in bed with him. He tickled her, tried to grab her nose between his knuckles, and actually had a pillow fight. He was trying to sleep with Brooke snuggled beside him, but she didn't stop talking, so Matt was twisting her finger, her arm, etc. Brooke said "Why are you being so mean to me?" Matt replied "Because you won't shut up." Oh my gosh, it's just like old times. His friend stayed with him Thursday night when we went to Brainerd and she asked Matt if she was asking too many questions, and Matt said, "Better you than my sisters."

Ella, the therapy dog, visited Thursday night and Matt petted her for quite a while. It's amazing to see the change with Matt and Ella–from Ella snuggling near Matt in ICU with no response, to Matt sitting in the wheelchair repetitively petting her. Matt continued to smell his hands every couple minutes while petting her, with her owner, Marlene, assuring him Ella had a bath last night. Marlene said "You've lost weight, not the way to do it though." Now I know it's time to leave the hospital–when the volunteers have noticed I'm losing weight. After she left, Matt was playing Candy Crush on the iPad, then wheeled forward to open his closet door with his left foot off the footrest, literally running over his foot. I said "Matt stop–what are you doing? What do you want?" Matt said, "My hands smell like dog." I asked him if he wanted a washcloth, and he said "yeah" and not only washed his right, but his left without me telling him to. Matt's awareness of his left arm and hand is improving a lot and this is very important (attending to the left side is huge for not running into door frames, and hopefully driving someday.) Matt has always been "a smeller." As a baby, to get him to eat any vegetables, I would bring a spoon of blueberry dessert for him to smell, and when he opened his mouth, I would swap it for like beans or peas, etc. He did catch on after a couple of months and then would spit it all over me, but at least he did get vegetables during this time. I looked at Matt's baby book tonight where I had written monthly journals of my memories for every month through his first year (as I have for all five of the kids) and saw under the title "cute doings and sayings" about how Matt would run to the TV and smell the flowers with Thumper (the rabbit) during the Bambi movie he watched a minimum of two to three times a day at age two. Oh–the wonderful flood of memories. Every time I see a baby boy or small child I miss all the memories of Matt as a child and want to go back just for a day.

Matt had a former basketball team member and his mom visit last night, bringing him a framed photo and a basketball signed by Blake Griffin from the Los Angeles Clippers. I told this to the PCA tonight, saying he was from the LA Lakers, and Matt corrected me, saying "The LA Clippers." Tonight, Matt's coach visited with some of the players and brought Matt a signed game ball from Kevin Love from the MN Timberwolves. We now have about five basketballs that symbolize so much love and caring, it's beyond describable.

This afternoon before I left the hospital I decided Matt should get up in the wheelchair because he had been in bed from one to four pm. The PCA, Michelle, and I stood him up and he was standing SO well with weight on both legs, so I told her I wished we could take him for a walk. She said "I'm comfortable with that." We walked him from his room to the dining room which is a long ways (maybe one hundred to one hundred twenty-five feet) and it was the best walk ever. Matt wasn't pushing to the left, was standing up tall, and was able to straighten his left knee the majority of the walk without me blocking it. Matt even stopped and looked at me intently during his walk and I said, "Oh Matt, give me a kiss" and he gave me a kiss on the cheek. It was so sweet—as the PCAs said "Ohhhhh." At this moment, I had this strong insight and knowledge that Matt not only would be at the boys basketball game on senior night, February twentieth, but would WALK onto the court. Michelle said "I work that night, but I could switch to help him walk onto the court." I then thought if Michelle and I can walk Matt, Bill or Coach Dahman could help me walk him onto the basketball court. I have no doubt.

Abby was at parent's night tonight for the dance performance, recognized, and gave Bill and I a thank you card. My heart went out to her, having to watch her team dance in her warm-up suit versus dance uniform, but she's alive, happy, and will dance next year for sure. Abby is doing good though, back in school full-time and says her test scores are getting better. She still gets tired easily, is frustrated quickly, takes longer to acknowledge Bill or I have spoken to her, but overall is doing amazing. I asked her if she would be willing to have acupuncture and she said "No. I don't want it." Laura tries to cheer her, or ask how she's doing, and Abby will say "What's it to you?" I know it'll continue to get better and I'm very thankful for how far she has come. God is so good.

I was given Matt's confirmation letter he wrote to our priest this week. Matt wrote about all he had done volunteering through youth group with Sharing and Caring Hands in Minneapolis, youth rallies, etc. Matt wrote these things had affected his faith because he felt like he was getting closer to God by helping people less fortunate than him. Matt said, "When I am older, I will live my life as a Catholic by trying to help with the youth group in the area where I live and raising my children in the Catholic faith. I would like to be fully initiated into the church so I can grow deeper in my faith and become a stronger

Christian for as long as I live." For as long as I live is the part that made me instantly tear up–why would he say that? Now it'll be to a ripe old age of ninety.

Wow. Now you fully understand my title of Tilt-a-Whirl—our life is moving forwards, backwards, clockwise, counter clockwise, etc. However, our faith is the foundation and is solid. May God bless you all and may you all encounter as many blessings as we have.

Girls-Laura, Abby, Brooke, Matt, and Kami

Jenn, PT at CM, Matt, and Mike, PT at SCH

Our Last Move Before Home—Country Manor

—◊◊◊—

Feb. 3, 2014

Today was a wonderful, yet exhausting day. I don't think Bill, myself or Matt slept well last night in anticipation. I wasn't going to journal, but it didn't seem fair for all the prayers and thoughts I knew everyone had for Matt today. I may have ordered ten dozen donuts, which we brought to the pediatric ICU, acute rehab, inpatient rehab and to Country Manor for staff in appreciation for all they have done and are doing for Matthew now. Dr. Derr had on the "I wear green for Matt" band which completely touched me. He said he loves green. We discussed medications and I wanted to be sure Matt would stay on his Ritalin and he also added fish oil which helps with brain healing. He set up a follow-up appointment at the Centra Care Health Plaza for April eleventh to look at Botox for Matt's left hand again as this will be exactly a day after he can have it again with the three month waiting period.

Uncle Kenny came to help us pack up and move to Country Manor–it was awesome and his smile was continuous. We brought Matt in our new vehicle and I told Matt someday he'd drive it and asked him if he knew that. He replied, "No" as my heart sank thinking he didn't think he'd ever drive again. I said, "No what?" and he replied "I didn't know that." Whew, I can breathe again.

Matt's memory continues to improve. Yesterday, he was restless in his wheelchair, asking to sit in a regular chair in the lounge. We repositioned him in the wheelchair and played a game of Crazy Eights. He was able to hold the cards in his left hand between his thumb and index finger. I asked Matt if he wanted to walk and he said, "Yeah." I told

Matt then we should go find Michelle to help us walk. Michelle came walking down the hall and Matt said "Michelle, would you walk with me?" It was so adorable. Bill said that after Matt had Reese's peanut butter cups last night, he told him "We should wash that down with something," and Matt replied "Yes, Daddy dearest." Gosh is that a blast from the past—and wonderful to hear.

Today as I was unpacking Matt's stuff, he said "Mom?" I said, "What Matt?" and he said, "Can you find my phone?" and then later said "I want to see if I have any texts." Matt was drinking water and said, "I'm going to have to piss." I asked if he meant right then, and he said, "No," so I asked if he meant latter because he was drinking water, and Matt said "Yeah." I continued to unpack Matt's belongings and asked where we should put his Ricky Rubio banner from Coach Dahmen. Out of the blue, Matt says, "Mom?" and I said, "What honey?" and he said "I love you." No prompting or me saying it first–I was very teary-eyed as I gave him a hug and Matt kissed me on the cheek twice. I went to get Matt's clothes from my office and told Matt I'd be right back, and as I was leaving the room he began wheeling his chair with his left leg off to the side behind him. I asked Matt what he was doing and he replied, "I'm going home." I explained he needed therapy for at least a few weeks so he could walk on his own and I wished I could take him home right now, but it wouldn't be the best decision for him. He nodded and agreed to stay.

Matt had OT/PT/ST evaluations today and I was amazed at how much he remembered of a three sentence paragraph the speech therapist, Melissa told him, and even more when given multiple-choice answers for the details. We walked in the hallway with PT, but he needs a bigger AFO, which I know they'll get very soon. We scheduled pool therapy at seven am tomorrow/ Before I left tonight, Matt said, "You'll be here for the pool tomorrow morning? You'll bring my swimsuit?" The OT, Steph, came in with a Reese's peanut butter cup, saying "I wanted to get on your good side right away. I'm sure I'll be bringing more." Matt also has a PCA who graduated from Pierz a couple of years ago. She even came in her jacket as she was leaving to tell him good-bye for the night. Matt will make friends quickly, always has, and many staff at the hospital promised to visit him at Country Manor too–which I think helped his transition, knowing he'd see them again.

I think life will be much more manageable with Matt at Country Manor for me now. I know he'll continue to get excellent care and to progress in therapy. I had Matt write his name today for Steph (OT) and it was as legible as it always was. I was OVERJOYED. When he signed the book we wrote with his classmate, it was basically a zigzag after beginning with an "M." Today, it was perfect and I was so thankful, it brought tears to my eyes. His coordination in his right hand has improved two hundred percent, thanks to all of your prayers. He even began to take notes from our conversation which was adorable. Matt wrote his response of "Yeah," progress, and activities of daily living skills as well as the date–spelling February correctly I might add. Matt continues to make my day, every day, and I am so thankful to see his progress. It's so difficult for words to do my heart justice. I feel guilty for focusing so much on him, especially when seeing Brooke had eleven of twelve words wrong on her spelling test last Friday. She usually does amazing, but forgot to look at her list. Guilt, guilt, guilt—I'll try to be better with her studying. She typically writes the words down and looks at them over breakfast and has them memorized by Friday, but we forgot last week. Be assured the new list for this week is posted on the refrigerator. It's such a juggling act to balance everything these days, and Brooke has the hardest time understanding this. She's upset she couldn't see Matt in his new room today, but will soon. Now that Laura can drive, she plans to bring the girls to see him at least one night a week.

Love Heals

Lord, daily you protect me from harm. I feel your love surrounding me, acting as a buffer against the world's evils. You take my defeats and turn them into victories. You turn my weaknesses into strengths and my sorrows into joys. All this you do because I am your child and you love me. I do not deserve your love, but you give it anyway. Re-create your love in me. Use me to help the healing of others.

The love for Matt Continues

—〰—

Feb 6, 2014

Matthew is adjusting well to Country Manor and continues to win everyone's heart. He is so busy. The nurses hardly see him during the day. He has three hours, forty-five minutes of therapy each day, in addition to three meals, a shower and visitors. He is much more awake now with a low dose of Ritalin back twice a day: however, he tired from his schedule. He likes his new room (no more white walls) and his therapists, but I know he misses everyone from inpatient rehab too. Matt wasn't feeling well at lunch and didn't even eat the burger and fries I ordered, saying his stomach hurt. He did have Reese's peanut butter cups and shrimp low mein for dinner, but then threw up. I'm so hoping he's better by morning and it doesn't last days as this will take a lot out of him. If only I could just kiss everything away–it's tough to see him deal with more. It will get better though.

Matt had pool therapy from seven to eight am the past three mornings. He has no objections to this time as he loves the pool and me being able to help Jenn, his PT, with the session. The floor comes up to ground level and we wheel him up to the bar. Matt stands so we can take the chair away, then we lower the floor of the pool into the water– it's super cool. On Tuesday morning, I'd say all three of us got a work-out. Matt wanted to push to the left, kept trying to lift his left leg off the floor and bring his feet forward in front of his hips, leaning backwards. Jenn is shorter than Matt and I therefore she stands on an eight inch step to be high enough to assist him. Today, Matt stood from the wheelchair with minimal assist and kept his balance, in the middle (correctly by leaning right) and

226

had both knees straight with weight pretty symmetrical. Jenn and both let go of Matt and he held this position for a few minutes. I was so happy and knew all the prayers for the pool to help Matt's recovery were in fast forward. Today he even "played basketball" reaching for balls floating in the water and tossing them into a clothes basket. Matt works super hard in the pool and is tired after an hour–but didn't even need to sit and rest today. Jenn let him pick what he wanted to do the final ten minutes of the session, and to my surprise, he said, "be done." Of course, I told him this was the wrong answer. He agreed with my idea just to float on his back. He rested his head on Jenn's shoulder and worked on kicking both legs with knees extended. After a bit, he totally relaxed and I think even fell asleep for a minute. It was difficult to find words to describe how I felt seeing him float, so relaxed and like nothing had happened–I think Matt felt the same way too for a few minutes.

I brought Matt his cell phone on Tuesday per his request. My heart sank as he checked messages from friends the night of the accident asking him if he was ok, and a text about the senior class trip airplane tickets. I'm not sure if he understood all of these, but know he was happy to know he had received texts when he didn't have his phone. Matt has figured out how to call and text me. He had a doctor's appointment on Tuesday in our Quick Clinic on Country Manor campus for his initial assessment (looking at his medical history, medications, etc.) While we were waiting to be seen, Matt looked at his phone and put it back in his pocket. I immediately received a text from him. Super surprised, I asked Matt if he had just texted me and he said, "Yeah." The text said "She left." I believe he texted it after the speech therapist left his room, to let me know, and hadn't hit send until then. I thought it was pretty good he wanted to keep me informed. I brought Matt back to his room and went back to work while he had OT. While at my desk, my cell phone rings and it was Matt. It was so good to hear his voice, although I was kind of in shock I think. Matt said "Moooommm?" I said "Hi honey, did you need something? Are you ok?" and he replied "No." I asked him, "What was wrong? What did he need?" and he replied, "To go to the bathroom." Matt had his call pendant near him, but decided to call me instead–how cute is that? I called the nurse's station and they thought this was pretty funny too and immediately helped him to the bathroom. I guess it's better than calling 911 as some confused residents have done in every facility I've ever worked in.

While at the doctor's appointment, Matt brought his phone to about a half inch from his right eye to try to read a text. I told the nurse practitioner that Matt complains of blurred vision. He asked Matt if he saw one or two of him, and Matt replied "one." He then took a pen in front of Matt and asked him to let him know when he saw two pens instead of one, as he brought it closer to his eyes. Typically at about two inches from your nose, you'll see two images. Matt saw two pens at about eighteen inches away from his nose. This has a fancy name called convergence disorder which is typical for head injuries and something Abby had to work on too in OT. Now it makes perfect sense why he keeps print farther away or closes one eye if it's close—to see only one image. They asked if this was assessed at the hospital and I said, by the time he could talk, Matt could open both eyes, visually track, and identify people. I never thought to further assess this like I should have—but it's hard to remember and address everything. They will continue to work on this in OT (as will Bill and I) and Matt has an eye appointment next week too.

Everyone is getting to know Matt and want to do whatever they can for him. The dietician is continuing Matt's favorite Magic Cups protein ice cream cups and a Boost or Ensure drink with vanilla ice cream for a shake. The recreational therapist met with me for ideas for one to one visits with Matt, thinking he wouldn't like group activities with primarily older patients. I told her he loved bingo at the hospital and she literally thought I was teasing. She did say it was a good coordination, visual and cognitive activity though. I had plenty of other ideas such as comics, the newspaper, bringing him to the piano, etc. The hardest thing will be finding time in Matt's busy schedule. When I asked about how often Matt would have showers, there were three nursing assistants in the hallway who all said, "Just ask and we'll give him one whenever Matt wants." He will have a shower at least three times per week after the pool too. Matt even asked for a haircut today while in the pool as his bangs were blocking his view of Jenn. I'm sure the beautician will give him a haircut tomorrow or Sunday. She immediately was trying to figure out the schedule for today, and I reassured her it wasn't that urgent, whenever it worked out for them.

The chaplain from the hospital already came to visit Matthew and called our chaplain to continue with the daily readings he was doing with Matt. I have been so overwhelmed by the love and prayers the entire chaplain team at the hospital have provided and continue to show Matt. He was worried about the transition for Matt and seeing him I know helped to lighten Matt's loss of the hospital staff. His PT, Mike, (from the hospital) plans to see Matt next week and when I told Matt about this he immediately nodded and said, "Yeah." I know he misses Mike, Kelly, Shawn, Sandi, the doctors, and the nursing staff too, so this is huge for Matt, as well as Bill and I. There are so many wonderful and kind people who have touched our lives since the accident. Something we never would have experienced (still wish we hadn't experienced of course) but I believe is part of the "good" that will come out of this journey we were given.

Laura and Abby worry about student council and school assignments. Kami is worried and excited about her basketball tournament this weekend, and Brooke about how she'll dress as an old lady for the one hundredth day of school next week as well as what she'll bring for her class for Valentine's Day. Although it's events we need to juggle and plan at times, it provides normalcy and keeps us "grounded." Bill brought the girls to see Matt on Tuesday night and I think this helped them to know where he was and that he was getting wonderful care and attention. It was like you could see their worry ease as they entered Matt's room.

Beloved, do not be surprised at the fiery ordeal that is taking place among you to test you, as though something strange were happening to you. But rejoice insofar as you are sharing Christ's sufferings, so you may also be glad and shout for joy when his glory is revealed. I do believe we have already seen Christ's glory revealed in the accomplishments Matt has achieved. Know with certainty, we have so much more that will be revealed in the days to come. I thought the following poem was awesome from Matt's view point.

The Rock

I rise like the phoenix from the ashes of my pain
And spread my wings to take flight once again.
With newfound wisdom, I rise into the sky,
And with clarity and focus, I shall fly
Higher than before with greater ease.
For I have survived: I have achieved.
And when I come again to rest on land
Upon the rock of faith I will stand.

XBOX

—⧆—

Feb. 9, 2014

When Matt was in the ICU, becoming alert for short periods of times, I brought his Xbox controller to see if he would remember or try to hold it, push a button....anything. He put it in his right hand and couldn't figure out why he wasn't able to use his left hand too. It broke my heart, so I took it back home for my sake, remembering all the hours he spent playing Xbox and how many times Bill and I told him stop playing and to come to dinner, or go to bed. One of the PCAs said a resident was going home today, and asked if he could bring the recreational therapy department's Xbox into Matt's room. I, of course, said, he'd love it (thinking of adaptations and how he could use the strength he does have to use the controllers too). Today when I arrived, immediately the PCAs said "You should have seen Matt's face when we brought the Xbox into his room." I didn't plan ahead this morning to think of bringing his games form home, but tomorrow's another day.

Yesterday after watching two of Kami's basketball games in Foley, I called Matt to see if he'd want me to pick him up something special for lunch. He answered his cell phone on the second ring and after I gave him some suggestions, he chose his favorite—pepperoni pizza. We had a really good day. Matt had therapy in the morning, pizza for lunch, then we had friends visit, as well as most of the basketball team and his coach. Matt loved this. It was a surprise, however perfect timing as he doesn't have therapy on Sundays. Matt stayed up in his wheelchair the entire time, listening to the guys, watching football, and continually appeasing Brooke's demands to tickle her, play basketball, etc. We all went to Subway (on Country Manor campus) and had dinner. Guess what Matt ordered?," pepperoni pizza again. The guys and Coach Poepping were so attentive to Matt's needs. They'd give him his glass (he'd open his mouth rather than take the glass), adjust his straw, and at Subway, one of the guys even wiped his mouth with his napkin for pizza sauce he'd missed. I thought to myself "that just so sucks to see Matt needing his help, and yet it was the sweetest thing I had ever seen." I think of how Matt's accident has most likely changed the team's compassion, and how thankful I am to see him eating pizza with his basketball team again. It no longer "sucks."

Matt has been checking his phone for texts, making sure I only see the ones he wants me too, and is responding short phrases back. He is improving so much with his memory games on the iPad, it's like anticipating a surprise watching him re-learn more every day. He just looked over from his Candy Crush game on the iPad and said "So what's the plan for tomorrow?" Isn't that is cool? I told him a shower at six forty-five am and five therapy sessions–no pool until Jenn, his primary PT, is back on Tuesday. He nodded his agreement.

Grandma visited today and commented on Matt scratching his dry skin. He continued to scratch even more and didn't want any help with this, or any lotion. Grandma said "Grandpa has the itch too–to go fishing and I think he caught the bug." After thinking about this, Matthew replied "I'm itching to get out of here." We all laughed, as Matt's sense of humor is coming back. I have yet to hear him laugh yet–even when he bumped the pizza box and literally showered me with a full glass of orange juice yesterday, from my eyebrows, my clothes, and the entire floor. Instead of laughing or saying anything, he looked at me with big eyes, waiting for my reaction, and then handed me a napkin as I was wiping up the floor. I know in time, this will be very funny to him—I may need to have an OJ shower in the future soley to see his reaction.

Matt's room is adorable—I've completed hanging up all his basketball items, including the Pioneer banner with tacky clay stuff. When staff come in, they say, "Wow! Look at this room" and it's only a portion of what we had at the hospital as we almost needed a U-Haul to move out.

Hopefully the week will be amazing in preparation for next Thursday night's basketball game. Matt wasn't sick at all after Thursday night–so he could have just had an upset stomach that day.

"Bless You"

—⁓—

Feb. 11, 2014

Matt continues to adjust very well and to progress in all his therapies. He started the day with pool therapy again and did well straightening his left knee even when putting weight through his leg. This is a huge improvement and will help his walking. Matt practiced going form sitting to standing with the bar in the pool several times to work on bending his trunk forward at that final range before sitting in the plastic chair and not to lean to the left during the transition. This is so much better with him only needing minimal assist and verbal cues. In the transition however, his swim trunks got air bubbles in them and of course I had to tease Matt about this as he completely seriously denied the bubbles were "him." He sat and his right leg had a huge air bubble in it as Matt "patted" it out from his hip to his knee with Jenn his PT was looking over his leg, her face near the water. The bubble came to the top right into her face with water even spraying her a bit. We of course had to laugh, and Matt smiled symmetrically on both sides of his face with a genuine smile. It was twice as funny. Matt walked around the pool and worked on straightening his left knee and keeping his balance. The pool is great feedback not to lean to the left or backwards as Matt does "on land." He denied being tired, even when his left leg began to tremor from muscle fatigue and for the first time ever, we had him stop walking when he wanted to continue.

Matt continues to have tightness in his left knuckles, but is able to actively open his fingers more often, and with increased repetition. When he works really hard with his right hand, his left hand gets tighter. This is challenging when I put a cup of pudding or ice

232

cream in his hand to hold; however, I have no fear of him dropping it. He was almost able to make a complete circle with the arm bike yesterday using his left hand. This requires shoulder, elbow and wrist motion while maintaining his grasp. Matt is now able to take his contacts out. He needs a little help to keep his right eyelid open; however, this shows how much his right arm and hand coordination has improved. Before he literally would have poked his eye out if he had tried, and now I have so much hope he'll be able to take care of himself again someday, one step at a time. I still cue Matt to put his utensils in his mouth "straight on" to avoid food on the left side of his mouth. Matt is now able to lean forward in the wheelchair, without using his right hand to pull, to eat over his plate, aware now of not wanting anything to spill. This seems small, but after two months of watching him struggle with food dropping, it makes me smile.

Matt continues to play Candy Crush as well as other memory and math games on his iPad. He was doing math problems this afternoon on his own, a program that switches from addition to subtraction, to multiplication, and to division. He needed some cues, but being able to switch at all is a huge accomplishment. Last night the therapeutic recreation gal came in and asked Matt geography questions from Trivial Pursuit. For the record, she and I didn't know a single answer. Matt was able to answer about forty to fifty percent of the questions correctly, including countries, cities, oceans, etc., especially if we told him a letter the answer began with. I asked her to repeat the ones he had wrong to see if he would remember the answers (working on short-term memory, which is the toughest for him.) He was able to answer all but two questions the second time around. Matthew needs to be reminded of the information he knew before the accident

Mike, Matt's PT from the hospital, today and Matt was very happy to see him. Matt took the *St. Cloud Times* from his dresser with the photo and article of them and began looking at it. Mike said, "Matt, I have the article on my dresser at home too." My heart once again melted. You could see the relief in Mike as he checked out the therapy gym, pool, and Matt's room. Everywhere we went, staff said hi to Matt and Mike said, "It feels so connected here." He was happy to know Matt was getting five sessions of therapy too and even walked Matt with Jenn, his PT. Mike could tell Matt had improved with how much help he needed to walk in the past ten days since being at Country Manor and also noted his memory was improving. It was wonderful to see his compassion, being so vested in Matt's recovery and promised he'd visit again.

At dinner tonight, as Matt was eating, he suddenly raised his right hand and pointed to a patient across the room. In the loudest voice I have heard yet, he said, "BLESS YOU" to a patient who had apparently sneezed, unbeknownst to me, as many things are these days. It was like he had the answer to the final question on *"Who Wants to Be a Millionaire"* without his "phone a friend." I had to look away and hold my breath not to burst out laughing, in part because he surprised me, but the pointing just topped it off. Needless to say, the patient didn't hear him. Matt has received many blessings since his accident from the chaplains, prayer group, priests, pastoral assistant, etc., and now he was blessing someone. How amazing is that?

We have asked Matt and checked his vision in OT several times, and since the very next day, he denies any double vision at any abnormal distance greater than a few inches from his nose. I spent the past five days and evenings with him (Bill became sick Saturday night and Kami since Monday) and have not seen Matt close an eye or bring his phone up to his eye to read it. He did have difficulty reading the journal the kids at school wrote for him, but only because the background was tiny squares and checkers. He loved the inspiration from everyone who wrote to him, asking me to continue to read their entries, knowing he is missed by his friends at school. My point, however, is that the prayers for Matt's vision were heard one-hundred fold.

My inspiration for today:

Decide to change the words "I hope" to the words "I feel very sure" or even "I have faith" that all will occur in perfect order. Later as you slowly eliminate "I hope" from your vocabulary, switch from "I feel sure" or "I have faith" to "I know." I know Matt will recover, walk, finish school, drive again, and continue to touch a lot of lives like he did before the accident and since that day.

God talks to everyone, all the time. The question is not: To whom does God talk? The question is: Who listens? Thank you all for talking to God and listening in Matt's behalf for healing.

Green Light

—ɯɯ—

Feb. 15, 2014

Matt's thinking continues to improve and his personality is coming back. He had a doctor's appointment with Dr. Halstrom at the Quick Clinic on Country Manor campus (super nice not to have to go out of the building) on Monday. Since Matt was doing much better being back on Ritalin two times per day and Dr. Derr gave the okay to increase the dose from five mg to ten or fifteen mg twice a day, I figured, "Why not?" We could always decrease the dose again if needed. It may just be healing, but I'm pretty sure with the timing, that the Ritalin is making a huge difference. Some examples:

Bill and I took him to an eye appointment on Thursday. I was so happy to see the increased ease with transfers as compared to just last Monday. We no longer needed a blanket on the seat to pull him over, and Matt was able to scoot in and back with very little help. He automatically grabbed the seat belt, opened and closed the door and was more observant of sights along the way. On the way there, we were stopped at a stoplight and Matt, who was riding shotgun said "Green!" I obviously wasn't paying close enough attention.

We had to wait with Matt in the exam chair for forty-five minutes while they obtained his hospital records. Needless to say, I didn't bring the iPad or anything for Matt to do. After having him work on bringing his ankle up several times, marching, etc. with his left leg, Matt just had to wait. He began scratching his legs, pulling up his pants legs, then his left arm, etc., which drove me crazy. I asked Matt if he itched, and he said, "No." I asked him "WHY are you scratching so much?" and he replied, "For shits and giggles." Hearing him say that, I no longer cared about how much he scratched.

The eye doctor grossly determined Matt didn't have a visual field cut on either side, or upper and lower quadrants. He had 20/20 vision in the left eye and "almost" 20/20 vision in the right eye with his contacts in. With prisms, he determined Matt's complaints of double vision was due to a convergence disorder related to an injury to his fourth cranial nerve. He said it was partially damaged and would just take time. He said there wasn't any benefit in completing eye exercises and that he should have a formal visual field test as he has a bit of difficulty looking to the lower left. I told him I'd like to know for future driving and to ensure we work on any deficits in OT. Matt was talking so much louder Thursday, naming off all the letters on the eye chart, fairly quickly too. I took out a piece of gum and Matt wanted one too. I cannot tell you how thankful I was to see Matt tracking with both eyes, being able to identify small letters, and to be chewing gum. I told him not to swallow the gum; however, later I saw he had.

Matt has been doing much more in the pool. He even was able to walk on the treadmill of the swimming pool floor for nine minutes on Thursday morning. It wasn't very pretty, as he tends to walk only on his toes with his right foot, but HE DID IT. Last week, we only turned it on for a few steps as this was too difficult to do. Matt corrects his balance and even marches in the pool. We walked in the afternoon Thursday and Jenn (PT) asked Matt to bend his knee as he brought his leg forward, giving him a visual target of trying to get his knee toward her hand. Matt brought his knee up, almost as high as his hip as both of our mouths dropped in amazement. Jenn said, "This is why I do what I do." Bill even walked Matt half way down the hallway by himself, walking on his right side. It shows how much Matt is improving, without needing assist to step with his left leg, to straighten his knee, and to hold it while stepping with his right foot. Last night, it was much tougher, but Matt was really tired. He wants to be able to walk on that basketball court next Thursday.

Matt continues to text and call with his cell phone. He called me to tell me he was thirsty one afternoon and he wanted a Diet Coke, rather than all the Powerade and Mountain Dew in his refrigerator. Kami texted him and said his responses were all one to three words long, but he answered her questions. I came into his room and his phone was vibrating so I told Matt he must have a text. Matt didn't even look up and said, "No, the battery is dead." Sure enough it was vibrating low battery. Matt texted me yesterday "I wanna get out." My heart dropped. I called him and asked why, and Matt just repeated it and said "Because." I asked if he just wanted to be home and he said, "Yeah." I told Matt it would be selfish for me to take him home now because he can't walk and wouldn't have so much therapy every day. He would need someone with him all the time if he went home now. I asked him if he understood and he said, "Yeah." I then asked him what he wanted for Valentine's Day, bought him two comedy movies on sale, Reese's peanut butter cups and Lay's potato chips. My solution for everything is food, which seemed to work just fine. It does make me realize how much better his thinking is to even text this and know he wants to go home now. The other night, I asked Matt if he was going to try his corn for dinner. Matt looked at me and said, "Eventually." Matt's OT, Steph, had a student with her this week. She said Matt asked her student "What sport do you like to watch the best?" Matt had initiated a conversation and asked a question, which is amazing.

Matt's short term memory is getting better too. He remembers what he had to eat about seventy-five percent of the time. He remembers who comes to visit and more about his therapy sessions too. He was disappointed the girls from his class didn't visit for Valentine's Day as planned, and asked "Who was coming today?" He wants to go to Jimmy's PourHouse again, so we may go on Sunday just to cheer him a bit.

Someone from the County came to visit yesterday regarding our guardianship, while I was at a continuing education class. Bill came for lunch and to help with the interview process if needed. He asked Matt to name some of his aunts and uncles. Matt named two of my sister-in-laws and one of my brothers. Bill believed this was to see if Matt knew some of his options for guardianship. He then asked Matt who he would like to make decisions for him, if he had to choose. Matt replied "Gregg," who is my brother. Bill said "I don't think he knows his options, that he's only able to choose aunts and uncles." He then said, "If you could choose, including Mom and Da. . ." Matt said "MOM." That was all the information he needed to know Matt was in agreement of us having guardianship "for now." We'll go to court in March. He asked Matt if he wanted to go to court too, and Matt said, "Yeah." Right now, Matt would like to go anywhere—even if it's to court.

Matt continues to be optimistic in his journey of healing and I am so thankful he's not down in the dumps despite wanting to go home

Singing Alleluia

—⁂—

Feb. 18, 2014

Matthew continues to surprise me with something new every day. It's like having a birthday present every day, only the gift is from God. On Saturday a classmate and her mom visited and I found out Matt is texting her "a wake-up call" at five-thirty am, six-thirty am, or this weekend at three-thirty am. His texts are usually one to four words long. His three-thirty am text simply said, "Goodnight." I thought he slept like a rock after four hours of therapy a day, but obviously I'm wrong. I thought about taking his phone at night so he sleeps. However, he has so little control of his life right now, I can't take his reaching out to friends away from him, even if it's in the middle of the night. His classmate and mom think it's great, I'm so happy he is able to text, so no harm done.

On Sunday, we went to the chapel at Country Manor with Father Stangl and Matt was attentive throughout the entire mass. He made the sign of the cross, said every response, and even sang the Alleluia. Matt didn't sing in church before so I could tell it was from his heart. Father Stangl came down to us for the sign of peace, talked to us after mass and gave Matt a small stand-up iron cross.

We then went to Jimmy's PourHouse for lunch and what a difference from about a month ago. Matt was sitting up perfect in his wheelchair, scooting himself back to reposition if needed. He fed himself his burger, fries, and root beer (unwilling to give Brooke even a sip of his after she spilled her soda) and asked to watch boys basketball versus the girls basketball game that was on. I was talking to Brooke or my Dad, when I heard Matt say something, so I asked him what he said. He continued briefly to sing, and said, "I'm

238

singing to the music." It was an older rock song, but he was enjoying it and remembered the words. Seeing him watching the game and singing to the music was incredible.

Yesterday was such a "scribbly" day if I could describe it. First of all, I got stuck in the driveway, needing Bill, my brother and my Dad to come to the rescue at six-thirty am, in a hurry to get to Country Manor for Matt's seven am pool therapy. I was out in about fifteen to twenty minutes; however, it took an hour to get there due to the awful road conditions. I quickly go to the pool and Jenn is in alone with Matt and he's walking on treadmill. Oh my gosh–it wasn't until last Thursday that Matt really tried the treadmill, and now was able to do this with only Jenn and looked 100% better—watching the underwater camera on the computer screen and straightening his left knee. In the afternoon, Matt walked with Jenn and I the entire length of the hall (about eighty feet I'd guess) and did not want to turn around before getting to the very end despite being given the choice to turn around sooner. Matt typically rests, then walks back, but he denied being tired and walked all the way back to his bed without resting. I looked at the clock and he had been standing for thirty minutes. Matt did not need help to advance or straighten his left knee at all during the entire walk, even when being tired. He does lean backwards with fatigue though and will hyperextend his left knee at times, but IT IS SO MUCH BETTER. I am so thankful Jenn is so vested in Matt's recovery, seeing him early, or at the very end of the day with new ideas every day. I thought about getting Matt a custom AFO (ankle-foot orthosis) if it'd help Matt's quality of gait and progress, but I know Jenn's goal is for Matt not to need a knee brace or an AFO by the time he's ready to go home.

In OT, Matt works on his left hand, sitting balance, dressing, and toileting skills. Matt was able to reach forward and back with his left arm more than I have seen and to push his arm into his P.J.'s top now. When I help Matt go to the bathroom, he transfers from his wheelchair to the toilet with only minimal assist and verbal cues, and can manage his clothing with me assisting for balance only, which is huge progress. Matt's coordination on his right continues to be evident as he uses his iPad and feeds himself—even the nurses comment on this. It seems to be like putting together a jigsaw puzzle where the pieces are finally beginning to fit.

Matt continues to work on math, memory, problem solving in speech therapy with Melissa and Rachel. He was answering math questions accurately and fast this weekend and is remembering so much more short-term about what happened earlier that day, what he had for lunch, etc. Matt is even asking people questions too, such as asking the acupuncturist what college he went to today. I asked Matt what movie he watched with my friend Saturday night and he said, "Jim Carrey." Anyone who knows me, knows I know nothing about actors and actresses so I asked her and she said Matt was right–"It was *Bruce Almighty.*"

Matt is asked to attend activities and surprises the gals when he does want to go. It's super funny. One of the therapists heard the therapeutic recreation gal ask Matt if he wanted to go to the trivial session on past presidents and of course Matt said yes, to which she replied, "Really?" Matt was involved in a discussion of past presidents and loved it. He played bingo this weekend too, much to their surprise and although he didn't win, he enjoyed it. He wants to go to the dining room to eat, versus eating in his room, as he's very sociable and is often in a conversation with another patient in rehab. He is so liked by everyone, it's adorable. The PCAs all seem to dote on Matt too–from bringing him movies, treats, or an extra shower, they are wonderful. Every spare moment they have, they are visiting with Matt or seeing if he wants anything. Father Popp visited today and brought Matt down to the rehab gym to talk to me. The first thing he said is, "Wow, everyone sure knows Matt. They were saying hi to him the whole way here." I foresee Matt making friends that he'll be in contact with for many years after he leaves.

Today, we had a new adventure. My friend suggested we try acupuncture again now that Matt is out of the hospital, saying she has such a strong feeling this will help his healing. We have nothing to lose trying acupuncture and this may be another gift in Matt's healing. I feel everything happens for a reason and this may be part of the windy path we've been given to travel in our journey. We had an appointment for two-thirty pm and I thought I knew the location. After several stops and calling for directions, we finally arrived. Matt was putting the windows down and said he was hot when I asked. I thought maybe he was just checking out our new vehicle—wrong. As I put the vehicle into park at the office—Matt threw up everywhere. Did I forget to mention that he just had a strawberry shake and red Powerade? Bill said, "We have to cancel," so I went in to tell them and to get paper towels or a rag—anything. She asked the acupuncturist, and he said he'd still see Matt, "and maybe even work on his motion sickness." What a wonderful guy I thought several times during Matt's session, as I continued to smell strawberries. He placed about fifteen to twenty needles and Matt said he could feel them, but it didn't hurt. I know nothing about acupuncture really, just that it can help with blood circulation in the brain, sensation, movement and muscle tightness or tone. I didn't know needles were going to be placed on Matt's right side to allow input to cross over through his brain to the left side. This was super cool as Matt's brainstem damage was to the area between his two hemispheres. As he moved Matt's left hand, the skin around the needles in his right hand became reddened due to increased circulation. I asked Matt what he thought of it on our way back, and he said, "It was relaxing." He wants to see Matt ideally three times per week; however, doesn't work on Fridays. It's tough to schedule around four hours of therapy, but I feel we need to try it. God has so blessed us with flexible jobs and wonderful bosses and management that have been supportive since the day of the accident and all that's been happening in our family life since. I would write this even if no employees from our work or management ever read this. It's not to "kiss up," it's the truth so we'll make it work. The results may be immediate or take one to two weeks to see changes. Matt was working on opening his hand on the ride back and his hand seemed more relaxed after the shower he had upon returning. We have several appointments set up and time will tell. I want him to be able to eat a sub, hold a basketball, play drums/bells, etc., etc., with both hands, so much that we need to try.

Bummed

—◊◊◊—

Feb. 22, 2014

On Thursday morning Matt was so excited for the basketball game, he could hardly sit still in his wheelchair. Jenn brought him to my office because he was so anxious he didn't want to go back to his room and had about ninety minutes until his next therapy. He kept trying to pull himself through the doorway and finally I asked what he wanted and he pointed to my candy dish and said, "Butterfinger." I told him he could have just asked for it and gave him a few to take back to his room. I found out in the early afternoon that the game was postphoned and went to tell Matt who was waiting for therapy in the clinic. He was playing a memory game and wasn't concentrating at all, pushing all the cards of the game quickly without looking at them—obviously very upset. I told him he had four more days to work on walking even better, and he reluctantly agreed. He did not do his very best in his therapy session which ended early per his request, or during his pool session Friday morning. I had lunch with him and told him he needed to do his best not only for the game, but to get back home. He acknowledged this and did much better the rest of the day.

In his PT Friday afternoon, Jenn asked him why he needed to work his hardest and he said, "To walk out on the basketball court," and she then asked him, "What about after that? Why do you need to keep working hard after Monday?" I loved Matt's response of, "To PLAY basketball." Sometimes, actually a lot of times, I know I want this for him even more than he does. Bill and I walked Matt last night the entire distance of the hallway and back to his room and he did wonderful. When we were leaving another patient's family member who had also been at inpatient rehab with us at the hospital, came to us and said she was crying watching how far Matt had come. "I went around the corner and started bawling." His nurse said, "I had to look away too so I wouldn't start crying." I can't imagine how emotional the game will be for Matt. He does get distracted by anyone in the hall, a sign, etc., while he's walking, (as he would have before the accident too) and so will need to focus extra hard Monday night, but he can do it.

Matt had another acupuncture appointment on Wednesday which focused again on his left side and also "dampness" per the Chinese medicine. Josh said it could be dampness in the brain, or in the mouth–such as phelm or salvia, etc., so I thought this was super cool as Matt does have a more difficult time, especially when he's too tired to remember to swallow. He leaves the needles in for fifteen to twenty minutes and lets Matt rest after his treatment. When he came back, all three of us were sleeping–I'm sure we were a sight and surprised him, but to his credit, he didn't comment. That evening in bed, Matt was pushing the left side of his mouth up and I immediately asked him if he had more sensation in the left side of his face, and he replied "I'm practicing my smile." My heart melted, as I'm always asking him to try to smile on the left side too.

Matt is making many friends at Country Manor. The older gentlemen at his table in the dining room are doing "knucks" with him, encouraging him and asking him questions. Matt totally enjoys this, wanting to eat in the dining room even when given the option to eat in his room. Much to the recreational therapy staff's surprise, he never turns down a game of bingo. My friend and her son stayed with Matt Thursday evening when the weather was bad so Bill and I could go home, and he wanted to go to bingo even though they were visiting. They went with him, and an elderly lady who cannot see very well, asked Matt to help her watch her card. He looked over at her and said, "Yeah." Matt has yet to win a game of bingo at Country Manor, but keeps going for the socialization.

"Your life has nothing to do with you. It is about everyone whose life you touch, and how you touch it." This is a quote from the book *"What God Said"*. It is definitely some-thing to ponder. I think of how all of you have touched my family's life and Matt's life in his recovery. Also, how our story has touched your life–I'll continue to ponder this statement and what it fully means. Two of our on-call therapists just yesterday told me that they continue to pray for Matt and our family every day—as I know many of you do too. That is so huge to me and definitely living out what God said, to touch other people's lives. It sure has touched ours—thank you.

TILT

—⟨⟨⟨—

Feb. 25, 2014

I feel like a pinball machine on "tilt" of emotions. I needed to "freeze frame" my emotions last night at the basketball game to hold it all together and be able to walk Matt onto the court. I never expected Coach Dahman to mention me at all, let alone thanks me for my strength, courage, love and faith, saying it has affected our entire community. That's when tears began and I barely comprehended what was being said, although looking at Laura and Abby's faces, I saw they were crying too. The community support is why our family has made it through the past four months. Every time I'd get a bit down, Matt's coaches, our priest, the chaplains, our families, and good friends would assist to renew my positive thinking and faith in God's healing. Many days, I'd ask God "for a sign" or an "improvement" in Matt's condition, whether it was physical, emotional, psychological, or spiritual, and I was never let down. Matt's healing I strongly believe is to renew everyone's faith, especially in the power of prayer. I can't tell you how many parents have told me their son and/or daughter pray for Matt every night, many under the age of seven. Coach Dahman and my friends have never let me falter in my hope and faith for Matt's full recovery—what a wonderful gift and he thanked ME.

I asked Matt where he wanted to eat on Sunday and of course he replied, "Dominos." Knowing there isn't much of an atmosphere there, we decided on carry out and had lunch with our friends at Country Manor before going out. We took Matt to see the movie, *The Monuments Men*. Bill warned Matt he had heard it wasn't that good, but Matt said, "I read the book." He transferred into a real movie theatre chair, sitting with his friend Lindsey, having popcorn and a Sprite. Every time I looked back he was having one or the other and would smile at me. It was so incredible to see him enjoying a movie again. Matt did say the movie was better than the book. I fell asleep for part of it and without a doubt will never read the book. I didn't care what we watched as long as he was happy.

Matt had an acupuncture appointment Monday afternoon and I told Josh how he said he was worried about the basketball game and all the people. Josh included treatment to take away worry, anxiety, and fear. I truly believe it helped as Matt was as calm as ever, loving every minute of seeing his friends, teachers, and the young basketball players who came to tell him about their season. After Matt's session, I barely touched his left fingertips and he opened his hand completely. I have so much hope that his treatments will speed up his physical and cognitive recovery.

Matt walked wonderfully onto the court. I didn't even have to assist his left leg at all, or to keep his trunk forward for balance. He stood for several minutes, up tall and even waved and gave the peace sign to the crowd. I was never so proud of him. He was in a standing picture with the team and wanted to instantly put on the signed Blake Griffin jersey he was given (in standing, over his Pierz jersey) on the court. His coaches stood with him for the *Star Spangled Banner* and he was able to sit on the bench with the team in his wheelchair, totally into the game. He received high fives from every player who came off the court, and from the opposing team after the game. It broke my heart to see him try to clap and knowing how much he wanted to be on the court, but the fact that he was there, clapping, and with the team in itself is a miracle. I asked Matt on Sunday if he still wanted to be a physical therapist some day and he replied "No." I asked him if he knew what else he'd like to do, and he replied, "Be a basketball player."

Bill dropped Brooke and I off at home after the game and took Matt back to Country Manor. Matt has not been home or even seen our house since November 1st, 2013. He immediately opened his car door and Bill told him to shut it, he wasn't getting out. Matt reluctantly shut the door and my heart sank. Then Matt said, "I wanted to pet Saddie" (our golden lab.) He opened the door and petted her for just a little bit until Saddie thought I might have food for her and walked away. I went into the house and had my emotional meltdown that was so long overdue. I know it was all the overwhelming wonderful emotional events that had happened in the past few days, as the tears were completely of happiness—it's difficult to explain.

Matt walked with Jenn, his PT, and a PCA today, both of whom told me "He walked SO good." He walked about one hundred and twenty feet in ten minutes, a record, and only needed verbal cues for his left leg placement and trunk positioning. I thought he would have been exhausted from yesterday, no nap, texting all the way home last night, etc., so I was very excited he did so well. Matt's shoulder, elbow and wrist strength is improving too. I noticed a significant improvement on Sunday and. I'm not sure if it's his OT, the acupuncture or the prayers, but I was ecstatic. Matt continues to amaze me with his improvement in memory, problem solving and thinking. A coworker was trying to think of a word to send out in an e-mail, saying "What is the word that means: typically, or traditional, or what we usually do?" wanting someone to help her out. She said "Suddenly I hear this voice say, 'customary' and it was Matt behind me." Matt asked his PCA, Noah, tonight "What's for lunch—I mean dinner?" without us even talking about it and correcting himself. Matt is more aware of his facial expressions and even literally pushed up the left side of his smile for a picture last night to make it even and was able to hold the smile. My heart went out to him, wanting his smile to look good and being aware it was only on the right side, but then I was triumphant he was able to figure this out.

This afternoon we took Matt for another acupuncture appointment (Bill and I now walk him in, including a step) and to an eye appointment to look at if Matt has any visual loss in any quadrant, right or left, upper or lower, or any deficit in visual tracking. The eye doctor came in and said "Matt's vision is perfect." He doesn't have any visual field loss or tracking problems. This is SO huge to be able to drive again, for safety, and for balance as much of our balance is influenced by our vision. After having gone to several courses on neurological visual deficits and low vision, I am very thankful Matt's vision is perfect. When I look at him, it seems like his eyes aren't completely focused together; however, this may be my imagination from weeks of comparing his pupils and watching his eyes track in PICU.

Matt continues to affect the staff and patients at Country Manor as he has a special place in many hearts I'm sure. Two of his PCAs came with gifts for him today. Noah brought him in *The Beatles* record he had bought in Nashville (I believe) and wasn't even opened.

He said Matt and him like the same kind of music and when Matt wore his Beatles shirt the other day, he knew the record he had was meant for Matt. Matt texted me Saturday and said "everyone likes my shirt"—how cute is that? Another PCA, Cassandra, went to the game last night, took a picture with Matt, and brought him king size Reese's peanut butter cups and kids sour patch candy today. The emotions continue. . . . .

Joy is closely connected to our expectations, what we think and believe. Don't look to the world to form your hopes, dreams, and expectations, because even if you get them, they won't be fulfilling. Look to God, who is able to do exceedingly, abundantly, above and beyond anything you could possibly imagine.

As you take steps of faith to be obedient to God, you will experience his faithfulness, and your faith will become strong. Don't let fear stop you because God will never leave you or forsake you. I am not afraid of change because it leads me to new beginnings.

Home at last and a new goal: Prom

—ᴍ—

Mar. 2, 2014

I am amazed by Matthew's improvement in cognition and memory, as well as seeing his sense of humor return. Some examples are:

#1 While in the pool, Matt lunged for the bar and when Jenn asked him if that was a sign he was finished, finding it really funny. I was turned the other direction and when I asked Matt what he did, because I didn't see, he turned his head toward me, smirked and said, "Your loss."

#2 Matt's PCA who brings him treats, asked him what he's going to do when she's on vacation for eight days. Matt immediately replied, "Die of Hunger." We laughed of course, but as I thought about this, it became even funnier to me. After all we've been through of Matt needing to be airlifted, not being able to control his body temperature, breathe on his own, having a tube feeding, etc., he thinks he'll die of hunger at this time? Enough said, it's funny.

#3 I told Matt the other day "he was my guy." He replied, "Then what's Dad?"

#4 I told Matt we needed a pool rule like the garden, and he immediately said, "What's said in the pool, stays in the pool." I would agree to this, but my journal is similar to what the kid's refer to as my annual "Tell-all Christmas letter."

#5 I told Matt "I was thinking." and Jenn said–"Imagine that, huh, Matt?" Matt turned and looked at her and said, with sarcasm, "Always."

Jenn told Matt she was doing the Polar Bear Plunge next weekend and he said, "I want to do the Polar Bear Plunge" with the most excitement and voice volume I've heard since the accident. He said he wanted to do this with her next weekend; however, we convinced him to practice jumping off the boat or pontoon this summer and do the plunge next year. Jenn asked Matt if it was something he always wanted to do and he said, "Yeah." It's funny how many little things you just don't know, even after many long drives home from basketball games listening to Matt's "bucket list."

In speech therapy, Matt also continues to improve. His therapist said they were doing word problems the other day and Matt subtracted something like five hundred eighty-one from six hundred ninety-eight in his head instantly and had the right answer, to her surprise. I asked him today what he had for breakfast and he remembered he had peanut butter toast and eggs. His short-term memory continues to improve.

In OT, Matt continues to work on his self cares and strength and function of his left arm. He can now open his left hand at times near his body, versus needing me to raise it over his head. His fingers aren't so tight and he continues to slowly get more shoulder and elbow strength to lift his arm from his side onto his lap and partially for me to put his transfer belt on before transferring or walking him. It always takes longer for the arm to rehab, but with the progress in his mobility and cognition, it'll come in time as I know healing is taking place and therapy gives him a huge assistance too obviously. I do believe Matt's acupuncture is contributing to his affect (emotions, expressions) as well as his increase in strength and thinking.

We have an appointment with the neurologist on Tuesday and I can't wait for her to see how good Matt's doing. Much of what he's doing already are things she said he may not be able to do because of the area of his brain injury. I have no doubt Matt's recovery so far will be a great surprise to her.

On Thursday night, the Mom of one of Matt's classmates called me to ask if Bill and I had any objections to Kailey asking Matt to prom. I had tears instantly. Knowing they have been close friends and she was one of the first people Matt texted, that it was sincere, not "just to be nice" was again overwhelmingly wonderful and a gift to Matt. Matt had been talkative on Monday, excited about the game, and had been a bit quieter since—but not "down." He now has an awesome goal for two months out. She visited on Saturday, coming into the room with a poster that had PROM on it, saying she had a question for him, "If he'd go to prom with her." Matt immediately said "Yeah" (as he nodded.) "I was going to ask you." We then took a picture of them with the sign and of a standing hug. How cool and emotional for me AGAIN.

We decided to take Matt home today for a few hours, knowing if we can do a step at the acupuncture office, we certainly could do three to get into the house. Bill went to get Matt himself as he no longer needs me to help. When they got home, Bill asked if I was coming out to help walk Matt in. I was making a spaghetti hotdish and wanted to quickly finish the onion I was chopping. I put on my shoes, opened the door to the garage and was shocked to see Matt already on the second step with only Bill helping him. WOW. Matt didn't even smile when I told him he surprised me. He's getting a bit of a cold and wasn't very talkative today as usual. He was able to sit on a regular kitchen chair for lunch (without armrests.) Bill grilled steak per Matt's request for lunch and Matt devoured it despite my repeated suggestions he slow down, chew more, and telling him we had plenty more and wouldn't run out. After lunch, the girls wanted to play Mario Party with him on the Wii. Of course, I thought if we could do three steps, we could fifteen. Our stairs have a landing half way which makes a huge difference to stop and stand for a minute. It went pretty good, until Matt surprised us and decided to go step over step versus putting his right foot on the same step as his left. Bill chuckled and had no fear of Matt losing his balance or falling. Again I'm thankful for Bill's height, strength, and that he hasn't had any back problems, etc. which certainly is a blessing in Matt's ability to go places at this time. After about an hour of being downstairs, Matt was getting tired. I asked him if he wanted to lie down in his bed, or go back to Country Manor. He replied, "Go back," much to my surprise. I think he was getting irritated with Brooke trying to literally feed him chocolate chip cookies, saying "left, right" behind us as Matt walked, wanting to sit on his lap, repeatedly asking why he couldn't stay home longer, and asking him who he was texting. Matt elbowed her and said, "Don't be so nosey." I think he felt bad seeing my surprised expression as he got mad at her, and a minute later he gave her a hug good-bye and tickled her. It's difficult to put in words how it felt to have him home again, even for a few hours. It was also difficult to have him leave again, but as we explained to Brooke, "He'll get better faster with all the therapy he does every day so he can come home and stay home doing much more." I know Bill and I say this as much to remind ourselves it is the right thing for Matt as much as to explain it to her. The wierdest thing about today, is I stayed home all day for the first time since before the accident. It has been a really long day and I even took two short naps, both of which Brooke woke me up countless times.

We finally took Abby to the dentist as she was complaining of a "sensitive" tooth. I thought, well she just had an appointment in August, so it may be a small cavity, but nothing urgent. We found out she broke off part of one tooth and sheered the enamel off of another molar during the impact from the accident. That's why her tooth is sensitive— oops, now I feel bad for putting her appointment off. She is getting a filling and a crown this week, and has begun orthodontist appointments we started before the accident for new retainers as her teeth had shifted since getting her braces off. She's going to chiropractic appointments and I need to schedule her for massages more regularly as I know this would benefit her too. She now is willing to try acupuncture too when we can schedule this. It's just a matter of fitting it all in with Matt's acupuncture, doctor's appointments and his court hearing next week, I think, for guardianship.

I am the Way and the Truth and the Life; no one comes to the Father except through Me.

There is ALWAYS a way. It may not be easy, it may not be convenient, it may not come quickly; but if you will simply keep on keeping on and to refuse to give up, you WILL find a way. Jesus is the Way, and He will help you find a way where there doesn't seem to be one.

Refuse to say "No way," Jesus is the Way.

Winter Blahs

—⚏—

Mar. 8, 2014

This week has been "status quo" pretty much. Matt and I have been fighting a cold and don't have that extra "energy." Matt has been a bit more down, actually saying "It's not going fast enough." He texted me one afternoon and said, "I feel like I'm never going to make it out of here." I know as he is more aware of everything, he is more frustrated, which is understandable. I know he's missing his friends a lot and is texting often. He had a doctor's appointment yesterday and she asked him if there were things he could do now that he couldn't do a month ago, and Matt replied "No." Of course, I began listing the things he could now do. A month ago we had just moved to Country Manor and wouldn't have dreamt of taking him home and down a full flight of stairs, having him do car transfers with only Dad, his memory, math, left arm strength, etc., etc. Matt agreed, but it wasn't heart-felt. The only real goal he is focused on now is "walking for the grand march at prom."

Matt had a doctor's appointment with the neurologist on Tuesday and she was pretty amazed at Matt's cognitive and physical progress. She asked Matt what was the last book he read, and he immediately said, "*The Lightening Thief,*" I have no doubt she was very surprised. She asked him other questions and to show her if he could move his left leg at all. Matt straightened his left leg out and then moved his ankle up and down too. He also opened his hand (near his stomach) almost fully, showed her how he could bring his hand to his chin and bring his arm forward and back using his shoulder muscles. She said "Matt you have made so much progress in just four months and you can make progress for two years. You can come back in six months, or as needed." Given the choice, of course Matt opted to come back to show her how he would be doing in six months, and I think she was pleased with his response. I liked Dr. Reike in PICU. She was personable, told me what the possibilities of deficits were for the areas of brain injury, but didn't take away all hope, stating we really wouldn't know for two years how Matt would be. When anyone asked Matt what she said after the visit, Matt said "She said there wasn't any damage." Well, if that's what he took away from her visit, I'm perfectly okay with that.

After our appointment we asked Matt where he wanted to eat—totally thinking Arby's, McDonald's, etc., and he replied "Jimmy's PourHouse." Bill and I looked at each other and he said, "Well, ask Mom, she's driving." We decided to walk Matt into Jimmy's PourHouse versus using the wheelchair. Bill transferred Matt out of the vehicle and I needed to back up to park and was coming back to help him walk. Bill proceeded to walk Matt in himself, including managing two doors without any help. Matt then sat at a regular table on a chair without armrests and was fine, enjoying his usual bacon burger and fries. As we waited for our food, I thought about our three visits to Jimmy's PourHouse and all the progress Matt has made. Initially Matt needed two of us to scoot him back in the wheelchair several times, sprayed Mountain Dew everywhere when coughing, and needed to have help eating—even to lean forward toward the table. Our second visit, a couple weeks ago, Matt was able to sit in the wheelchair at the table, bring himself forward to eat, watch the basketball game and enjoy visiting. This week he WALKED in, sat on a REAL chair, and no one walking by would have had a clue how he has spent the past four months. God has certainly blessed Matt, Abby and our whole family.

Matt continues to be "famous" at Country Manor, everyone saying hi to him wherever he goes and several patients who I know are eighty to ninety years old, wanting to do "knucks" or "high-fives" at every meal, cheering him on. The therapeutic recreation staff ask Matt to every game of bingo and he never declines (even winning fifty cents today.) Our music therapist brought Matt sheet music for his right hand—songs by Elvis, which we haven't had time to even try yet. Matt's PCAs continue to dote on him as well, coming in just to talk when they have time, and leaving him treats. Cassandra left several treats before leaving on vacation so "he wouldn't die of hunger" as Matt had teased.

In speech therapy, Melissa was having Matt work on word problems and commented that "they were getting pretty hard." She said, Matt replied, "Lay it on me." They played Scattergories and Matt needed to identify an article of clothing of that started with the letter A and Matt replied "Ascot." I had no idea what it was, but of course Matt and Bill did It's so fun to see Matt's personality return, and how it was before–including little smirks that are more frequent lately. Bill gave Matt his phone and he said "Thanks–I mean thanks Daddy dearest" a long-standing statement between them. It was absolutely wonderful.

It is tough for me to see Matt struggle emotionally with all the changes he's been dealt. God has a plan for Matt and hopefully we'll know what it is some day.

TWO WORDS–5 LETTERS

—⚬—

Mar. 15, 2014

I was still a bit "down" this past week even though Matt is in better spirits as he's feeling better. I've been thinking how I wanted him home for Thanksgiving, then Christmas, and now it's been Valentine's and we're talking about Easter. I had hoped Matt would go back to school for a couple months this spring, now I think he should continue his intensive rehab as long as insurance approves. Matt has been participating in almost four hours of therapy a day, acupuncture three days a week, increased to four meals a day, and never turns down any activity he is asked to attend. The activities are wonderful for Matt and I know it keeps him from getting down; however, as I sit in them, the reality of how life has changed hits like freezing rain in my face.

We went to bowling the other night and one resident said "He's not even smiling, doesn't even like bowling and doesn't want to be here." She is a bit confused and of course doesn't know Matt's spontaneous smiles are rare (but increasing) as Matt proceeds to get a strike. It's a bowling stand where you push a rubber bowling ball down to the pins across the room. Matt loved it and took it all in, scaring me as he joined staff and other residents who said "Go Louise!" with his loud deep voice next to me and clapping by slapping his right hand on his left arm for anyone who did well. It was heart-warming and yet sad for me to watch, thinking we should be at a basketball game, youth group, anything. The next night we played card bingo and Matt assisted to yell bingo for another resident in his loud voice, raising his hand and pointing to her, four times. I know Matt felt good to help her out, and he even won a game. Myself, I was in pity-land doing a reality check. Yesterday, Bill was coming over so we could take Matt to get an iPhone as he's been wanting his iPod to listen to music and had asked for a new phone days before the accident. I went to Matt's room, only to find out he was playing bingo. I asked Matt if he wanted Dad to pick out his new phone or if he did. He said he wanted to pick it out, then changed his mind when I said we were leaving and he wouldn't be able to play bingo. I repeated "You want to stay and play bingo rather than go to the MALL and pick out a new phone?" He nodded yes, opting for Bill pick out a new phone for him. Unbelievable! That's how much Matt enjoys the many activities he goes to.

Matt has decided he wants another full meal around eight or eight-thirty pm after his nightly activity. He initially asks for a Snickers ice cream bar at the Country Store on Country Manor campus, then changes his mind and wants a meatball marinara sub, Lays potato chips and an ice cream bar. I was pushing Matt back from the Country Store/ Subway Tuesday night and Matt says "Hey Mom!" and I said "Hey Matt, what?" totally thinking he'd say we should get more food, or tell me about wanting his iPod, etc.; and he says in a loud, deep voice—"I love you." I know my heart ached from feeling his love at that moment. For weeks in PICU, I wondered if he'd ever know how much I loved him. Now to hear him randomly, whole-heartedly yell it out, overwhelmed me in a way I'll never be able to describe or have you know how I felt.

It's been close to ten pm before Matt finishes eating and I get him ready for bed. I'm thankful I can do this as it lets me feel like a half-way decent Mom and like I'm not just leaving him—he's usually snoring before I leave the room. Of course, it did take longer when Matt dropped a meatball out of his sub and we had to stop and sing "On Top of Old Smoky" together, it was uniquely cool in it's own way.

Laura and a friend visited Matt last Sunday evening. I asked Matt if he had a fun time with Laura and he said "No." When I asked him why he didn't, what had happened, he replied, "I wanted to play basketball with her and we didn't." Bill asked if he told her that, and he said "No." Bill was staying Monday evening with Matt, so I told Matt he could play basketball with Dad tonight. He had played basketball in the pool that morning and also while working on standing balance in the afternoon during his PT sessions. Matt replied, "No, I think I've had my fill today."

Matt went to the year-end basketball get-together Thursday night at Old Chicago with the team. Dean said they were going "non-traditional" this year, but I know they came to St. Cloud to make it easier for Matt to attend. We did not bring Matt's wheelchair even in with us. He walked in and out, sat on a low, hard wooden chair without armrests and even stood with Bill to watch a game go into overtime. Matt hardly said a word the entire time, but instead listened to his friends and took it all in, having pizza. They gave out the awards for the season and even a plaque to Matthew for "Being the Hardest Worker" on the team. It made me think of how hard Matt is working and not to focus on the now this week, but how far he has improved.

Matt is walking now with his PT, Jenn, being on his right side only. He's correcting his balance often automatically without being told in sitting and standing, is able to put on both socks and his right shoe, and is engrossed in the new games Melissa, his speech therapist downloaded—"Stack the States" and "Stack the Countries." At an acupuncture appointment this week, I had this feeling Matt could reach up with his left arm which was at his side. I asked Matt to try to reach for my hand, and he did. He was able to reach up with full elbow extension over his head similar to a "bench press." We showed Josh when he came in and he proceeded to place needles in Matt's right side and to have me work on active-assisted movement with his left arm. It was super cool and I'm pretty sure Bill was a bit teary when he came in and saw Matt able to do this.

Okay—I've kept you in suspense long enough. Let me explain my caption tonight. Mark, the chaplain from the St. Cloud Hospital visited on Thursday with another staff member from the hospital, a priest from Scotland, and another man from Chicago who has been living in Ireland. They were coming to Central MN to go to Cathedral High School, where they incorporate readings and books from Saint Anne, the books Matt liked to have Mark read to him at the hospital. I knew they were visiting; however, didn't know they were flying in until the day before or from that distance until I met them. Mark said he had asked them to include Matt in prayers right after the accident with my permission. It's a blur now, but I do remember him asking if Matt could be on a prayer list early after the accident. Matt showed them (with my prompting of course) how much he could move his left arm and leg and Mark had tears, saying "He couldn't move that side at all before." It was super cool and to have one of the visitors say how much he could feel the love and support in Matt's room with the poster, balloons, photos, banner, etc. He said it was an amazing feeling just walking into his room. My spirits were boosted as Mark told Matt how far he's come, never to give up, etc. I told Matt to give Mark a good hug, and he did, patting his back, as Mark said "you not only made my day or my week, you made my month." The priest from Scotland came over to shake Matt's hand good-bye, and said "God Bless You." Matt didn't let go of his hand, and said two words I will remember for the rest of my life and will keep everything into prospective for me no matter what the future holds—Matt replied, "He has." I said, "What?" thinking I had heard Matt wrong as he repeated it again and Mark said "He said God has blessed him." OH MY GOODNESS! I wanted to burst into tears thinking how awesome it is Matt realizes he has been blessed despite watching basketball every spare waking minute, looking at his basketball pictures and all the things he wishes he was doing. He still knows he has been blessed—-wow. I now think I'm a complete loser in my faith compared to Matt. Those words will change my life and my view on everything forever. Take a moment to ponder this—-I'm sure I don't need to add any inspiration to this, Matt has it all covered for me.

Progress continues

—⁓—

Mar. 22, 2014

This week seemed slower, but as I compare it to last week, Matt continues to make good progress. We brought him home last Sunday again and had the grandparents over for lunch and to play cards. Matt went up and down the flight of steps to the basement, and we could certainly tell the difference in his strength and our comfort level as compared to three weeks ago. He played the Wii with two classmates, with his feet kicked up in the recliner, and loved it. Upon walking back up the steps, he surprised us by going step over step versus putting his feet on the same step, three steps in a row, needless to say, bringing a smile from Bill and I. It was a very good, fun, "normal" day.

In PT pool therapy the next morning at seven am, Jenn asked him how his weekend was, and Matt replied, "Better than ok." She asked him what he did and he said, "I played cards and won and played the Wii." Jenn lowered the pool deck and of course, the famous air bubbles occurred in her swim shorts, as she pushed them smooth and told Matt she had bubbles this morning. Jenn said Matt was holding onto the pool bar, got his balance, let go, looked at her and said "Yeah, bubbles" as he made quotation marks in the air with his right hand. That was the story of the week, as Matt continues to get better physically and to enjoy making people laugh again. One morning this week, as I walked into the clinic, Matt said "Hi Mom" from across the room. I hadn't even noticed he was in the gym as I was looking for my office key in my bag. I went over and said hi and talked to him a minute and asked why Jenn was so quiet. She said, "Tell Mom, Matt" and he replied "Because I told her I didn't want her to talk." I couldn't believe it, but then Jenn explained how Matt doesn't like her constant cues for perfection, so she asked him if he wished she would just be quiet and of course, Matt replied, "Yeah." I explained to Matt he needed to listen to Jenn so he gets better as quick as possible and that she was his ticket home. He nodded his agreement and I believe they've bonded quite a bit more this week. Jenn gets Matt to smile more than I do—and has it all figured out if it's his "cheesy grin" to pacify her, versus a smirk, versus a real smile. He did smile agreeing Jenn was funny, saying Dad was funny, and I wasn't. Oh well, it was worth seeing a smile.

Yesterday afternoon, I was able to watch Matt walk with Jenn walking backwards in front of him, for the longest distance ever, about two hundred and fifty feet. Matt did let Jenn know when he passed his room, to her surprise as she tried to sneak in a little more distance. I think having Matt's friend watching gave him extra motivation too, but it looked awesome.

We were supposed to go to court in Little Falls on Tuesday when the weather and roads were awful, but got the okay to have a phone hearing instead. Matt received a phone call from a public attorney asking him a few questions about guardianship and if he was in favor of this. Matt replied "I'm all for it." Bill and I went to our attorney's office and called at two pm; however, the judge was still in another hearing. We waited for almost an hour, then it was strange to have him ask us over the phone to stand and raise our right hand. We gave him information why we felt Matt couldn't make medical decisions at this time, and he agreed with us. After they complete a background check to make sure Bill and I don't have any criminal history, it'll be complete. It's a relief to finally have this over. Guardianship will be reviewed in one year, at which time hopefully we can give all decisions back to Matthew. The crappy weather in the end, saved us a considerable amount of lawyer fees, not having to travel from St. Cloud to Little Falls and back, and to wait an hour for the hearing. I believe God gave us the snow for a reason.

Matt continues to love his acupuncture appointments and I believe it is a good adjunct to his therapy. Josh has been stretching his neck to help with muscle tightness to improve nerve innervation to his left arm. Matt is now able to open his left hand in any position if he's relaxed, however it still tightens with effort. I noticed is arm is not so tight when he's walking as it was a week or two ago. Matt is able to bring his arm out to side for me to put a gait belt on him, and to bring his left hand to his mouth without difficulty. I noticed about a half hour ago, he's been chewing his fingernails on his left hand. Now that is progress. Matt never would have been able to open his fingers bringing his hand to his mouth a few weeks ago. We have Botox injections planned for April sixteenth to relax his finger flexors and allow him to open his hand functionally. Matt is able to place his left hand on the bar in the pool without assist in standing, so his strength is getting better.

In Speech therapy, Matt continues to work on memory, problem solving and speech articulation as Matt is difficult to understand at times, especially when he's tired. Yesterday, Melissa said, they went over three syllable words, a list they do every few days and only have done two or three times total. She said Matt repeated the word she said on the list, then began saying the words in order, without her saying them first, without looking at the list. She said "I was like –you've got to be kidding me." This is completely how Matt would have been before the accident.

Talk as much as possible about your blessings and hopeful expectations, and it will increase your joy. Be sure each day is filled with words that fuel joy, not anger, depression, bitterness, or fear. Talk yourself into a better mood. Find something positive to say in every situation. Be positive and good things will happen. I know everyone's positiveness has helped our family to not only be hopeful, but confident that Matt will make a full recovery.

Get Out of Therapy Free Pass

—⁓⁓—

Mar. 30, 2014

The past week has been super busy, but overall, a very good week again. We bring Matt home for a day every weekend and try to plan things he wants to do to keep him in good spirits, motivated and knowing he continues get better. Last weekend, Matt came home for dinner and Abby's play. We had chicken for dinner and Matt and Brooke pulled at the wishbone. Matt won and Brooke asked what he wished for, and despite the other girls telling him he wasn't supposed to say, Matt immediately said "For a good Prom." It was wonderful to see Abby in the school play even though her part was fairly small, and to have Matt enjoying the spaghetti dinner and watching the play, even picking the murderer correctly. (It was a murder mystery play.) I was touched to see some of the cast wearing Matt's wristband with their customs. I can just feel the support wherever I go in Pierz, it's difficult to describe, but I know Matt feels it too.

We had an all school band concert on Tuesday night and I wasn't sad this time because Matt wasn't up there playing. I was thankful to see Abby playing her flute, thinking of when she couldn't with the stitches through her lip and the loud noise, and now she's smiling and giving it her all.

At acupuncture on Tuesday, Josh stated, "His left leg is coming back. There is more sensation than before." Matt can feel the needles in his left foot and ankle and jerks his foot back now, not because it hurts, but because it tickles. He's moving his toes and ankle with much more ease, quickly now, rather than with effort. Bill has also been getting treatments for an ongoing sinus infection and has been avoiding certain foods for a day

263

after a visit. He was told he couldn't have any dairy products for a day and said, "But we're having tacos tonight." I told Bill it was only for a day and he'd be fine. Bill says to Matt "Hey bud, do you feel sorry for me?" Matt replied, "Yeah." Bill said, "Thanks bud," as Matt adds "Someone has to," knowing he was being funny with a grin. Later that day, I don't even remember why, but I said "It drives me crazy." Matt replied "What doesn't these days?" I was pretty surprised, yet happy to see his personality come shining through.

Matt is now walking with Jenn in front of him without a wheelchair following behind for two hundred fifty feet with less help and less fear of falling. He has gone from "death grip" on Jenn's shoulder, to placing his hand on her shoulder, to moving his hand down closer toward her elbow. This shows us Matt is more comfortable and trusting his balance too. Matt even walked with Steph (OT) about twenty feet with Jenn coaching them both and she's only about 5'2". Steph is hoping to soon have Matt walking with her in his room while getting ready in the morning. How cool is that? Matt agrees with Jenn that she nags him, but will not agree with Steph about this. Steph asked if he felt she was more fragile and Matt said, "Yeah." We have a new PT student with our PT, Brian. Matt was watching her in the gym this week and Jenn jokingly said, "She wants to be like me someday," and Matt says to her "Don't do it." Jenn asked if she should be like Brian someday and Matt said "Go for it." I asked Matt why he gives Jenn a hard time and he said, "Because she gives it back." It's good for Matt to have humor to make his therapy more fun as this is such a part of his personality.

Matt had Brooke stay with him while Bill went for pizza last weekend. I received a text picture of Brooke smiling on his bed, and another text that said, "I'm stuck with Brooke." I found out later, she had instructed him to take the picture and to text those exact words, and of course Matt humored her. Bill and I had take-out dinner last weekend, with friends visiting and Matt did not want to eat with us in his room. I couldn't believe it, and was a bit embarrassed he didn't want to stay with us, so commented, "You like eating with the guys in the dining room, right?" Matt nodded and I asked him who was his favorite person in the dining room and why. Matt said a man's name without hesitation, and his rationale was "Because he's funny."

I was putting in Matt's acupuncture appointments in his schedule and noticed on Friday afternoon he had a cancelled therapy session with a comment he had refused therapy to play bingo. I told Matt this would not happen again. He only had one "get of therapy free pass and he used it." He wasn't very happy with this and gave Jenn a glare when she came in the room. I told Matt I saw it in the schedule comments and Jenn didn't rat him out. He was then okay with Jenn, but knew he was busted because she knew too he had used up his one and only free therapy pass.

Yesterday, we took Matt to get fitted for his tux for prom. It was fun and they were super accommodating with trying on his tux and shoes, including his left ankle and foot brace using a shoehorn. Bill and I walked him in the tux shoes and I could definitely notice a difference. I'm a bit leery about him walking without having the extra ankle support of his basketball shoes for the grand march. I packed regular tennis shoes for him to practice in PT with Jenn and although we ordered the tux shoes, I'm sure everyone would be just fine if he ended up wearing basketball shoes as a back-up plan. We still have five weeks to work on this. Matt's arm continues to slowly get better. He can bring his elbow up out to the side about half way to his shoulder, (like you would to put on deodorant) onto his lap if it's down by his side, and on the pool bar without help from his right hand. Matt is able to hold onto the grab bar in the bathroom with his left hand for balance to be able to manage clothing with his right hand, which is huge progress. When Bill transfers him, he always gives Matt a hug. On Friday, Matt gave him a two armed hug, without any cueing or help, for the very first time. It made my day! Matt and Jenn are working with the PCA's to start a walking program in the hallways and also to transfer with only one staff with nursing.

We have the senior basketball conference game next Saturday night in Pierz. I told Matt Dad would be gone on a golfing trip, (I had to convince him to go to get a break after five months of going non-stop) so it'd be him and I getting in and out of the vehicle. Matt said, "Can I go early so I can shoot around before the game?" I said, "In the wheelchair?" and he said, "No, standing." My heart ached for him. I decided to call Coach Dahmen to make this goal for Matt happen. Of course he said he'd be happy to help. I can't imagine going through the past five months without all the support Coach Dahmen has given our family. I continue to tell him, he's my "rock" and he says, "I know."

We took Matt to play bingo today at church for the Lions Club. Matt enjoyed this, especially when Grandma got four corners and gave the card to him to yell, as well as the cash price. He was getting frustrated being one away, two to four places. on a single card almost every game. When someone called bingo one time, Matt hit the table with his fist. This made me jump and Grandma said, "I think I need some toilet paper. You scared me so much Matt." He smiled of course, no longer mad. When Grandma told Bill about Matt hitting the table and to tell him what she said, he replied, "She shit herself" in a calm, matter-of-fact way which made it even funnier.

"Lord, if You lead me, I will follow". If you make that commitment and truly mean it, then you can expect God's guidance in your life. It may not always come immediately when you ask for it, but it will come. While you are waiting, continue to thank Him. He has a plan and will reveal it to you at the right time. I listen to God, and He leads me every day, in every situation in my life. As I was looking for my inspiration, I found this immediately and I know this was meant for me as I've been struggling with the "patience" of God revealing his plan with the accident and Matthew's full recovery. I have no doubt Matt will recovery ninety-nine percent or more, get married, have kids, etc., it's just waiting that's the toughest. When I really think about where we started at though, I know God's blessings for Matt's healing has been in warp speed.

"TMI" (Too Much Information)

—⸬—

Apr. 5, 2014 1:12pm

This week has been one of more humor–no surprise where Matt's concerned. Matt had fun playing some April's fools jokes on the staff at Country Manor, which was funny because I never mentioned it or knew he even knew it was April Fool's Day. He was with Steph from OT and she asked him if he could open his left hand. Matt replied "No." She said "I was surprised and said 'you can't?' and then Matt smiled and said April Fools" How great is that? In the dining room that evening, Matt said to two of the PCAs he was so tired. They commented about it and he said "I'm tired of you two," as they were both shocked by his announcement, until he again said "April Fools."

We went to Wheel of Fortune one night this week and of course, this is so up Matt's alley as he's calling out letters and answering the puzzles (winning six times.) He even figured out "*Butch Cassidy and the Sundance Kid*" and "Zeus and Athena," both of which I had not a clue. It was just like old times. Matt would always then explain things to me in a matter-of-fact way and never make me feel stupid for not knowing trivia questions. I had really missed this, so it's great to have this ritual back. We also played bingo again this week, and although Matt didn't win, it was super cool as he was texting a classmate, playing bingo and helping Brooke with the "Stack the States" game on the iPad, all at the same time. I did help him with a few numbers he missed, but didn't have him give bingo his undivided attention as the therapist in me was ecstatic he was able to divert his attention to multiple things simultaneously.

I brought Brooke with me to see Matt on Thursday after Kami's afternoon play. I never see Matt's frustration or anger unless it's with Brooke pestering him. I feel awlful for her as she misses him and loves him so much. She therefore over stimulates him to the point of him becoming upset. We stopped at Subway and picked up dinner before seeing Matt and Brooke was super excited about her "Miss Piggy" Muppet bag she got with her kid's meal. She says, "Matt, do you like Miss Piggy?" "No." Brooke exclaims, "You don't? You like the *The Muppet Show* though right?" Matt replied, "Yeah." Brooke asked, "Do you want my Miss Piggy bag?" Matt stated, "No." "Do you want another Muppet bag?" Matt said, "No." Brooke continues, "Do you want a bag with all the Muppet's on it?" That was the final straw as she repeated these questions each about three times. Matt attempted to stomp on her feet, obviously having had enough of the interrogation. We then ate our dinner in the conference room and Brooke coughed, announcing proudly she had farted when she coughed. Matt calmly says, "TMI." Brooke continued to ask Matt which games she could play on his iPad or iPhone. She asked to play a particular game and Matt replied, "Knock yourself out." She was coughing and coughing with a tickle in her throat despite having a cough drop while lying in Matt's bed. Matt was getting more and more upset saying, "Don't cough in my bed." Whew—I almost needed a referee.

Matt continues to improve physically as well. He has progressed to needing only minimal assistance walking with Jenn two hundred and fifty feet. She walks backwards in front of him and his job is to let her know if something is behind her. She told me Thursday he walked amazingly and even told her when the vitals cart was behind her so she didn't trip. She added when she thanked him for letting her know, he said, "Well, if you fall, I fall." Jenn said it was still cool that he told her, even if it was for self-preservation. Matt is improving in being able to go from lying down to sitting and from sitting to standing too, only needing minimal assistance as he continues to build his trunk strength. It seems so slow, but then when I look back a week or two, it's all huge gains. Our insurance approves two weeks at a time, and so far hasn't said a word about not continuing to cover Matt's stay.

Matt is super excited about the conference basketball game tonight. He'll be able to see the senior players from all the teams he's played with over the years. Coach Dahmen is planning to help me get him down the steps and to the game early as Matt so wants to make a basket while standing today. Matt texted me several times today–so much for my request he sleep in today for the game. He texted saying "I'm kinda nervous for tonight." Then he texted, "But I might fall, that's what I'm nervous about." I reassured him Dean and I would not let that happen. He could shoot a basket with his right arm under the hoop and then he can watch the girls' and boys' game. Everything would be just fine. He replied with, "Okay, can I play Xbox at home?" I told him we weren't going down the basement with dad gone, but I could bring him games back to play in his room at Country Manor. He replied, "I'm just itching to play Call of Duty." Matt was playing this when Abby called him for a ride the day of the accident. He hasn't played it since November 1st. Reading this text brought back a flood of memories, as well as a smile, as it's a sign to me yet again of Matt's full recovery.

I was at the grocery store this week when a young man rather cautiously came up to me and somberly said, "Can I ask you how your son is?" I told him some of the above events from the week and he said, "Oh that's so good." Yet, he remained very serious. I couldn't stand it any longer, so I asked him who he was, thinking he knew Matt. He told me he was one of the first responders at the accident. He said, "I've been at many accidents, but that was by far the worst I've ever seen. Even the police chief of Little Falls said so too." I didn't know he was at the scene. I said Matt had to be re-intubated at the hospital and the staff said it was tough to do and they didn't know if he'd live at one point. Matt has two chipped teeth from the intubation too. He said, "Yeah, it was bad," and I could tell he was "re-living" the scene in his head and had multiple times over the past five months. I asked him if he read my updates, and he replied, "No, but I pray for him all the time." He asked how Abby was doing too. We brought her to her first acupuncture appointment this week and she seems to be less frustrated overall and more patient with Brooke. Abby says "I feel like a mother goose with Brooke following me everywhere I go." Brooke is having severe separation anxiety and won't be a single room in the house unless someone else is with her. Abby is busy with softball practice and is currently obsessed with having Gary's Pizza every time we go to St. Cloud.

I was teary-eyed the rest of the day, thinking of this first responder and his sincerity and continued prayers even though he doesn't know Matt and Abby personally. It's wonderful how people care. A classmate of mine, a couple weeks ago after Abby's play, told me he and his kids pray for Matt every day on their drive into school.

Shooting basketball – Coach Payne, Matt, Coach Dahmen, and Mr. Rochleau

SHAKE IT UP

—〰—

Apr. 13, 2014

Our journey continues at a gradual pace, but in the right direction. Matt is now walking with Jenn, using a rolling wide based quad cane with her on his left side, versus holding onto her shoulder facing her. He will veer to the left with the cane, but has the balance to pick it up and reposition it on his right side. He even walked with two PT staff with his right hand in his pocket (no arm support), needing more assistance, but showing us his fear of falling is improving to trust himself to do this. He continues to improve with his transfers and several of the PCAs are transferring Matt with another staff just standing by as they both increase their confidence. Jenn is meticulous in how Matt walks, making sure he isn't compensating or substituting the muscles he should be using with his trunk or left side. Matt tells Jenn she is "picky." Jenn says, "And why am I picky?" Matt replies in a monotone voice, "So I get better." Jenn, then said, "And what happens when you get better?" fully expecting him to say he could then go home, as Matt replied, "You get pickier." Jenn had to smile as there was truth in what Matt said. I am so thankful for the skilled therapists who work with Matt, dedicated and giving him two hundred percent in every session. One of the nurses from a long term care wing at Country Manor came to my office on Friday to ask a question. She said, "I just saw Matt on his way to bingo. You know everyone loves him." How cool and amazing is that? She doesn't work with him, but can tell by staff bringing him to activities how much everyone cares about him

Steph, OT, asked Matt to rate his therapies from most to least favorite. Matt picked OT as his least favorite as Steph said "Really, I'm last?" Matt replied, "Sucks to Suck" much to her surprise, of course getting the reaction he wanted from her as he smiled, knowing this was pretty funny. Matt really likes all his therapists, especially teasing them, and seizes every opportunity to do so.

Matt continues to text me, saying he could use a particular t-shirt, who came to visit, etc. I smile as I think of the texts he sent yesterday morning. He texted me at four thirty-two am saying, "I'm awake." Then texted again at six thirty-nine am saying "Now I'm asleep." I asked Matt about this when I got to Country Manor yesterday and he continued to smile, thus letting me know he fully knew the humor in his text.

Several people have asked me if Matt made a basket at the conference game last Saturday. He stood with two of the coaches and the athletic director as he tried to make a basket. He had difficulty with positioning and coordinating his right hand to shoot the ball, but improved with repetition. He did not want to rest even as his legs became shaky until Coach Dahmen told Matt, he needed to rest. Matt rested several minutes and then tried again getting the ball stuck under the hoop. Coach Dahmen told Matt several times to look at the basket versus Kailey (his prom date) who was watching. When the seniors were warming up before the game, Matt wanted to go out and practice with them too. Dean and I reassured Matt we'd try again in a few weeks and he'd get run over with so many players out there. Matt was agreeable; however, it was tough to watch him wanting to be on the court so much. Dean and I walked Matt onto the court when his name was announced for the Pierz senior player. Matt literally bolted leaning forward and taking the highest, biggest steps I've since yet. Dean said "Holy shit Matt, are you in a hurry?" Matt gave each player a high five on the court and led the team back to the bench. Matt did not want to sit in his wheelchair during the game, but sat on the padded folding chair, at the edge of his seat. I don't think his back ever touched the backrest of the chair as I watched nervously and was beyond thankful of the trunk strength Matt had gained and was working on during the game. He gave every player a high five as they went on and off the court and was very happy to see the senior players from all the teams in our conference, since he hadn't been able to see them this season. Matt was able to name the players, first and last names, without difficulty and even was in a picture with two of the guys holding his hands in the back row—smiling hugely. It was super cool. Some of the mom's from other teams visited with me and gave me their support and encouragement which lifted my spirits as well.

My Dad had a hip replacement on Thursday at the St. Cloud hospital and we surprised him by bringing Matt from Country Manor to visit. Matt pulled on the bedrail when we wheeled him up to the bed. I asked Matt what he wanted, and he replied, "To get closer." We positioned Matt closer so he could shake Grandpa's hand and give him a high five. Matt agreed with Grandpa he was in better shape than Grandpa was. On the way home from the hospital, Matt said, "This wouldn't be a good song for a pop commercial". I said "Why, was it banned after the Super Bowl?" I listened closer and realized the song was "Shake It Up." I then caught on as I asked Bill if he knew what Matt meant and of course Bill replied, "Yeah". I asked Matt why he let me struggle with the reason and he replied, "You have to learn some time."

Matt's left arm and hand continue to gain strength. He is able to pull down the pulley handle with his left arm straight, turn his palm up and down (even to get communion today) and to bring his hand to his mouth and straight again. Josh is able to press on trigger points throughout his left arm–pectoral muscles to forearm and Matt will open and close his fingers. We have an appointment with Dr. Derr this Wednesday to have Botox injections to Matt's wrist and finger flexors. The goal is to decrease the tone (or spasticity) so Matt is able to strengthen the wrist and finger extensors to use his hand functionally. It typically takes seven to fourteen days for the full effect of Botox, however in the past several months I've realized how God listens and answers with power in numbers of prayer for specific healing in Matt's recovery. I know he'll continue to improve in every area, but I'm so hoping Botox will help Matt to use his left arm and hand in the near future.

For you have the need of steadfast patience and endurance, so you may perform and fully accomplish the will of God, and thus receive and carry away what is promised. This quote from Hebrews so fits Matt and our family's patience as we continue to pray for healing and his recovery.

What else did you expect?

—⁓—

Apr. 19, 2014

The highlight of the week was going to see Dr. Derr on Wednesday for a follow up and Botox injections. Dr. Derr was amazed at how well Matt looked (he's up to two hundred pounds now–the first time he ever has been) his thinking, and his physical improvements. He said, "You've done really well at Country Manor. Is everything going ok—are you treated well?" Matt immediately shook his head yes without hesitation. Bill and I walked Matt so Dr. Derr could see how his arm tightens up when he walks, look at his balance and the improvement in his left leg strength. I do believe he even said "that is amazing–or incredible." I was so proud of Matt and all the effort he's been putting into getting better. When Matt stopped, he asked him if he could straighten his left arm and Matt did–much to his surprise and delight.

Matt is used to needles from acupuncture; however, the Botox injections do hurt, unlike acupuncture needles; however, Matt never flinched or said ouch. He contracted each muscle Dr. Derr asked him to do to be sure he had the right site. Matt received injections to his biceps, wrist flexors, finger flexors, and his thumb. It was triple the amount of Botox he got in the hospital, but was dispersed throughout all these muscle groups with multiple injections. After completing the injections, Dr. Derr said, "We don't know how much it'll help, but I will say a prayer that it does–I'm not sure if you guys are into that or not, but I'll say one." He has no idea how "into that" we are. The Botox wears off in three to four months; however, in the meantime, Matt will be able to work on strengthening all his left arm extensors to overpower the returning tone and tightness of his flexor muscles. As we were leaving, I told Matt he did awesome and he replied, "What else did you expect?" He did have a very good point.

On Wednesday, it was our 20th wedding anniversary with a foot of snow. When we were waiting in the doctor's office, I asked Matt if he knew what day it was and he said April 8th. I told him it was the 16th and asked him if he knew what day it was. His eyes lit up and he said in a louder, excited voice "It's your anniversary." We hadn't mentioned it before this, so I thought that was pretty cool. Bill and I had planned to go out to Mongo's Grill for dinner, but with the roads bad, we stayed and had Gary's Pizza with Matt–which he was all for. It was perfect in its own way and we were thankful we have each other and for Matt and Abby's recovery. It's far more important than going on a trip or even out to dinner. We are so lucky.

This past week, I've been thinking non-stop about the future. Our insurance policy covers 120 days in a skilled nursing facility which, as far as I calculate, will be May 30th or 31st. It's ironic the timing will be almost exactly when the girls will be home for the summer. Isn't it funny how some things fall into place?

I've been wondering whether to purchase the wheelchair Matt has now, as it's in good condition, has a great cushion and fits him well (and they are giving us a good price for it) or to wait until Matt is discharged as insurance would then most likely approve a light weight "regular wheelchair." We need to also begin adding railings to get into the house, additional railings on the steps to go downstairs, as well as to look for furniture upstairs that Matt can easily get up from. He'll need a bedrail, and possibly grab bars in the bathroom; however, I'll know more as its closer to him coming home. I've thought a lot and plan on adding on the deck we've wanted for many years off the upstairs laundry room so Matt can go outside during the summer without needing to do any stairs. Can you tell how my mind is spinning? I know Bill is too as he's awake multiple times every night, but has no trouble falling asleep at each acupuncture appointment sitting up in a chair within two minutes. I told him he should sit in a chair at night and he'd probably get more sleep. We need to put it all in God's hands and the future will fall into place.

We are going to Bill's sister's house for Easter today, to my parents tomorrow and are bringing Matt to both gatherings. It'll be good for him to spend time seeing all of his family again as he missed this at Christmas. Matt knows all his friends are busy and has been getting less texts and visits lately. He used to check his phone multiple times a day for messages and never have it out of his possession; however, now will leave it on his tray table and only checks it a couple times a day. When I ask him if he's texting his friends, he replies "they're busy." Matt needs encouragement as reality is sinking in with graduation near. Matt is a bit more discouraged; however, still denies being down in the dumps to me and tries very hard in all his therapies. Prom is in two weeks so I think as excited as he is, he's realizing that he may not be able to walk with only Kailey for the Grand March. He may be able to with the rolling quad cane—one day at a time I guess as the day gets near. I'm planning to ask the insurance company if we can have an overnight pass for prom—doesn't hurt to ask, all they can say is "No."

Shrimp Tail? Back At You!

—⚍—

April 26, 2014

Easter was a wonderful weekend. Matt played cards at the Athman gathering–even Texas Hold'em. I could tell how much better his walking is improving. Bill walked with Matt and his brother, and then his brother-in-law who had never walked Matt before. On Sunday, we sat outside and played cards at my parents so Matt could spend some time outdoors as it's been months since he's been able to do this. It was two full days, and Monday morning at seven am pool therapy, Matt was pretty tired. Jenn asked him if he wanted to be finished early, but Matt said "No" and then put his face in the water to wake up. What a trooper.

On Wednesday, we took Matt to the dentist in Pierz to fix his chipped teeth from the accident. They were very accommodating and scheduled more time for actual work versus just a check-up. She was able to fill both his front teeth, top and bottom, without needing any crowns at this point which was awesome. Matt has been very sensitive to cold with a bottom tooth when eating cookie dough blizzards; however, had no hypersensitivity when she tested it. We won't know if any of his teeth have fractured roots and will need a root canal in the future–time will tell, but they took x-rays for a baseline. Matt did great having Novocaine and was able to watch "*Family Guy*" on the iPad with headphones while they fixed his teeth. Gosh have times changed, huh?

My friend and her daughter went to Red Lobster one night this week with Matt and me for dinner. We were able to walk Matt to and from the vehicle without difficulty–still getting used to everyone watching us, but Matt seemed okay with it. He had breaded shrimp, fries and five biscuits. I was peeling my shrimp, pinching the tail off when it slipped and literally flew at Matt. He picked it up in like a second and whipped it back at me. I told him it was an accident and asked him if he was mad because it wasn't on purpose; however, he shook his head no with a grin. I said something funny during the meal and my friend laughed. Matt looked at her and said, "Don't Laugh." She tried not to, but laughed again as he repeated, "Don't Laugh," then added "It only encourages her." She then burst out laughing, knowing he wasn't upset at her for laughing. On the way home, Matt identified every song and artist, showing us how well he knows them all. I covered up the radio screen which says the song and artist and asked him who sang the song that was being played. Matt said what I thought was "Art." I said, "Art who?" Matt repeated it again twice and then started pounding on his chest and said, "Heart" which was what he was saying all along. I said, "Gosh Matt, I thought you we having a heart attack" and my friend said she thought he was having a seizure as we both laughed and Matt smiled. It was pretty funny. I love to see his personality come shining through more and more.

Matt has made huge gains with his left hand since Botox last week. He can now open his hand in any position and no longer has his fingernails digging into his palm. Matt has been able to reach and grab items and to keep an open hand on a ball in OT. Of course, the therapist in me may be encouraging his left hand function as well. He even ate a breadstick with his left hand Thursday night. With a little help, he was able to open and close his bingo numbers with his left index finger and to reach, hold and squeeze his toothpaste. I have a renewed faith his left arm will continue to progress with everything he does functionally–with a bit of encouragement. Matt was able to hold his cards in his left hand and is now able to bring his thumb to touch the tip of all his fingers on his left hand except the little finger. This is absolutely wonderful and I am so thankful. I notice too when Matt walks he can push his left arm straighter without his elbow and wrist flexed up toward his chest. As his balance continues to improve I know he won't kick in the tone in his left arm for stability like he tends to do now. Time and patience, perseverance and prayers will make all the difference–I have no doubt.

Kailey, her Mom and another classmate came over tonight to discuss prom. They plan to go bowling and out to eat during the day. I asked Matt if he wanted to go watch them bowl and he said, "No, I want to bowl" as my heart sank and my mind thought of adaptations. I wondered if we helped Matt, if he could throw the ball standing, or from a chair sitting behind the lane. I guess we'll have to see the day of prom what's doable and how much drive Matt has to join his classmates. I've been thinking of the Grand March and asked Matt if he would like to walk with Kailey and the rolling quad cane. He said, "I don't like that cane" and prefers to walk with Bill and Kailey instead. I found out they will be the first one in the Grand March so he doesn't have to stand in line. We practiced with them walking Matt in the house tonight and I think Matt was so excited he forgot to bring his left leg with. After telling him to slow down and bring his left knee up, he did one hundred percent better walking back to the kitchen. I'm now certain having Bill walk with is a great idea and necessary. Matt is getting better every week. We noticed this especially on the stairs today–going up and down, it was much easier and a lot less scary for Matt. I called the insurance case manager from HealthPartners this week and left a message about an overnight pass for prom. She called me back within hours and said she had "goosebumps" when she listened to my message. She had already called the Medical Director to get approval and said he told her "I can't believe you even asked. Of course it would be okay." She said, "If he hadn't said yes, I was going to strangle him through the phone." She talked to me for a while and actually has a son, who is a senior in high school this year (how ironic) and commented on Matt's progress from her reviews. She said his last skilled nursing day is June forth per our policy—ironically, school gets out June third for the girls. Tell me God doesn't have everything planned out and I can give you so many examples of how he has everything in his hands and has since the day of the accident. God is hearing all of our prayers and it replaces my worries and fears with extreme peace. It'll all work out as it's meant to be. This week, one of the nurses at Country Manor asked Matt how things were going for him. She said he replied "I'm getting better." Matt has had visitors and more texts this past week and I can certainly tell the difference in his mood and determination. It's huge for him.

Faith is not about wondering whether something will occur, or thinking it could happen, it is about feeling sure it will happen. This is a quantum leap from wishing. It is a much higher energy, a much more powerful one. Faith has more pulling power than Hope by a factor of ten.

Matt and Kailey at PROM

Mitchell, Katelyn, Kailey, and Matt

Matt and Lynn

PROM

—〰—

May 4, 2014 2:06pm

This week has been a blurr—from Brooke losing a tooth, Kami having a mini-retreat I didn't know about, Laura doing a Polar Plunge (telling us the day after,) running out of gas (after I told her she'd have enough to go home), hair appointments, three acupuncture appointments for Matt, one for Abby, my birthday with everyone going out to Jimmy's PourHouse for dinner Thursday night, signing up for year-end field trips and summer activities and sports (convincing Kami to do some versus being worried about being home with Matthew), tux fittings, and prom last night—whew.

I have dreams I can fly sometimes—they are my ultimate favorite. Over trees, houses, in the clouds, etc., it is simply amazing. Well, Friday night I dreamt I was flying in the house like a bat. Up to the ceiling, almost into the wall, down the banister a few times, swooping down to give Brooke a kiss and then back up again trying to burn energy, circling over and over at one hundred mph it seemed, never getting outside. I woke up–of course not rested, and thought my dream summarized the chaotic week. Hopefully this week is a bit more mellow.

Matthew continues to improve with problem solving and memory. Bill and I are trying to have him figure out how to turn and position his feet for transfers and getting in and out of the vehicle and it's certainly improving. Melissa in speech has told me Matt continues to progress as well with math skills and problem solving–even identifying the bills and coins needed when given a large amount of money, such as one hundred and sixty-eight cents, without difficulty. Matt continues to show his wittiness and sense of humor. He sat back down after not positioning his feet correctly, looked at Jenn and said, "That was shitty." The progress with Matt's balance and mobility continues, but at a slower rate. When I asked him to sit up on the edge of the bed Thursday to get ready for Jimmy's PourHouse, he surprised me and sat up the quickest I've seen and I was across the room. His confidence and trunk strength is improving for him to even attempt this.

After Matt got all dressed up in his tux, we took pictures at Country Manor. He was able to stand with only Kailey assisting for balance. We went through the facility, per request of nursing staff on other units, and to see the therapy staff too. Matt was very excited about prom, having everyone see Kailey and his friends, and knowing he had a pass until Sunday. We went bowling with Matt, Kailey and another couple from Matt's senior class yesterday. Matt used the adapted bowling ramp for most of his frames, but did try just throwing the ball sitting in his wheelchair too (the wheelchair wheel did get in the way for this technique.) Matt's friends were amazing—helping with the ramp, getting Matt's ball for him and cheering him on. We ate with Matt taking everything in—talking very little, but thoroughly enjoying himself. Matt took a thirty to forty-five minute nap at home before going to the school for pictures. Pictures went well and Matt and few classmates walked in the hallways for the senior farewell video. I couldn't let go with them never having walked with Matt before, so snuck behind them with the transfer belt, avoiding being in the video. Matt was able to get many pictures of classmates sitting in the wheelchair and in standing. Near the end of almost two hours, I asked him if he wanted a picture with another couple who had come over to say hi, and Matt shook his head no. I was embarrassed and asked him why he said that. Matt's reply was "I'm all pictured out." I told him he didn't have to smile so much, but it was rude to say no when someone asked. He then agreed and took the picture. He'll have many photos for memories—it was super cool.

Matt and Kailey were first for the Grand March. After Bill and Kailey had Matt standing, I brought the wheelchair to where they would be sitting after the Grand March. I was so nervous to be on the side watching, I didn't even clap and wanted to yell out how he should be walking ("big steps, left knee up, step on your heel, etc, etc.") I don't think I took a breath until he was sitting in the wheelchair—but Bill and Kailey were calm and had it all under control. Matt decided to wear his basketball shoes until the Grand March; however, after his coach said, "nice basketball kicks," Matt did not want to change to his tux shoes. It was fine with Bill and me, therefore Matt wore his basketball shoes with his tux. Matt told both of his coaches he "was ready for Wisconsin Dells" in June without us even talking about this at all. It's wonderful to give him goals to look forward to–the basketball games, prom, going home, Wisconsin Dells, etc. I know it will help keep him motivated. After the Grand March, Matt transferred to sit in a regular chair at the tables by the refreshments. Initially Bill and I were by him and he didn't want to eat anything. Matt looked at me and said, "I don't want to stay. . . .very long." Then Bill brought him chicken strips, he had another beloved dose of Ritalin, and friends started coming over and sitting by him. Bill and I backed off and let him listen and enjoy his classmates that he's missed so much. I went home about 10 pm and Matt and Bill stayed the entire prom, getting home close to 12:30 am. I asked Matt why he decided to stay, and he replied, "I had a change of heart." Matt had pizza when he got home and wanted to go downstairs to his bedroom. The steps continue to get easier each time he comes home. We gave him the house phone to call my cell if he needed anything after he rattled off my phone number. Matt slept until seven am and then called to go to the bathroom, and again at eight am to get up because he couldn't sleep. I know he was excited to play Xbox. We walked Matt barefooted and he was hyperextending (snapping his knee back), therefore decided to have breakfast downstairs. Matt tried playing Xbox and couldn't without using his left hand, so played Super Mario Bros. 3 with the Wii instead and enjoyed this.

Apparently God knows we may need more assistance when Matt comes home June fourth. I talked to Matt's head basketball coach last night who said he has the summer off and to let him know if we wanted him to help out with Matt. I was emotionally drained and teary-eyed on my drive home. The entire town is so supportive and good to our family. I had never realized and felt how much good there is in people until the accident. I will never take all the kindness we have been shown for granted, but instead I thank God every day for all the blessings that we have had in the past six months. I thank God for you.

Plate versus Platter

—∿—

May 11, 2014

Monday at work was super busy and I needed to run to Target to get items for Kami's time capsule project before going home for Abby's band concert. I drove into the yard at six fifty-six pm with groceries and other items to unload quickly before getting to the school by seven pm. I changed clothes, leaving my purse and phone in the truck. When I got back, Abby had answered my phone and said, "Here, it's Laura and she's crying." Laura said "Mom, I need to go to the emergency room, I hurt my knee. It's the worst thing that's ever happened to me and I think I might bleed to death!" I started driving to the high school, thinking Laura was hurt by the baseball fields in town after doing stats for the boy's game. By the time I was a mile from the high school, I found out she was a mile and a half the other direction from our home and had been rollerblading. I dropped Abby off and she said she would have her friend drive her home from school after the concert.

When I got back home, Laura had towels on her knee and it was gashed open–to the point I didn't think the skin would be able to reach with stitches. Wow–she really wasn't exaggerating. She was ready to pass out, her ears were ringing and she was pale. I tipped her seat down, put an ice pack on her forehead and decided to go to Little Falls to St. Gabriel's Hospital because it was closer and she was very anxious about getting there quickly. At the ER, they attempted to get some of the dirt out with a syringe of saline and a brush; however, when the x-ray revealed the dirt and gravel was down to the bone, they aborted this plan. The orthopedic surgeon was called in and she had surgery to debride

285

and irrigate the wound. Laura hadn't torn any tendons or ligaments and hadn't gotten any debris into the capsule. After having stitches placed internally and externally, it looks better than I expected and she can put full weight on it. She doesn't need to use crutches or anything. We were very lucky as this was the best possible outcome.

As I was waiting in the emergency room, the lobby, and in the recovery room, I thought to myself, Okay, really God? Don't you think our plate is full already? I know the bracing and therapy required after a torn ligament and all the outpatient therapy Matt will be doing after he returns home, and just couldn't think of adding more to our busy days. I then had the realization that Bill and I had started out with a platter, not a plate. God did hear my plea and I know he only gives us what we can handle—apparently, he agreed with me. Laura applied iced and elevated her leg for two days, still doesn't walk with a normal gait pattern due to pain, but she'll be okay. She said, at least I stopped myself from falling backwards and I didn't hit my face—we certainly didn't need her to have another backwards fall and concussion again. We are lucky—no broken bones, again. Laura said one of the teachers at school said "Tough year to be an Athman, huh?" That about sums it up, but I know many people out there are dealing with far more than we are. I need to keep that into perspective and be thankful again for all the blessings we have been given.

Matt continues to make progress with his left hand as the tone decreases and the strength to open his hand improves. He even tolerated being on his hands and knees on the mat with his left elbow, wrist and fingers fully extended. His standing balance continues to improve especially with self-cares and he corrects his balance more automatically. Jenn said one day that Matt got out of the pool and was waiting for Steph from OT to shower, she was just picking up equipment and out of the blue, Matt said, "Jenn?" She said, "Yeah, Matt?" He replied, "Thanks for everything." It made me teary for as much as he is frustrated at times with what he's asked to do and how difficult things are for him physically, he still is grateful.

Matt continues to improve with his speech articulation and I can understand most of what he's saying in longer sentences without having him repeat it. Melissa, from speech, reports he is making very good progress with problem solving and memory. Matt has begun to drink from a glass or cup much better without needing to use a straw to prevent spilling. He also has a more symmetrical smile when it's automatic, rather than with motor planning if he's asked to smile. I have heard him chuckle a few times—not a lot or real long, but it is wonderful.

This week I have a field trip to the zoo with Brooke, and Bill is going to Camp Foley with Kami for two days of the week too. Next weekend is Matt's graduation mass and breakfast. We still need to wrap up equipment needs for home—grab bars, railings, bathing equipment and having someone with Matt pretty much all the time. I know it'll all fall into place as we now have a good idea of what we'll need initially when he comes home.

All of the support and prayers have gotten us through this past week again. That's how Bill and I can handle our full platter.

Graduation Mass

—✺—

May 19, 2014

On Sunday we had graduation mass in Pierz for our parish, St. Joseph's. Of course, always busy until the last minute possible, we went to the mall Saturday late afternoon to get Matt some new dress clothes, and then arrived at the church at seven forty-five am for eight am mass, only to find out we hadn't ordered a cap and gown for him to wear like his classmates. Luckily the principal was working at the breakfast brunch, so went to the high school and got Matt one to wear. Matt was first in the procession of mass (gotta love having the letter A for a last name.) We pushed him in his wheelchair, but he wanted nothing to do with sitting in it during the mass. Matt sidestepped into the pew and stood every time but once during the mass; however, sat instead of kneeling. It made me thankful for all the practice he gets in therapy with sidestepping, and also made me think of many future goals including keeling, genuflecting, etc. Matt stood on the altar for a class photo after mass with two friends on either side of him for balance, with a genuine smile. I continued to flip from one extreme emotion of sadness for being at his graduation mass in a wheelchair, to being so ecstatic he was really there, sitting in a regular pew, and participating in the mass. It was an emotional roller-coaster–again. I was asked to speak at the brunch last February; however, Bill said he would do the talk. He wouldn't let me know what he was going to say which really made me more nervous than actually speaking, so I wrote up an introduction, only to have him say he "wouldn't and couldn't, follow my speech." Bill was okay with talking first, so we shared the guest speaker role. I wanted to include it in my journal as many of Matt's classmates belong to other parishes, as well as his friends from other schools. You will soon find out God definitely gave me guidance through Brooke for my speech. My voice was so shaky and my right leg too. I was surprised I could stay standing—bu made it through what I had to say, noting a few teary eyes as other mom's listened, totally unexpected for me. Here is what I said:

"Diffuse Axonal Shearing was the diagnosis Matt received after the accident. My friend told me about three months later she had researched this after the accident, and since it was a mote point now, she would tell me what she found out. I did some research too to confirm the prognosis and every article I found said ninety percent of patients with this diagnosis do not come out of a coma, and those who do often remain in a vegetative state. This in itself is a huge testimony to the power of prayer. If there's one thing that's been so important and consistent since the day of the accident, it's the prayers our family received. I wanted to focus my talk on remembering this power of prayer as you venture into the new changes of your life. Whether it's worrying about taking a test, having money for groceries, gas, a broken relationship, or whatever trial you face, remember to say a prayer and God will get you through it. You may not understand how and why things don't happen the way you want, but believe me, there is a reason and someday you may know what it is, but even if you don't, trust that God has a plan. I had huge plans for Matt's senior year and college. His plan was to be a physical therapist and play basketball, and although I don't know why, I know his plans were changed for a reason. Already I know so many people have strengthened their faith because of the accident and that in itself is amazing and has already given us some answers.

Brooke was writing in a notebook yesterday, drew a picture and wrote this story: "Once upon a time there was a cross that would grant wishes and one day a girl went for a walk and saw the cross and then wished for stuff and she couldn't see what the cross did, but it granted her wishes and when she ever had wishes she went for a walk." Her story brought tears to my eyes as I realized my seven year old "gets it." She knows to go to the cross for her wishes and they will be granted. She didn't pick Santa, the Tooth fairy, a wishing well, but instead chose the cross. I thought to myself how much the past six months have changed her view of the world and her faith at age seven, and have such a sense of peace that she too is on the "right path." Think of this as you venture out to college and jobs, and remember to take a walk to the cross whenever you have wishes as Brooke describes, or difficulties in your life, requiring guidance. You will never regret taking that walk or asking others to say a prayer to help through trying times. Be there for each other, keep your family and friends close, and help others in need—that's what life is all about."

The past week has been a blur of planning for Matt coming home. I made an appointment for him with a vendor to get a new light weight, collapsible wheelchair, an appointment with the orthotist to get Matt a custom AFO (ankle-foot orthosis) to prevent his knee from hyperextending, (snapping back,) talking to the Social Security office, and looking at equipment and home modifications we need to decide on and obtain yet. I told Brooke we were going to switch Matt's bedroom upstairs and she'd be downstairs and she had a complete meltdown, despite my telling her it'd be temporary until he could do the steps more easily. My heart goes out to her for yet another change in her life, but she does understand the reasoning. Bill and I looked at furniture Matt can get up from more easily with the girls while we're at work (including a lift chair with other power options) as well as adding railings, grab bars, shower adaptations, etc. It's a bit overwhelming and we haven't purchased anything officially yet; however only have until June fifth to "pull it all together." I know as much as he loves everyone at Country Manor, Matt's excited and ready for the transition back home. I can't imagine how it'll be to have everyone home at night for dinner—that in itself will be a gift.

Matt continues to show his personality. After going to Subway for dinner last week, he told the worker, "My compliments to the chef." He's posting on Facebook early in the morning and continues to post with humor. Matt has been playing "Who Wants to Be a Millionaire" on his iPad and to participate in any trivia activity he can at Country Manor. He even tried to figure out a scavenger hunt during speech for a special activity by the recreation department. Matt is improving his left hand coordination and can now touch his thumb to each finger and even has the pinch strength to finally open a piece of candy–something that seems like no big deal, yet is huge not to have to ask for help. Every accomplishment is a milestone and greatly appreciated. Matt played cards with his grandparents on Sunday and was able to pinch and hold the cards with much more ease. Grandpa even commented on how much better his left hand was from a few weeks ago.

"The Waiting Place"

—◊◊—

May 26, 2014

This past week has again been busy and emotional. I'm looking forward to having Matt home and being in a routine–graduation behind us. On Wednesday night, we took Matt to the senior youth group party at Pizza Ranch, disc golf, and to the DQ. Matt enjoyed the pizza–of course–but was quiet and had a tough time looking at photos of all the events and activities their class had done over the years. He looked at each photo, then began flipping them over and wouldn't, or couldn't say why. Bill said he thought seeing all the things Matt could do before had to be tough on him. We went to disc golf and in about thirty seconds all the kids were long gone in the field. Matt and I went with the adult youth group leaders and he had a tough time throwing the disc, but did get better with practice. (I wasn't very good at this either, but Matt's discs went the shortest distance, which was frustrating for him.) Matt's sole goal whenever we went golfing was to beat my score. He used to "adjust" his score to his benefit when he was younger (until Bill also kept track and busted him,) but before long after joining the golf team he didn't need to, beating me honestly without effort. He did enjoy seeing all his friends again and literally fell asleep drinking his vanilla shake from the DQ on the way home. On Thursday night, Bill and I went golfing and I felt guilty leaving Matt alone, but knew he was busy with bingo and in perfect caring hands, and that it was "okay" to have a night out. As we continued to golf, I knew I wasn't feeling guilty Matt was alone, but rather that we were golfing and he couldn't. Matt was on the varsity golf team at school and really enjoyed this. The golf team, like the basketball team, has also been so supportive. They visited and had Dominos pizza with Matt when the season started. I'm sure it's a mixture for Matt's emotions too, being happy not to be forgotten, yet sad he can't be out golfing with the team this year. I'm positive by next summer he will be golfing and hopefully having this goal will continue to motivate him to keep working hard in therapy.

The wheelchair vendor came out to see Matt at Country Manor on Wednesday to begin the process of having Matt get a new light weight wheelchair for home. Matt was able to propel the wheelchair much easier and really liked the cushion he brought to trial. It typically takes four to six weeks to get, but I'm hopeful we'll have it for the Wisconsin Dell's basketball trip mid-June. His OT, Steph, wrote the letter for medical necessity the same day to speed up the process when she had a cancellation. I read the letter on Thursday morning and it was written perfectly to justify the deficits present for insurance to pay for this higher priced wheelchair, needed for long-term independence with mobility. As I finished the final sentences, I had to fight back tears as this "wonderfully written letter" was about my Matthew. I needed to focus on our plan for his wheelchair to be only temporary—hopefully collecting dust six months from now. I thought about how encouraged I was seeing Bill walk with Matt alone on his right side this week. Matt was able to walk with minimal assist from Steph and I on Wednesday, without holding onto anything with his right hand, a huge improvement from when I've last seen him try this. Matt continues to use his left hand more, but needs reminders to do so. He played cards again on Saturday at home, placing and holding them in his left hand without any cues or help to "organize" or grasp them for the first time. Laura asked Matt what games he wanted to play this summer and he replied "games that make me look smart."

On Saturday, my best friend, Joan, came over and helped us clean and move bedrooms all day. It was amazing how much needed to be cleaned after months, how many things had accumulated under beds, and how many clothes Brooke had outgrown. She did better than I had anticipated with the move when she had her mattress, sheets and blankets brought down as this was a concern for her. It's such a huge relief to have that project completed. Now we need to finish our decisions about furniture and get the equipment Matt will need. I've been thinking non-stop about Matt's routine once he gets home, exercises he'll be able to do with PCA care or the girls, (possibly even at the fitness gym in Pierz–even in the evening with us) what we'll do if no one is available, being able to get him outside, doing some educational studies on the computer, etc., to keep him busy and getting better versus playing Candy Crush and the Wii or Xbox the majority of the day. It'll definitely be a new chapter in our journey.

Matt came home for Abby's fifteenth birthday. When anyone asked him what his plans were this weekend, he'd reply "It's my sister's birthday." He saw his new room upstairs and was okay with this. He went downstairs twice to play Xbox and the Wii (good therapy, but also a good reminder how additional railings will make it much easier too) Matt went on our computer in the afternoon and as I checked on what he was doing, he had posted on Facebook, "I'm coming home June fourth." Actually, I believe it's June fifth, but didn't correct him, as my heart melted, knowing he was excited about coming home after seven months and wanted to share this. He looked at other things on the internet, but kept going back to read any responses he received. The encouragement and praise everyone gave him for all his hard work to get home again is what motivates him and keeps him from getting down.

We had four girls stay overnight for Abby's birthday last night and many times I thought about how special this birthday was to us, knowing she's doing good and able to celebrate with her friends–evident by non-stop laughter. I took them to AirMax and even though it made Bill and I nervous to have her jumping with all the jaw, neck and hip pain she has been having, it was wonderful to see what she could do. Her balance, coordination, and strength have improved SO much–again making me thankful for the blessings we have received in Abby's recovery. She is going to acupuncture, the chiropractor, massage when we can fit it in, and I'm planning on having her possibly start physical therapy again to strengthen her back and pelvis muscles to prevent her hip from being out of alignment. Realistically, this won't happen until Matt is going to outpatient therapy too, but it's less than two weeks away and she'll be finished with school so scheduling will be easier.

As I was waiting for girls to jump at Airmax (Bill took Matt to the new *X-Men* movie instead,) I was looking for a new book to start on my kindle. I had downloaded several religious books a long time ago for my Mom's kindle which also went on mine; however, I had never read them myself yet. I began to read, "Waiting on God." It was amazing. I have been going back and forth about the disappointments we've faced and the wonderful miracles we have encountered since the accident. Now, it seems like we are in a "stale mate," just waiting for the final pieces of our life to fit together from the accident. This book "struck home" for me. "It's in our most desperate, darkest hour that we cry out countless questions to God: Why are you allowing this? What is the purpose of this? Are you there? Do you care? The answer from God sometimes comes in the form of a question. . . Where is your faith?

"While you're waiting, God wants you praying, drawing nearer to Him, and resting in the peace that He provides in the midst of a raging storm. As you wait, God strengthens you because you begin to realize God IS at work. . .He's growing your faith and He's purifying your heart. And faith is rarely grown with anything other than overwhelming circumstances, and typically not found in any place other than the 'waiting place'. There's no other way to purify gold than by the fire—it's part of the process. . .and it's necessary. God knows what He's doing. He's in control even when life isn't. Trust that when your world seems to be falling apart. . .it's really falling into place in the hands of your Almighty loving God. Trust. Wait. Rest. God's help is on the way. Wait in faith and don't let doubt get the best of you. The outcome of our trial depends upon one thing: Our faith in God. And it's the "waiting place" that tests our faith and strengthens us so that we have a testimony that says "My God is faithful." He's increasing our faith by threatening to destroy it. "Faith isn't Faith, until it's all you're holding on to." Your times of trials, your times of "waiting," are teaching you to lean longer and harder on God than you ever thought you could. He's growing your faith in ways that you cannot conceive. When hope is gone, there is faith, and faith brings about God's presence and power.

I cannot describe how refreshing it was to read a small portion of this book and feel that our "waiting place" as Matt is recovering at a slower pace now, will have an amazing boost if we all keep that faith. His blessings have been revealed many, many times already, but in faith it'll continue. I think I'll read this book to Matt too and it'll help him understand his circumstances and to keep his faith strong.

Family Graduation Photo–Abby, Lynn, Bill, Laura, Kami, Matt and Brooke.

Graduation

—ᨓ—

Jun 2, 2014

Last week was of course our usual "beyond busy" but in an exciting way. Matt had an appointment with the orthotist on Thursday—the same one Kami has seen for years, and I literally felt sorry for him as he was "shocked" to see us with Matt. He couldn't find his words initially and apologized as he knew "nothing" about the accident prior to entering the room. He did; however, give his assessment and plan two hundred percent, I have no doubt. He watched Bill and I walk Matt, read the note from Jenn, his PT, and discussed putting an adjustable hinge in his brace to prevent Matt from hyperextending his knee, having clonus (shaking of his left leg when fatigued) and making the heel portion out of a soft cast to provide Matt with increased sensation to his heel to encourage heel strike when he's walking. He also discussed building up his right shoe to have Matt step on his heel and asked that we bring in an another pair of shoes that fit him for him "to practice on." He could have just given us a molded plastic brace; however, is so vested in doing what Matt needs best. Another blessing given to us through the many people who have had a part in Matt's recovery.

Thursday night was Kami's graduation from grade school. They had a beautiful mass, including songs, diplomas and each child's plans for the future. The slide show afterwards was certainly a reminder of how fast the kids grow up. Kami has grown up more in the past seven months than I care to admit, as I want to keep all the kids in a bubble of protection these days. I thought about Matt's graduation ceremony for Friday night, his many dreams, and how his class will be "moving on" as I sat through the service and knew it'd be a tough night. I focused on the positives and went home to check out Amazon and medical vendors, ordering a shower chair, suction grab bar, a rolling quad cane, bedrail, and a hand exerciser. The future will turn out wonderfully.

After a busy Friday at work, frustration trying to set up an account for Matt's Social Security, getting Matt changed and to the high school, with the heat and humidity, I was physically and emotionally exhausted. Matt was so excited for graduation all day, telling the therapists, "I'm graduating." He chose bingo over PT again, much to my dismay, but I didn't say too much to him as his spirits were soaring. Matt even got the director of housekeeping's attention and told her he wanted to talk to me, proceeding to borrow her cell phone. I rejected the call as the number was unfamiliar. She came to my office to let me know "the scoop" and I called him back. Matt was very excited to see and get pictures with his friends as well as to "graduate." We don't know where Matt is at without further testing this fall, or how many credits he'll need to get his diploma, but knew it was vital he graduate with his class and then quietly complete high school requirements. Matt walked with Bill and me in the procession. It was not his best walk by far; however, better than prom even with the distractions of the crowd and clapping. Matt sat in his wheelchair for the ceremony, wanting to stand for the pledge of allegiance, and for the diplomas to be given. His classmates reassured him it was okay to sit. I was teary-eyed as the senior band members got up to play with the band and I told Bill "Matt should be playing with them" as he shook his head and said "I know," watching all the graduates walk up and down to get their diplomas, and having Matt receive his in his wheelchair with a heart-felt hug from the superintendent. The ceremony was almost completed with only a few tears, as I had sweat and make-up somewhat running down my face. The principal got up for the closing talk, beginning with "That afternoon on November first when the police called her, trying to locate parents, she knew it couldn't be good." She talked about how "the accident has influenced the graduates and the entire community. Who would have thought in November, December, and January, that Matt would be walking in tonight?" She thanked Matt for his hard work and perseverance, as well as our family for our faith and the impact we've had. Bill and I then began to hear nothing as I had tears streaming. Kami, and Laura (across the gym) were sobbing and Bill was looking down, trying his hardest not to break down too. The crowd all stood, except for our family, as they clapped and clapped. It was so overwhelming to feel all the support—as I'm teary now—for once at a loss for words to describe how God's love filled the entire gymnasium and gave us strength for our continued journey. Bill did tell her afterwards we were going to press "bullying" charges because she made us cry. Again tears mixed with laughter—what a combination.

Matt had a great time, having pizza, giving out his graduation pictures, asking his classmates to sign his year book, and even participating in the interview of "what your plans are for five years from now"—of course his answer being "basketball." I left early as I was emotionally "tapped out" and needed to breathe. Bill stayed with Matt until eleven-fifteen pm to make sure Matt was back by midnight due to insurance regulations. I believe he must have told me "how great everyone was to Matt at the grad bash" at least six to eight times yesterday. "They would sign his year book, get a picture with him, loved his pictures he gave out, and many classmates would come over to talk to him or just say "hi."

I know that Matt has shown tremendous progress every time we've had many people praying or thinking about him—such as the adorations when he was in a coma, the benefit with Matt getting his left leg strength back that night, and even the progress since his graduation mass—as he now answers questions about foreign countries with near perfection, and I can understand his speech so much more now—even on the phone. Saturday night Matt ate a burger with both hands after I helped him get a good grasp position (the first time I haven't had to physically help him bend his left elbow) and yesterday he walked from the chapel at Country Manor to his room with Bill and I (approximately two hundred fifty feet,) the best he's ever walked yet. He stood tall, kept his balance with little assist from us, and took in all the staff's comments about how good he looked and was doing. Matt has so much support from staff throughout Country Manor—not only therapy and nursing, but dietary, housekeeping, laundry staff, maintenance, activities, etc., etc. It's truly amazing and I know it's a HUGE part of Matt's determination. I worry a bit about him not having this when he comes home, but he'll continue to be surrounded by family and friends who love him and we'll be back for outpatient therapy three times per week beginning next week so he can still say hi to everyone.

Tonight Matt looked through his year book for at least an hour, holding it with both hands and not only looking at the photos, but reading every word his classmates had written to him. It was so therapeutic for him and touching to watch. He also watched *Ace Ventura: Pet Detective*, played a basketball game on his phone, and Candy Crush on his iPad simultaneously after putting his year book down. I figure it's wonderful attention to task, diverted attention, and cognitive re-training all at once. Who am I to interrupt a great therapy session when I see it? I asked Matt if he wanted me to get him ready for bed, but he wanted the PCAs to help him as they always joke and have him smiling the entire time. He'll be stuck with Bill and I soon enough.

"Faith is to believe what we do not see, and the reward of this faith is to see what we believe." When you learn to trust God, you don't have to "see anything". You just know with all certainty He's there.

NO PLACE LIKE HOME

—w—

June 7, 2014

This week was busy getting ready for Matt to come home. On Wednesday Matt had acupuncture and was much more energetic in anticipation of going home. While waiting for "the needles" to take effect, Matt and I were alone in the treatment room. Matt looks at me and says "Mom, what was your reaction to my car accident?" I was so surprised he asked this—as he has probably has been thinking about this for months. I told him I had never been so scared in my life, how difficult it was to eat anything when he couldn't eat the first three days, and how awesome he is doing based on the "diagnoses" he was given. He then asked "What was Dad's reaction?" I told him Dad was "taking it all in initially because we didn't know how he'd be, but after the MRI results we cried and cried on the phone because he was with Abby in ICU in the Cities." (I figured Bill could tell Matt more of his "reaction" himself.) Matt was quiet for a while, then lifted his head off the pillow again and said "What about the other guy?" I had told him many times in ICU everyone else was okay, it was an accident and no one's fault. This is the first time he has asked—seven months later. I told him the driver of the other vehicle was off work a few days because he was pretty sore, but was okay and felt really bad. He even brought a bouquet of flowers to ICU a few days after the accident and to check on how you were doing. That seemed to be enough information—he put his head down and fell asleep for a while. When Abby and I were walking him out (Abby had a treatment too,) Matt stopped and looked in the chiropractor's office as usual. He looked up and said: "Here comes trouble. Someday you and I are going to go one on one"—of course talking about basketball. Matt replied; "HOLD ME BACK." How amazing is that?

Thankfully, all of the adaptive equipment was delivered before Matt came home. The railings on the entrance steps and extra set on the basement stairs were a huge help and make the stairs less fearful for Matt. On Thursday, he went up and down fourteen steps twice, once yesterday (we tried going down backwards with Kami and I and it went pretty well.) I don't think it was much different for Matt, but I was less afraid of him losing his balance going forward down the steps without Bill helping. Matt's head basketball coach (who I'll refer to as Coach Poepping as Matt and Matt is really confusing) came over yesterday to see how Matt does walking, on the stairs, what meds he needs, and exercises to do with him. Matt was very motivated to do the exercises with his coach, and I know his coach will do everything to get Matt's left side stronger, improve his balance, and his walking. I had this really good feeling, it'll be therapeutic for both of them. I tried walking Matt with the rolling quad cane in the morning yesterday and it was pretty tough first thing before his meds. His coach walked him with the cane and also only being on his right side. I told him and the girls to help for at least the first week until everyone was more comfortable and when Matt gets his new AFO, this should help his walking too.

The first night Matt slept like a rock—all night until five forty-five am, snoring away. Last night was another story. Matt knocks on his headboard and "we" can hear him being on the other side of the wall. Well, really Bill would hear him, wake me and say, "Matt's calling." I got up and his legs were hanging off the end of bed—he is used to the extended bed at CM, so we positioned him diagonally on the bed. The next time he called, he wanted the blankets over him. I then told Bill he didn't need to wake me up each time. He woke up a bit after six, but wanted to get up to the bathroom. Bill and I began walking him without his left foot brace and decided to sit him back down as it wasn't going well. He had a super tough time walking, not standing up, or straightening his left knee—which I haven't seen him do in a couple of months. I think he was physically tired from all the transfers, stairs and walking—not to mention the exercises with his coach yesterday—yeah, we may have over did it a bit. We sat Matt on an office chair and wheeled him back to bed—creating memories. I told Matt we'd remember this after his first basketball game someday. He slept and took his meds, played the iPad for a bit and when he got up again, you wouldn't have known it was the same Matt from earlier walking. I decided I may give him his meds at seven am, then when he gets up at eight am, it'll be so much better for the coach and the girls.

Matt, Abby, Kami and I played cards after dinner last night and I have not seen Matt actually laugh so much in one sitting since before the accident. It was super cool. We had spaghetti for lunch, made chocolate cookies, grilled for dinner, played Wii downstairs, cards, and then I made popcorn for a movie. It was already almost nine pm when Kami said "Mom, we don't need to do everything all in one day." I thought of my boss saying "You don't have to be super women," and opted to save the movie for another night. Matt's personality is certainly still evident. Bill cleaned his glasses and when Matt put them back on, he said "Ahhhh" looking at Bill, since he could see him better. Abby put her bowl in the sink, and with a smile, Matt points and says "dishwasher" as Bill and I are forever telling the girls to put their dishes right into the dishwasher versus the sink. I asked Matt after lunch if it's more work to be home and he said, "Yeah."

Overall, it's going really good. Matt even stepped into the shower this morning, surprising us by stepping both feet in easily versus sitting. It'll all be trial and error as we determine what works easier. Matt did not get out of working on getting dressed either day, or helping with every transfer as much as he can. It's tough love, believe me, but it'll be for the best looking back a month from now.

"How's Matt?"

—〰—

June 17, 2014

It's been tougher to find the time to post over the past week, but I certainly still know people care. I've been getting more texts asking how it's going, and it seems everyone at Country Manor, in many different departments have asked how Matt is doing and to say "hi." I come home with a list of people who said to say hi, or Matt gets to see them when he comes back for outpatient OT/PT/ST on Monday, Wednesday, and Friday afternoons. It's so obvious how Matt has touched many lives and continues to stay in their heart.

I checked into our insurance regarding homecare services, however if we did, it would need to be therapy as well as PCA care for a limited time only. Matt will progress much quicker participating in outpatient therapy, having the equipment and the continued pool therapy, that I didn't even consider home therapy. I checked into the Traumatic Brain Injury and Community Alternatives& Disabled Individuals (CADI) programs; however, we need to apply for Medical Assistance to be eligible. It's all overwhelming, and for now we are fortunate to hire Matt's head basketball coach for part of day. He comes over for the mornings, later on Tuesdays and Thursdays when Matt doesn't have therapy, and both Matt and his coach seem to very much enjoy their time together. Bill came to get Matt for therapy and he was outside dribbling a basketball. How cool is that? Coach Poepping helps Matt get ready in the morning, eat breakfast and lunch, and do all his exercises. At first walking Matt was a bit "off" for both of them; however, in just a week you can see how comfortable they both are and how much Matt has improved. So much so, I think I could help him up and down the stairs without any help–that's huge in such a short time.

His coach texted me one day and said "Matt finished his chocolate milk for breakfast, slammed the cup on the table and said 'Damn that was good.'" I laughed for hours—he is certainly regaining his personality and emotions.

Wednesday was completely crazy for us. Matt had an orthotist appointment, acupuncture, OT/PT/ST, and then went back for his orthotic. Laura had her wisdom teeth all cut out in the morning and I had a dentist appointment in the afternoon. Thank goodness Grandma brought Brooke to and from softball. Our orthotist came in the treatment room and said "I have a surprise for you today." He does the orthotics for the Timberwolves and said he had extra pair of team shoes and was going to adapt and give Matt a pair. He said all the great players are like size eighteen, but he found brand new size fifteen basketball shoes and modified it for Matt with a two to three inch lift. I think Matt is almost seven feet in them. Between thinking of Matt's coach spending quality, more than "just a summer job," devoted time with him, and his new unexpected basketball shoes, I know God is still looking out for Matthew and continues to bless our entire family.

On Matt's birthday at the hospital, his head basketball coach invited him to the Wisconsin Dells for their annual tournament. True to his word, and to Matt's delight, we went to Wisconsin Dells. Matt rode with the team and shared a room with the coaches. Coach Poepping transferred him onto the bench for every game and Matt was totally engrossed, even yelling out "box out" and "Make them earn it." We went to a water park both days and even helped Matt into the pool and hot tub. He loved splashing Abby–his teammates didn't splash back, but she sure did. He went with the team out to eat, to play mini-golf, to the games, and the water parks. Everyone is so good to him and our entire family–asking if we need help often. I've notice how much easier the car transfers went on this trip–guess lots of practice has really improved his balance in addition to his new brace. Matt's coach and I transferred Matt into a lawn chair at the edge of the wave pool. It was great to see him enjoy this–after figuring out the correct placement of the chair and keeping the wheelchair from floating away. Then the staff came over and said Matt couldn't be there–the chairs had to stay in designated areas so they wouldn't get "washed away." We helped Matt stand up from the very low lawn chair (about ten inches high) without his brace on, and he literally bounced up to standing. It was a wonderful surprise, even though I was upset he had to move. Matt didn't want to go into the indoor pool, but played *Wheel of Fortune* on my Kindle instead while Brooke played. I think he enjoyed being outside, with friends, and watching people. After seven and a half months, it's amazing Matt is able to go on a vacation. It is certainly a well-deserved vacation for him, the girls and even myself, as I had a massage yesterday. Brooke continues to be jealous of the attention Matt gets, wanting to spend time with only me in the pool or hotel room, and yesterday said "I wish the accident never happened." I told her we all wished that, but it wasn't anyone's fault and Matt is getting better—we are so lucky. She understood and agreed, but still "doesn't like it," however it happens to be reality for all of us.

Matt has been in good spirits, texting, posting on Facebook and looking forward to friend's visiting. He corrects Kami's spelling when she texts him with errors. I sat up really straight when we went out to eat, to cue Matt to do the same with his posture, and he loudly said, "Who are you?" He didn't look confused, but I couldn't read his affect. I asked Matt what he meant, and he said, "Who are you, Whitney?" She is a PT Matt knew from the hospital, now working at Country Manor, who is always encouraging his posture, trunk control and positioning. It was pretty funny as he sits up taller every time he sees her.

I am anxious to see how Matt will do with testing at the high school this fall to determine his classes, the assistance he'll need, and how many more credits he'll need to graduate. It all work out in time—right now I'm ecstatic to spend more time with him and to have him finally home with us.

Tough Love

—⚏—

Jun 24, 2014

I had seen such an improvement in Matt's transfers and walking over the first week he was home. At the end of last week; however, Matt wasn't putting forth his typical effort. I initially thought it was due to being tired from Wisconsin Dells; however, when he wasn't even straightening his left knee on Saturday, I knew it was much more and he was a bit down. Bill and I had a heart to heart with him and told him we would always be here for him, but couldn't do it for him. "We would if we could, but we needed him to meet us half ways for him to continue to get better." Bill asked him if "he wanted to be like he is now—is this as far as you want to get?" Matt shook his head "no." He stood from the shower chair and managed his clothing in like two seconds (without me asking him) for the first time ever. He walked very good out of the bathroom as compared to walking in, and has been putting more effort forth since.

Laura showed me what Matt had posted on Facebook Sunday night. He wrote something like this: "Don't take anything for granted, not even for a second. I woke up this morning, got dressed, and walked to the kitchen with my right hand on my Dad's shoulder to have breakfast. All for a chocolate chip waffle. You may ask if it's worth it and I say 'don't take anything for granted.'" Oh my goodness, with teary-eyes I realized once again how "in there" he is. He had another post about how some days he feels like giving up, but then remembers how far he's come—and that he needs to prove some ____ wrong. I couldn't believe it. I know that I've told him many times he's doing things doctors didn't think he ever would. If that's what motivated him, I'll take it.

Matt tried playing Call of Duty on Xbox last week and I think it's the most frustrated I've seen him since the accident. It was heart-breaking to watch as he tried to use both hands, to help his left thumb with his right hand, and finally to swear and say, "It's so hard. I hate this game." (that would be the edited version.) Of course I tried to encourage him and say it'll get easier every time he tries to play, it's okay to get mad—it's normal and I'm surprised he hasn't been angry more often. Bill helped him with the navigating of the game and they won two matches before Matt became frustrated again. I did tell Matt he needed to not swear in front of Brooke. Bill said it was enough for the night and Matt replied, "I'll be good." I felt so bad for him. It wasn't about being good, but about not having him so frustrated. Last night, he played again for a while without a "live" match, so it wasn't as competitive so he wasn't as upset. It'll just take time. I remember all the times I tried to get him to stop playing to come eat or do a chore—it's so ironic now I wish he could play like he did. Like Matt said, "Don't take anything for granted."

Bill and I are getting into a new routine and adjusting to having one of us or his coach help him with all his self-cares. It's odd to be sure to have one of us to get Matt ready at night for bed as the girls don't walk him alone and never help him go to the bathroom. Matt wakes up at three-thirty am like it's an internal clock. Often he asks for his phone, which is denied, as he needs to get rest too and will never nap during the day. Sometimes he needs to go to the bathroom, be-repositioned in bed, or last night merely pointed to his uncovered feet. I have returned to the memories of getting up with the kids when they were babies, thankful they were able to wake up versus having SIDS during the night. Every time Matt "knocks"on his head board for us and I get up, I am so thankful he survived the accident and he's finally home with us. I think I may gratefully develop an internal three-thirty am clock too.

Matt is checking his texts and Facebook all day long not only wanting, but needing the socialization. He was getting ready for bed this weekend and I saw a text conversation he had with the assistant basketball coach of Augsburg College—where Matt wanted to attend college and play basketball. I was surprised Matt was texting him and overwhelmed with his kindness of saying they were following his CaringBridge and continued to pray for him. Today he called me after Matt had texted him, telling him he wanted to talk. He said they had an encouraging conversation and Matt had given him my cell number with

"with a little help from his coach to understand the number." He called to let me know if they could do anything, to please let him know. I fought back tears for at least two hours. How incredible to have him take the time for Matt after seven and a half months to still see if we needed anything. I told him the encouragement he is giving Matt is what he needs more than anything. It would motivate him more than listening to me all the time. Having Coach Poepping work with him every day while we are at work is also a huge gift in motivating him. I told him I couldn't thank him enough as I thought to myself how thankful I was for the wonderful people God has put in our life during this journey.

I took Matt to Walmart after work yesterday. Bill was working late and Matt had been at outpatient therapy. I tried to figure out how to push and pull his wheelchair as well as the shopping cart on the drive over. Matt told me he hadn't had lunch because he had a late breakfast and nodded when I asked if he was hungry. We went to Subway at Walmart and I set him up at a table with his favorite meatball sub (only I was smart and had the worker cut up the meatballs and the sandwich into fourths–wow, it only took me five months to think of this.) By the time I finished shopping, Matt had eaten an entire twelve inch sub and a half a bag of chips. I parked the cart and took him to pick out a Batman Xbox game and candy he wanted. Now how to get Matt and the cart to the vehicle? There was nothing to it. I pushed him with one hand and the cart with the other, helped Matt into the Acadia and then unloaded the cart. It felt like a small victory as I disassembled his wheelchair, knowing the two of us could go pretty much anywhere without a lot of effort. On the way home I think Matt felt it too as he sang along with the 80's music from Kool 108. It was wonderful.

My greatest worry or concern is getting Matt's left arm and hand functional again and having him try to use it despite the frustrating effort it takes. I'm forever putting his arm on the table, putting items in his hand to hold–such as a bag of chips or his iPad with both hands. He only spontaneously seems to incorporate his left hand when playing cards without any coaxing. His shoulder is getting stronger–he was able to hold it over his head in sitting after I helped him get to this position for the first time yesterday versus only when lying down. He opened a tootsie roll, pinching the end with his left hand the other day without me telling him "to use both hands." I've thought of that tootsie roll, and although it was a tiny bite sized candy, it renewed my faith he will continue to get better with time and lots of love and encouragement. Matt's balance continues to improve. I'm able to walk him with the rolling quad cane myself (without a lot of assist and less cues for where to position the cane) even barefooted tonight. This is encouraging for me, especially without his brace, shoes, and at the end of the day when he is super tired. It will only continue to improve. I am hopeful he'll be walking on his own by fall and can return to school, even if for a shorter day initially.

I went to three stores on Saturday and at each I was asked how Matt is doing. Our caring community, family and friends are so overwhelmingly wonderful—- and the reason we have the strength we have to balance work, the girls, appointments and Matt's needs.

Church

—m—

July 5, 2014

I have noticed Matt's progress the most in church over the past few weeks. During his graduation mass mid-May, Bill's cousin and I helped lift Matt to standing and both of us held him to keep his balance. He needed to sit during one part of the mass because his legs were getting tired. Three weeks ago, we brought him to church in the wheelchair and he sidestepped into the pew. I held onto his transfer belt every time he stood, and he leaned over, holding onto the pew in front of him. After communion, Brooke was standing next to us and she proudly held onto the belt too—it was so sweet as she wouldn't be able to help him if he lost his balance. Matt realized she was holding onto the belt, let go of the pew with his right hand and began tickling her of all things. Both had smiles and Brooke never let go of him.

Two weeks ago, Matt WALKED into church from the truck and went up all the steps with Bill and I (at least twelve to fourteen I'd guess, plus a platform.) He stood holding onto the pew for part of the mass, then leaned his right thigh against the pew for balance. Matt is now able to stand the entire time everyone else does, but doesn't kneel yet. It's tough to get his feet so far under the seat with his left leg brace, and his long legs at six foot-eight inches. Makes me wonder how he did this before the accident. Last weekend Bill was at his brother's cabin, so it was only Laura, Brooke, Matt and me that went to church on Sunday. I offered for Matt to take the wheelchair in, but he wanted to walk in. Laura and I walked him, went up the steps and Matt sidestepped into the pew as the first song was playing. We stayed standing with everyone else, and although I asked Matt if he needed to sit for a bit after getting into the pew, he shook his head no and stood for several minutes for the introduction of mass. I no longer need to block his left knee when he's standing, or hold onto the belt. Matt leans against the pew with his right leg and lets go with his hand and stands super tall–I am so proud of how far he's come. Matt did scare me two times during the mass however last Sunday, as he reached for the guy standing in front of me on the left, turning toward his weaker side to shake hands with him for the sign of peace and lost his balance. He regained it and then shook hands with him–not giving up on his mission. At the end of mass, I totally thought he lost his balance again as the priest walked out of church, but instead realized Matt was GENUFLECTING. Oh my goodness–how cool is that?

Matt continues to improve with his thinking and to show more emotions. Laura has been calling Matt "Bud" ever since the accident (Bill's nickname for him.) She came upstairs a couple days ago and said "Hi Bud. How's it going?" Matt became upset, hitting his leg and said "That's not my name. Don't call me that." much to Laura's surprise. I told her it's good that he's gotten so much better he now doesn't want to be called "Bud" by her–it's Dad's name for him. Although Laura was somewhat taken back with Matt being upset, she understood.

Matt was watching "*The Lego Movie*" and as the credits came on after the movie, he said "Pause." He wanted to see who played the voices of the characters as each screen came up. He also noticed it was "Gary Cooper" that was starring in an old western movie on TV. I had no idea, but it's bonding time like before with Bill and him. The speech therapist was not in one Friday because her son was sick. Matt was eating dinner the next night and he asked me "Why wasn't Melissa at Country Manor yesterday?" I told Matt her son was sick and he nodded. When Matt went to speech therapy on Monday, he asked Melissa how her son was–she said "it was so sweet." I thought it was awesome he had remembered, and Melissa said, "That didn't surprise me, but it was sweet that he cared to ask right away." That's my Matt.

We've taken Matt to a couple graduation parties this year so far. Matt was eating dinner after being at his friend's graduation party and my heart sunk as he said "I was thinking about my graduation party." I told Matt he should finish high school first, right? He nodded and said "I was thinking we could have my party on my birthday (December thirty-first.)

I thought this was an excellent idea to have a "double party" and gives Matt a goal to finish all the classes he needs to graduate by Christmas break. I thought this was really good planning and insight on Matt's part and it is wonderful to have him looking forward to future events.

Someone asked us how Matt was doing last evening and Bill replied, "He's always getting better, but sometimes it's a bigger progression that's more noticeable." I was so glad to hear his response, as sometimes I think I'm the one who really notices all the "baby steps." Last weekend I walked Matt by myself standing behind him, without Matt holding onto anything. He usually holds onto the rolling cane or one of the girls when I walk him. I was so excited it took me hours to fall asleep that night. Matt was able to get both feet into the truck for me for the first time last weekend–lifting his left leg with his right hand–but having the trunk strength to keep his balance and lifting his leg mostly on his own.

We took Matt golfing with us last night. I was sure he would love the independence to drive the golf cart, but I was SO nervous and did have second thoughts as he had difficulty steering for corners and hit the gas at the same time. Kami rode with him and I had her hold onto him so he wouldn't lean out of the cart. Matt continued to get better with practice; however, Bill then rode with him–just like his driving lessons, and helped with the shorter turns, much to my relief. Matt watched every stroke and kept score for us. We had burgers and fries afterwards and it was a great family outing. We came home and had a bonfire with smores—what a wonderful Fourth of July. It was our first holiday at home together since last November, so that in itself was a gift.

We are invited to Bill's brother's house for the annual Fourth of July get-together. Matt looks forward to going places and it's good for him to get out with people. He had friends visit one night this week and I know it was the highlight of the week for him. He's looking forward to playing cards and just being outside by the lake. His coach asked if he could come get him and take him to the varsity basketball scrimmages on Tuesday night. Of course, I said yes and we could bring him. He said, "I'll come pick him up and take him." His coach has been the greatest blessing to us since Matt has come home. He even went to physical therapy to have training in walking Matt with the cane and to learn activities to strengthen his trunk. It's more than "just a job" for both of them. We are so fortunate.

I continue to tell Matt how lucky we are that his thinking is so good. The physical abilities will come in time, "I have faith in you." Matt nods as Brooke says, "Do you have faith in me?" She is forever trying to put food in his mouth, cover him up, etc., but Matt seems more tolerable with her lately and she's in better spirits as a result.

New Wheels and Shoes

—〰—

July 19, 2014

Co-workers and friends ask, "How's it going?" and my answer over the past week has been "It's slow–but we'll get there." As if knowing I needed something, over the past few days, I've noticed more strength in Matt's left arm. He was able to reach and grab keys on the counter, last night in his recliner, he reached for "knucks" (bringing his arm up and out—versus just elbow extension, the highest I've seen him lift his arm with shoulder movement yet) and he opened all the automatic doors at Country Manor after therapy with his left hand. This was the sign I've been waiting and praying for. This morning when Matt knocked at five am for a glass of water, he yawned and his left elbow straightened versus bending up to his chest–for the first time. I barely touched the top of his hand and he opened all his fingers too. Typically this only happens when I begin to open his fingers from his palm. My thoughts were that we are moving out of the "Waiting Place." I am so thankful.

Matt finally got his new wheelchair on Monday— it's red for the Pioneers. It's wonderful as far as the height, longer cushion, back support and larger footplates. His left leg doesn't go out to the side anymore and he's not sliding as much. I was so excited to get a good wheelchair for him. At the same time, I was sad this is a permanently approved wheelchair for him. I needed to keep reminding myself he'll only be using it temporarily and we haven't even brought a wheelchair into the house yet.

Matt went to the orthotist yesterday and had his shoes adjusted so he doesn't lean so far forward. His Coach Poepping helped me walk him four times before and after adjustments so the orthotist could assess Matt. The three of us discussed his balance, with how much help Matt needed, as John (the orthotist) looked at how much his knee over extends, how he catches his toes, etc. Matt is now officially back in his Timberwolves shoes. It is getting easier to walk Matt—I'm no longer afraid he'll lose his balance with me. I can walk him without him holding onto anything with his right hand now, and with very little help using the rolling quad cane. The toughest correction is to get Matt to bring his left shoulder forward and to lift his legs up with hip flexion. I'm hoping the changes in his shoes will help his balance and also to avoid using compensatory patterns such as leaning backwards to advance his left leg. Matt is doing so much better barefooted at night or the early morning without snapping his left knee back, and I pretty much helped him DOWN the church steps myself last Sunday using the railing as Bill held onto the transfer belt too.

Getting ready for school this fall has so many unknowns. I texted the principle and asked how many credits Matt needed yet, if he would have physical help during the day, about registering him in classes, not knowing if he'd be there a half or full day, etc. I found out Matt has forty-eight of fifty-nine credits toward graduation and the quarter he finished the day of the accident doesn't count as far as credits (but I'd think if he finishes some of these classes for an additional quarter, he'd get the semester credits.) Anyway, we will have a meeting and get a plan soon. I told Matt he needed to work on reading again and to pick a book he wants to read, or even one he already has read.

Well, two classmates visited last week and were talking about the book, "Divergent" and when the movie would be out. Matt then changed his mind from wanting to re-read a Harry Potter book, to reading Divergent. HE'S READING A BOOK. I'm so excited about this. He read twenty-five pages the first day and less a couple times after, but wrote a good summary statement about the book in speech this week. Matt definitely is my hero.

We've gotten into a new routine since Matt has been home. His coach comes over every morning Monday through Friday at seven thirty am so we can be to work by eight am. He does exercises with Matt, has him work on getting himself dressed, walks him into the kitchen, gives him breakfast and lunch. We are lucky this has worked out for the summer. Coach Poepping or Laura brings him to Country Manor for acupuncture and therapy. (Acupuncture two times per week and therapy three times per week,) and then

Bill or I bring him home after he's finished at the end of our work day. Matt is so patient when I need to finish up things at work. He'll quietly wait and play his iPad or go on his phone, or when the batteries were completely dead this week, silently wait without complaining a single word. Matt has always had more patience than the girls, which is another blessing in his recovery for sure.

Matt wakes up one to three times a night, and sometimes not at all. One night he woke me up at two am to show me he had taken his left hand splint off which was lying next to him. I told him he could just throw it on the floor and didn't need to wake me, and the next morning it was on the floor. He woke us one night to ask for a smore shake from the DQ. After trying to understand him for about twenty minutes, I finally asked him if he was uncomfortable, needed to go to the bathroom, etc. and if it was something that could wait until tomorrow, which he agreed to. When I asked him in the morning again what he had wanted, to find out it was a smore shake, we had a discussion about what "warrants" waking us up. Matt had a huge smirk/smile and completely understood. He hasn't woken us up regarding food any more, but does if he wants a glass of water–which is perfectly fine.

Thinking about updating my journal, I knew I needed to comment about Matt's speech. It's much easier for me to understand him, not only when I'm with him, but esp. on the phone. Last night he said "Mom?" and it was a normal voice tone, not deep and dragged out. This is the very first time I've heard it since he began to talk again. He wanted to know about the graduation parties today and also the Freedom Feast concert tonight. It's so cool to have him looking forward to things.

The youth group leader sent me a text about a book she was reading. It was about a mother who's son had been in a car accident with injuries similar to Matthew's. The mother said even though her son couldn't walk, eat, or talk, she was so thankful for his existence. When I'm feeling down, or that things are slow, I think of this often and do a complete hundred and eighty degree turnaround and I'm SO thankful for having more than Matt's mere existence. He is aware of everything, keeping up on the latest movies that are coming out, still wanting to go to Augsberg college, etc. We cannot say "We've been lucky" as his gains are beyond "luck," rather divine intervention. Matt has exceeded all expectations already and every gain he continues to achieve is yet another gift from God.

Really Matt? Spanish?

—〰—

Aug 5, 2014

Laura has been in the cities for 2 weeks (our driver), Brooke and Kami finished summer sports, Abby has been busy with tennis, the Steubenville weekend retreat and appointments, and Matt had his usual routine, plus several graduation parties. In addition to both of our jobs being super busy (I've been seeing more shoulder outpatients—but find I love my caseload and the normalcy as I've been mostly doing management since coming back to work in January,) the garden, etc. I haven't had much time to journal and don't want to bore my readers as Matt's progress had been slower until the end of last week.

Bill and I were very concerned as Matt began dragging both feet when he walked (even his right foot), not straightening his knees, leaning to the left and seeming to be in a lull. I know after nine months he's tired of working hard at everything and I can't blame him. I scheduled an appointment with his doctor to discuss an anti-depressant to give him a little boost. They had a "depression screen" for him to complete and he denied any and all feelings of any negativity—hence, we left with a recommendation for Vitamin D and an MD signature for a handicapped parking spot. I finally caved and decided it's not the distance to the store, but having the room to open the door and transfer Matt that is tough in a regular spot and when Laura brings him to school this fall she will have parking spot that will make it easier for them. The doctor checked six years for the time frame of the parking permit—I believe we will not need it two years, so we have another goal.

When I told Jenn (Matt's PT) about him dragging his feet at home, she immediately said "It's behavioral." I told Matt this and he improved quite a bit with his walking afterwards. I go into the pool with Jenn and Matt for PT on Wednesdays, and asked Matt to tell Jenn what I had told her about his dragging his feet. With a HUGE smirk, Matt says, "I don't remember." Jenn burst out laughing and said, "Even I'm not buying that." Matt then said, "It's me" and I asked him to explain what I told him and he said, "It's mental." I corrected him by saying it was behavioral, but we all had a good laugh and Matt has been doing one hundred percent better since. How smart to pretend he didn't remember on purpose to avoid answering the question–deep down I was ecstatic. Matt walked on the treadmill in the pool (the floor is a treadmill) for over thirteen minutes, without resting and very little assist, watching the camera with Jenn for heel strike versus toe walking, and even walked backwards on the treadmill last week for the first time. I find I'm not coordinated myself to do this, so turn and walk forwards–which doesn't surprise either of them. Matt walked in the pool a few steps to retrieve floating basketballs to shoot into a basket without holding onto the bar, edge of pool, me, or Jenn. He missed the long shot, getting mad and fisting his right hand into the water—scarying the daylights out of both of us. I tell Matt it's ok to get frustrated. I'm glad he's showing this "normal" emotion (not to swear though) but he needs to keep giving it his all. Jenn then said "I tell him it's good because it means he's not satisfied with how thing are and gives him a reason to get better." I thought about this many times since and I really like her rational even more than mine—making it such a POSITIVE reaction to being frustrated. Yesterday Matt walked with Brian in PT without any assistive device, bent down in standing to touch his shoe, sidestepped and walked forward and backwards to open cupboards. To Brian's surprise, Matt held onto the TOP of the cabinet to sidestep—as I heard him say, "Well, that's not what I had in mind, but it works." I don't think we ever had a patient use the top of the cupboard for support. Abby told me she walked Matt alone today, walking in front of him while he used the rolling quad cane, then with his hand on her shoulder "like Dad does" and he walked "really good." I've been able to walk Matt without any support too, holding onto him from behind, and trust me, he walks without dragging his feet and gives it his all—not wanting to fall. I've seen a lot of progress over the past week with his walking and it is very encouraging.

In church a week ago, Father Popp had a homily about when someone has a "near-death" experience, or survives cancer, they realize fame and fortune don't matter as much as family and friends. He continued on as he described our life over the past nine months, not the fame and fortune part, but the family and friends part having a priceless value. I saw Matt lean over and whisper to Bill, then he poked me and leaned over, saying "I love you." As I became teary-eyed, like now thinking about it, I don't think I could have loved him anymore. It wasn't a reply to me saying "I love you" first, and I know in a way it was his way of saying "thank you" for being there for him since his "near death" experience.

Okay—now the story behind the title. When Laura, Abby and Kami were all gone last weekend, Bill, Matt, Brooke and I decided to go out for dinner after therapy in St. Cloud Friday evening. We asked Matt to pick where he wanted to eat—we had a gift card for Red Lobster or Olive Garden, or we could go to Jimmy's Pourhouse. Matt was having a tough time deciding and then said something we totally could not understand. Of course, I have him swallow, clear his throat and try again, and again to no avail. I gave him paper to write where he wanted to go to eat. He quickly writes in Spanish—accents for pronunciation and everything—and underneath it writes, "Why not both?" Really Matt? He knew he was clever with a huge smile as Bill and I know absolutely no Spanish—it was super cool and a glimmer not only of Matt's personality ten-fold, but assurance that his future will be amazing. It changes hope to faith for me—again, and I am so thankful. Over the past week, I've still been told by several people how they continue to pray for Matt every day and how surprised I'd be if I knew how many people did. I tell my patients and even strangers about the accident and how Matt and Abby are a testimony to the power of prayer—it's so emotionally overwhelming to us in a wonderful way—thank you.

As several people have asked lately, "How's your daughter doing?," I realized I haven't written about her for a long time. She is still receiving acupuncture treatments once a week, going to the chiropractor and re-started physical therapy last week. Abby's pelvis/hip goes out of place, causing her leg length to be different, along with pain more and more often. She gets adjusted, however due to tight muscles, her pelvis/hip goes out again. It's been long enough now, I knew she needed to get adjusted and then have PT to strengthen the muscles to keep her alignment. Needless to say, she is going to Country Manor too and very much looking forward to her first pool session with Jenn. Little does she know what a work-out it's going to be on the treadmill with jets for resistance. I think I'll have to sneak a peek. Overall, Abby's personality is slowly returning. She's so much more caring than right after the accident and literally dotes on Matt, which is so sweet. I often wonder if she feels guilty the accident happened after he picked her up from dance practice, but they have always been close and I don't ask as I don't want her to think she should feel that way. I am very thankful she is physically and emotionally continuing to get better. She is quilting with Grandma and laughs non-stop with her. When Abby sets her mind to something, it's in your best interest to just stay out of her way. No matter if it's school, a sport, or another activity, be assured Abby is very strong-willed and will give it her all. She recently got her driver's permit, somewhat to my dismay as I worry and won't let her drive with me yet and asks to drive nearly every night. She is literally counting her driving hours—daytime, nighttime, city, country, etc. as Abby doesn't do anything less than one hundred and ten percent of what's required.

As always, I continue to thank God for his blessings through your prayers as Matt and Abby continue to heal. Remember to appreciate your family and friends as well as to say "I love you" to someone you may take for granted—you'll never regret it.

Fishing

—ww—

August 18, 2014

We went on a family vacation to Kavanaugh's Resort the beginning of August. It was SO wonderful to have time together as a family and the weather was wonderful! We were fortunate to have our friend's offer their pontoon for the entire five days—dropping it off and coming to get it on the day of check out, despite their busy lives and the travel time involved. I had mentioned I wasn't sure how we'd get Matt into my Dad's boat, or planned to rent a pontoon for a day or two, (not knowing they even owned a pontoon) and they insisted they would bring it for is to use—"end of story." We would bring Matt to the dock area in his wheelchair and he'd walk down the steps, through the sand, dock, and onto the pontoon with Bill. It's difficult to put my feelings into words to actually have him with us on a vacation, much less on the water and fishing. Matt sat in a chair on the pontoon the first day. I'd bait and cast for him, place the pole in his left hand and hold it as he'd reel in a sunfish. He did get the most and biggest fish; however, when reeling them in, his tone would "kick in" (meaning he would extend his left leg and bend his left elbow some) leaning to the left. We held him on the chair as he became tired, then Matt loudly said, "I'm Crippled!" I told him, "Oh no you're not!" I told him the fact he was on vacation, on the lake, and getting better was incredibly wonderful and every time he went fishing from now on, it would only get easier. The therapist in me needed to brainstorm. . . .hmmm. . . .as I placed his transfer belt around his chest and around back of his chair to keep him centered at midline, not having to use so much his trunk strength to maintain his balance. I told Bill, "Tomorrow, we need to put the wheelchair on

321

the pontoon," which we did and Matt was even able to reel in some fish himself, without so much frustration.

Matt played video games with my nephews (getting the highest score on a baseball game,) went into the indoor pool, threw water balls at everyone with a smile, went into the hot tub, sat at the picnic table to eat, played cards, and enjoyed a campfire. When we made the reservations, I thought four full days would be enough, if not too much for him, but I think he would have continued to enjoy the vacation for weeks. I didn't feel guilty missing therapy while we were gone as I know he did got a lot of therapy every day. On the way back from the pontoon one day, not only did Matt walk step over step (versus putting each foot on the same step) he SKIPPED a step with a huge smile. My sister was watching and had tears running down her face instantly—what an amazing moment to remember.

One morning Bill took our vehicle to get the oil changed and Brooke crawled into my bed. Matt had the other bed in the room and was still in bed. Brooke sneezed and Matt immediately said, "Shhh." Of course, I laughed as I thought he was sleeping. Brooke sneezed again, and again, and again with Matt "Shhing" her louder each time—for a total of seven sneezes. I laughed about it all day—it was priceless. Brooke would randomly put food in Matt's mouth when she wanted him to try something, if she didn't want something, or merely because she could. She put a marshmallow in his mouth and I told her to ask him first if he wanted it. She shrugged, throwing up her hands and said, "I always feed him." I came home one day last week and Brooke showed me a picture of a caterpillar she had drawn with segments and had Matt color two of them. Matt doesn't seem to get upset with her anymore which makes her much happier.

Bill took Matt to a movie one night last week after work and therapy. He said after they pulled up at the theater Matt said, "Dad?" and he said, "Yeah Matt?" to which Matt replied, "I love you." Bill said, it breaks his heart every time. I said "but it's a good thing and should melt your heart." Bill said "But he should be starting college." He will start college, just at a later date. Bill agreed, but at times I guess we feel so bad for him, despite his wonderful progress, that he has to go through this.

I'm still waiting for Matt to have testing to determine what classes he'll be in when school starts, how many hours a day, to schedule his therapies, care after school, etc. I haven't been sleeping well as Coach Poepping goes back to work when school starts again too and we don't have a "back-up plan" yet. I need to trust it will all work out. I asked Jenn in PT to work with the girls on getting Matt in and out of the van, going up and down steps, and walking today in preparation for school. She said Laura and Abby did amazing. Both of them did a van transfer and helped him on the stairs by themselves. One more wonderful accomplishment for Matt, Laura and Abby and less stress for me. Laura actually brought him home and got him out of the van, up the steps and into the house herself afterwards. I asked Matt if he can tell he's making progress and he replied, "No." I then remind him of things he can now do that he couldn't a few weeks ago. He nods his head in agreement, but I know he's looking at the entire task of walking, dressing, going to the bathroom, etc., so "baby steps" aren't as rewarding for him as they are for everyone else around him. I continue to have friends, neighbors, family members comment on "how much better Matt looks." It's so encouraging to have others notice this too–that it's not just me in my "bubble" noticing the little accomplishments. At church yesterday, a neighbor who was ushering came up to us and told Matt "I pray for you every morning and night." Needless to say I'm teary-eyed just typing this. I believe my sister-in-law was right when she told me I had no idea how many people still pray for Matt every day. I also have to say I was so touched to see that Mark, the Chaplain from the St Cloud Hospital, had signed the guestbook in Spanish after my last journal entry. I didn't know until Laura interpreted for me, but my smile lasted for days–knowing he still remembers and prays for Matt, following his progress. He did tell Matt and I several times that "Matt couldn't get out of his prayers even if he wanted to." What an amazing guy.

Matt continues to show his personality, only talking when it's something funny, or really important. I was pouring coffee into my mug and thermos on Saturday morning as Matt was eating breakfast. I didn't spill on the counter for the first time in months and commented about this to Matt who replied "Praise the Lord and his Miracles." He calls to Brooke if he needs the remote or the Wii turned on, Kami to take off his brace and shoes, and Abby typically if he wants something to drink or eat. He continues to dream about ice cream, I'm so sure of it. I went into his room one day last week and Matt asked for a Chips Ahoy blizzard from the DQ, with a huge smile when I said "How can you wake up wanting ice cream every day?" He has a vanilla shake every night before bed, so it's not like we are withholding ice cream from him—it's just funny to me.

I do believe Abby received prayers after my last post. She is seldom complaining of jaw, pelvis and neck pain. She is enjoying pool therapy and says her pelvis is staying in alignment so much better. She's busy with tennis (non-stop on vacation too) and goes for a run every night. I dropped her off at church for choir practice this week, and as she got out of the vehicle, she said, "Love you Mom." I haven't heard a spontaneous "love you" from Abby since before the accident. I was relieved to know she's getting back to being how my Abby always was personality-wise. What a gift. She's super attentive to Matt and Brooke and continues to be more and more caring as time goes on. She complains of being tired a lot, but even this seems to be improving over the past two weeks.

"As soon as we start wanting anything so much we try to take matters into our own hands to get it, we are asking for trouble. Be patient and wait on the Lord to work out things according to His perfect will and timing. Nothing is going to work out right unless it comes from God and is carried out in the Spirit in accordance with His divine plan and purpose."

School and Knocking Wars

—∿∿—

September 1, 2014

The past week has probably been the busiest and the most emotional of the summer for me. We had open houses, (including Kami's orientation to high school with Abby volunteering three days to assist with this), orthodontist appointments, therapy, acupuncture, Laura's work schedule, Matt's Botox appointments, Bill and I taking turns staying at work late to catch up, and going to the high school Wednesday, Thursday and Friday to get Matt and the staff ready for his return tomorrow. Needless to say, the three day weekend was wonderful and appreciated to take a break as we celebrated my parents fiftieth Wedding Anniversary.

I met with the school OT/PT/ST, director of special education, Coach Dahmen (general education teacher), school psychologist, nurse, the TBI (Traumatic Brain Injury) specialist from Mid-State, our principal and assistant principle. It was a good meeting, discussing our plan for Matt, physical adaptations needed, support staff, testing that would be completed over the first month, medication administration and requirements, and Matt's current level of functioning. We set up training for the next day to bring Matt to school to train the paraprofessionals who will assist Matt to the bathroom and to look at the desk and classroom set up.

When I arrived Thursday morning with Coach Poepping (along to assist with the training and letting staff know what he sees or works well for Matt after spending the past three months with him) the doors were being held open for us before we even got to the sidewalk. It was such a welcoming gesture and in no way did I feel like having Matt back at school was "putting anyone out," but rather the complete opposite of being excited for his return and looking at every possible way for this to be a positive, successful venture for Matt. The first emotional moment was to see one of the paraprofessionals arrive in Matt's t-shirt and finding out he had no idea the training was even happening that morning–how cool is that?

We looked at three different bathrooms to find grab bars on the right side, looked at desks and tables, (how did he ever fit in a desk at six feet, eight inches, before the accident is a mystery to me) and the lunchroom set up. At one point in our journey around the school, Mrs. Boser, (Carrie) our principle, even pushed Matt to the next destination and I was completely touched. We found an adjustable table to use at lunch and three other tables that Mr. Otte, (Tom) the assistant principle was going to have built up higher with blocks for Matt. Coach Poepping worked on training the paraprofessionals on toilet transfers and also transfers into our van at Mr. Otte's suggestion in case Laura needed help transferring him after school. I never had thought of this as being an option, but as it turns out, with Matt needing to get to St. Cloud Mondays, Wednesdays, and Fridays for outpatient therapy, Grandma can bring him if she can have help to transfer him into her vehicle. Mr. Otte said to tell Laura to find one of the guys or himself to help transfer Matt whenever she needed. He even went with and observed the transfers into the van–I was so amazed he would offer to help himself if needed.

He asked Matt who he wanted to eat lunch with as Carrie and Tom want this to be a social time with normalcy for him. Matt quickly identified four senior friends he played basketball with. Tom called each of them the next day to give them the "heads up" and to ask if they would be willing to leave class a minute early (or go to the head of the line), help Matt through the line, set up the table, and eat with him so he'd have more time. All the boys were very receptive to this and I know Matt's excited for school to be with his friends again more than anything. This extra step and concern by Carrie and Tom, to ensure Matt's social interaction, was above and beyond what they needed to do. How wonderful for Matt and reassuring for me to know he won't be left out at this important time of the day for him to be with friends.

I met with the academic advisor and Carrie to figure out Matt's class schedule. They decided Matt could have half credits for the first quarter of school he finished last year, the day of the accident, so he only needs seven credits to graduate; however, can have more. We decided Matt would have school until one forty-five pm each day so he could get to CM for therapy by two thirty pm. The other days he will have time for homework with his paraprofessional, to be in the library, have speech with the school therapist twp times per week, or can leave early. There is a "Performance Improvement" class for working out in the gym and Matt will be able to exercise and complete stretches, etc. with the paraprofessional who'll be working with him for the first hour every day. I think this will be awesome because honestly, having Matt complete a home exercise program would be very difficult to fit into the evenings—with dinner, dance, piano, tennis matches, youth group, homework, baths, and so on–every family knows how this time of day is, never long enough to get everything needed done. Matt had the choice of World Literature or College Comp II—both of which he was taking last fall, and either psychology or band. Matt picked World Literature without hesitation, and then Psychology. I told Matt that taking Psychology would mean more reading and homework and that he could play drums, bells with his right hand, etc., and told him how I cried the first time I went to a concert last December when he wasn't on stage. He agreed to "think about it" overnight. I asked him in the morning and he told me he'd take band. Yay! Yahoo! Can you tell how excited I am?

I came home from bringing Abby to a tennis fundraiser Thursday night and Brooke came running out of the house saying she had to tell me her idea. "I gave Matt my froggy piggy bank and I told him that if he walks good for three days, I'll give him a nickel. If he walks good for five days, I'll give him a dime. If he walks good for a week, I'll give him a quarter so he can get a gum ball at the video store." When I went into the house, sure enough, Matt had a froggy piggy bank (about two inches by two inches) next to him on the counter with some coins already in it for incentive. Brooke says, "Matt you're going to walk like a champion now, right?" Matt nods yes. "You're going to get a quarter, right?" Matt nods yes. "You're going to get a gum ball, right?" Matt nods yes. Brooke then attempts to shove the last bite of her cookie into Matt's mouth; however, he wasn't having it. It was so sweet to see her try to motivate Matt and to care about his walking too.

Let me explain the "knocking war." Every morning Matt will knock on his headboard if he wants something. He has learned that we say "Just a minute Matt" and fall back asleep, sometimes two or three times. This week he decided to knock, and knock, and knock, and knock until we literally are in his room, I'm sure to avoid the wait. One morning I went into his room, turned on the light, and asked him what he wanted. After knocking for a full minute straight prior, he kept his eyes closed and didn't respond. I decided to knock above on his headboard "back at him" asking him what he wanted as a smile slowly grew bigger. He opened his eyes and said "your breathe smells." In my defense, it was first thing in the morning but I laughed and laughed as he ended up with the upper hand despite my idea to have him understand how irritating non-stop knocking is first thing in the morning

Matt's humor continues, much to my delight. I asked Brooke to get some hamburger out of the freezer one day and she came up with a roast. I told her the hamburger was in the same white paper, but had hamburger written on it. She asked what hamburger started with and I told her an "H." She left the room as Matt replies "and it ends with an amburger." Laura brought Matt to an acupuncture appointment and jokingly told Matt and Josh that she was Matt's favorite sister. Matt shook his head no. Laura asked him who was his favorite sister and he replied "Abby, she's the quietest." Laura then said "but I'm second, right?" Matt then put all his sisters in order with her being last with a big smile at how clever he was as Josh and Bill laughed and laughed (per Laura's report.) He so enjoys making people laugh.

At my brother's house this weekend, they have decorative words on the wall that I've thought about several times. "Worry ends where faith begins." How true this is. Remember to put your faith in God and all your worries will be taken care of. I need to remind myself of this often as I worry about the new changes in our routine, Matt's arm, etc., etc. When I slow down, I realize without any doubt, everything will work out with the amazing people in our lives. Take time to count your blessings too, so much of our day—work, friends, family, etc., we take for granted.

Scrabble in Church

—m—

September 14, 2014

A lot has happened in the past two weeks as we settled into a new routine and adjusted to several "surprises" along the way. Matt has truly loved being back with friends again, has been talking more and in good spirits at home too. The first day of school was the toughest for me. I brought him to school—ecstatic, nervous and honestly very sad he has to return in his wheelchair—versus walking as I had hoped by this fall. I brought him to physical education with his paraprofessional, and Matt was wheeled into the line of students. I went over the exercises (arms and legs) that she will do with Matt during Phy-ed. I brought his medicine, school supplies, Gatorade and a couple snacks. It brought me such relief and gratefulness to know everyone was excited and happy to have Matt back. As I drove away; however, I needed to fight back tears, realizing this was way more difficult than watching him get on the bus his first day of school. It certainly has been one new beginning after another for months now, but all in a positive direction.

I went to work and came back to pick Matt up at three pm. He was in the media center with his paraprofessional and Laura who didn't have a class last hour. Matt had an awesome first day. He had answered several questions in World Literature class per both of their reports. Laura said "Mom, kids came and told me Matt knew all the answers no one else did." This was super cool as the kids then realized Matt "truly is in there," but needs time to express himself. On Wednesday after school and therapy (pool therapy for PT), a shower, the drive home, and dinner, I gave Matt his homework and he literally fell asleep with the pencil in his hand.

On Friday last week Matt played pep band at the football game. Bill took him to McDonald's on the way home after therapy and to the game. It's quite a hillside to get to the field in the wheelchair so he could play the cowbell. I didn't get there until half time and was touched to see his friend, Kyle, hand Matt his cowbell and drumstick, as well as to turn the page for Matt after each song. Matt struggled to keep the cowbell on his lap in a good place so he could hit it as I wanted to leap over the fence and hold it for him (Who am I kidding? I could never leap–maybe walk fast?); however, he needed to do this on his own. It was SO bittersweet, thinking of years with him playing the bells, drums, piano, and now trying to hit a cowbell on his lap in the wheelchair. I always then think about how wonderful it is that he's home, back in school, and able to play in the band again which makes it totally and only amazing.

This past week has been trying, at best, for myself, Bill, and Laura. Bill has been at work late every night and I've felt ready to apply for the "funny farm" just to get a break; however, in hind sight everything worked out well and we were once again lucky for a week of blessings. I took Brooke to the dentist on Tuesday to find out she needed to see the pediatric dental specialist due to a large cavity requiring a root canal and a crown, as well as two other smaller ones. She hasn't been to the dentist for about a year and a half. We cancelled an appointment last fall and then never rescheduled after the accident. As I was getting this information, I receive a text that Laura had a flat tire at school with Matt. Laura tends to solve any problem she encounters, going to the shop teacher who didn't have class that hour and having him put air in the tire so she could drive to the gas station. I went and helped Matt from the van into the Acadia, home and into the house, then went back to town to register and get Brooke's new dance outfit at class, and then to pay for two new tires on the van. We were lucky they were able to look at the van right away so we had all the vehicles for Wednesday morning.

On Wednesday after school and therapy, Matt wanted to go to youth group with Abby. I tried to convince him to just rest after his long day; however, he repeated, "I want to go to youth group too." Abby said, "If he wants to go, let him." I brought them both to youth group at church and then went home to get Brooke showered and ready for bed. Mass had just finished when I went back and they were about to have pizza in the church basement. Abby came to me and said, "Matt took his phone out and started playing Scrabble during the homily. I had to tell him to put it away." Everyone thought this was pretty funny.

Thursday, I received a text from the school nurse that Matt was so tired he even had to lie down. I told her about his busy day Wednesday and being up late last night. In the back of my mind, I was worried about Laura getting him into the house after school, but had hoped the nap did him well and it'd be fine. I was able to get Brooke into the specialist for her root canal and crown. I took her for ice cream because she did so well, and as I pulled into the DQ, Laura called crying and near hysterical saying Matt fell in the garage when she was getting him into the house. I called my brother, who is less than two miles away and was just leaving his driveway. He came right over and helped Matt up and into the house. Matt fell on his bottom and didn't get hurt at all. Laura was by far more upset, stating she wouldn't ever walk him again. Honestly, if she's that fearful of helping Matt, it isn't safe for either of them. Laura said Matt sat on the floor petting our cat with a smile waiting for Uncle Russ. Afterwards he told Laura "Thank you," and she asked Matt "for what?" Matt replied, "For staying with me until Russ got here." I was beyond stressed at this point. When I got home, Matt texted me before I went to talk to him "I'm okay." I totally melted thinking how he knew I would be very worried and sent me a text versus talking to me since texting is easier for him than getting the words out. I tried to figure out if Brooke was going to Kid's Place after school on Friday or coming home and Kami didn't know if she had tennis practice. I texted Coach Poepping, who is also coaching her tennis team, to find out about tennis practice. I told him Matt had fallen and I needed to get a new plan to get him into the house on Tuesdays and Thursdays. He immediately texted that he gets to Pierz at two forty-five pm after work and could come help Matt into the house. Okay, now I literally had to fight back tears as he said "No problem—that's what I'm here for. When basketball practice starts, he can go to practice with me if he wants."

Matt's left hand is getting more function with encouragement to use it. He becomes angry when I ask him to do things with his hand; however, does it and I know is pleased as he can see the progress too. I asked him to hold a plastic cup in his left hand last night, to spit in after brushing his teeth. Hhe opened his hand and grabbed it so hard that it cracked all the way down the side, surprising both of us. I try to make it positive and encourage him every time he uses his left hand and did get a smirk from him afterwards. Matt finished his first book today, and his fantasy football team won today. At church today, Matt was able to go step over step on the way in and out of church with the railing and minimal assist with much more control—it was awesome. I no longer have to even touch him while standing in church—-the trick was to have him at the end of the aisle to hold onto the wooden post that's higher than the pew so he doesn't have to bend over to hold onto it for support. He only needed a little boost going from sitting to and from standing. Matt even asked for the wine today during mass which surprised me. I could only think this will significantly help his healing as it's almost been a year since he's had this at mass.

At my Uncle's wake this afternoon, many people asked us how Matt was doing. Bill and I say he's always making some progress, but it's still a long road yet. The prayers for Matt continue more than realize. My cousin's wife told me today she prays for Matt every day and I haven't seen her in years. I know with all the prayers and God's healing, Matt will continue to get better and better without a doubt.

Abby finished physical therapy this week and no longer complains about her pelvis going out of place or needing to go to the chiropractor. She is busy with tennis, just received a part in the fall play, started "behind the wheel," and also ballet yesterday. She had four friends stay overnight last night and seems to be pretty happy overall when she's not super tired.

I found my inspiration tonight in a book by Joyce Meyer which seemed to fit where we are at right now "in the middle." I thought it had a good reminder for myself and possibly others with children—looking at each accomplishment as a gift and rejoicing rather than always looking and wanting more before it passes by.

There are many stages we must go through in the course of our spiritual growth. We need to learn how to enjoy the glory we are experiencing at each level of our development. It is true we are not yet where we need to be, but, thank God, we are not where we used to be. We are somewhere in the middle, but we are making progress toward our goal—and ought to be enjoying each stage. Often young parents delay enjoying their child until he has reached a certain stage of growth, "I'll be glad when he gets out of diapers, quits cutting teeth, learns to walk, starts, school, or graduates." On and on it goes until the child is grown and gone, and the parents have never really enjoyed any stage of his life. They were always waiting to be glad "when." We need to learn to rejoice and be glad in the Lord this day and every day along the way toward our goal.

Angels Among Us

—⁓—

September 30, 2014

The past two weeks have calmed down "just a bit"—other than the night I burnt my arm frying chicken, right before our kitten attempted to jump into the oven (pouncing on the hot oven door—wanting the chicken) and Brooke found my missing bracelet in the Cheetos bag. Bill's been super busy at work, as September always is for him and I'm so grateful for my job being flexible to come home to Matt when I need to. Both of our jobs have been amazingly so supportive and wonderful and continue to be so even after ten months. My boss makes a point of talking to Matt every time he comes in for outpatient therapy, and her boss, Becky, continues to post her support and prayers frequently even though I may not see her during my day. We have been so blessed to have Country Manor and Trim Pac for our employers and are both very dedicated to our jobs as well.

Matt continues to make progress physically and cognitively. When I think about the past two weeks, I surprise myself noting several gains once again. Matt's left arm flexor tone continues to improve as we work on increasing his strength to straighten his elbow, wrist, fingers and thumb. Last Saturday morning I handed Matt his deodorant and he lifted his left arm to put it on, put the deodorant in his left hand without any difficulty (opening his hand—yay!) and was able to reach and apply it under his right arm for the first time. I reminded Matt of how I used to pry his fingers open to put it in his left hand and help him lift his arm to reach the right armpit. Matt was frustrated with the effort it took to do this and said "but I could do it before my accident." I told him the accident wasn't anything we could control and yes, it's a nightmare, but "YOU ARE GETTING BETTER" to which Matt quietly nodded his agreement. Matt even reached back for the recliner to sit this weekend with his left hand for very first, again letting me know he's aware of his left side and beginning to increase his function. He is able to hold on to the grab bar in the bathroom and in church on Sunday I placed his hand on the pew to help him pull up to stand. Matt played the cowbell in pep band at the volleyball game and it was like watching a different person as compared to the football game three weeks ago. He held onto the cowbell with his left hand and kept beat nearly perfect. He looked so good–as many of my friends commented.

Matt stands in church without me holding onto him anymore, leaning against the pew in front of him for balance to use his right hand to shake hands, make the sign of the cross, etc. The girls and I went to church without Bill (he was working and went to an earlier mass last Sunday) and friends/parishioners offered to open the door for use, asked if we needed help on the stairs, etc. Everyone is so supportive and encouraging to Matt, commenting how wonderful he's doing to use the steps rather than the elevator. Matt then proceeded to go down the steps, alternating each foot on a new step. Matt is walking better with me at home too. He was willing to use his rolling quad cane last weekend for the first time in quite a while and I only had a hand on him for balance the majority of the time. He's also walking faster and more confident without his cane—not even holding onto me with his right hand. His new goal is to walk well enough that we sign him up for the senior class trip next spring as we need to decide by November.

Matt's personality and thinking has made me smile many times over the past few weeks. Laura called him to see if he had gotten in the house okay with Coach Poepping, and Matt answered the phone with, "You rang?" In church last Sunday, my nephew was across the aisle and Matt proceeded to wave to him, do the Star Track sign for "Live long and prosper," peace sign, and then to my horror and humor, he places his thumb on the end of his nose and wiggles his fingers. I told him he couldn't do that in church, but it really was funny. I told his PT about it today in therapy and he said I had a big mouth. This certainly lets me know he's getting better. We shut off the TV so Brooke could concentrate on reading her book Sunday night (Matt was on his phone anyway,) and when Bill came home he went downstairs to watch TV and eat dinner. Matt calls "Dad?" Bill came back up to the landing and asked him what he wanted. Matt replied "I thought we could watch TV together." Of course, Bill came back up and put football on, even though Brooke then complained. A part of me knows Matt just wanted the TV back on, but how clever is that? Bill and Matt continue to be very close. Bill gets him up and ready in the morning, makes him breakfast, gives him his showers and is always discussing fantasy football, movies, etc. with Matt.

I've noticed Matt talking in much longer sentences too now. He wanted to go to the Homecoming coronation and said "I was thinking I could go to therapy Tuesday, Wednesday and Friday this week." Last night he said, "Sorry mom, but I used up all the data again on my phone." He wanted to go to the away football game in Kimball last Friday night and said "So who's going to take me to Kimball?" We went to Grandma and Grandpa Athman's on Saturday and Matt went from playing "Dirty Clubs" to "Gin 13" without any difficulty, which I think was super awesome. The special education director at school called to tell me Matt did so well with all his behavioral and cognitive testing that they decided he only needs physical modifications. It makes me want to go back to PICU at the St. Cloud Hospital soon to show them how far he's come since his time there when the future was so unknown.

Matt's grandparents have been and continue to be wonderful too. Grandpa Ed (soon to be eighty-five years old) offered to help get Matt into the house with the girls if we ever were in a bind. I know he could do it without a doubt, and it was so sweet for him to offer. My mom brings Matt to Country Manor two to three times a week for therapy so we don't have to take off work. She gets time alone with Matt, even though he hardly says a word, playing his phone or iPad most of the way there. We are so lucky to have family support, which never falters.

I received a call at work from Holy Trinity yesterday, thinking, "Oh no, Brooke wasn't sick this morning." It was the school secretary telling me she had good news. My first thought was that Brooke won a spelling bee. She said someone came in and paid Brooke's tuition for the year this morning. He wanted to remain anonymous; however, but had given a large donation for our family's tuition, another family, and for repairs the school needed. I fought back tears for an hour—angels among us. Every time we take from the benefit account, I am beyond grateful for all the support we've received. It's unbelievable to think in two months it'll have been a year since the accident and the third time we start all over with deductibles. I never did get to send thank you cards out to everyone who helped us out, but think of you often—know our family is still and always will be very thankful.

If you've been able to watch the movie "God is not Dead," they say many times "God is Good, All the Time." and "All the Time, God is Good." Remember this as you look at the wonderful people in your lives and the many gifts you have received. I say this often and continue to see the "proof" through so many people.

School Rocks

—⁂—

I typically wait until I have "news" to post and the time of course. I found myself unable to sleep last night—excited to let everyone know how awesome the past two weeks have been. I went to conferences for mid-term last Wednesday night and it was amazing to talk to not only Matt's teachers, but the girls as well. Matt had four A's and one B in his classes. The teachers were all very caring and excited to tell me how they have noticed such a change in Matt since school started—being more awake, his affect, thinking, and physical abilities. They were very accommodating, asking me to let them know if anything would make things easier for him in any way. His Phy-ed instructor said Matt wants to be with the kids and even participated in a Yoga video with the class. He said "I am amazed at Matt's thinking. Every Monday we talk fantasy football and Matt's right on—he even pulls up the scores on his phone." One night Matt was typing a two paragraph summary for World Literature and after working on it for about an hour and a half, our internet shut down and he lost everything he had typed. Matt made a fist and was ready to slam it into the keyboard when I told him, "Don't even think about it," and he stopped. I was as frustrated as he was and then Laura came over, gave him a hug and asked him to tell her what he had written and she typed it for him. Laura then set him up on Google Docs so Matt wouldn't lose anything he had written if the internet went down. Matt was given a computer last week to use for homework assignments. It has predictive text to speed up his ability to type with one hand. It's similar to cell phone texting, letting him choose the word you are looking for as you type. Matt has only used it a few times with help from his paraprofessional at school, but it's much easier for him.

We had a meeting with twelve people at the school last Monday—not including Bill, Matt and me, to go over test results and gather information to establish an IEP (individualized education plan) for Matt. I was a bit overwhelmed having so many people contribute, as well as care about Matt's future. The testing determined Matt didn't have any cognitive deficits, just communication difficulty and the need for physical adaptions. This was SO huge for me. His reading skills were assessed to be "average or above average." I am SO thankful for all the healing and progress Matt has shown with his thinking—words do not do my feelings justice. The school psychologist who assessed Matt started her report with "I told myself I wasn't going to cry when I gave my report. I brought in Mountain Dew for Matt when I met with him for my testing and even though I gave him the option to be finished, he didn't want to quit. He did so well with everything and at the end of my assessment I gave him a word and asked him to tell me the opposite of each word. One word was synthesis and Matt quietly said 'antithesis'— I couldn't believe it." Do I know what either word means? The answer is NO." The adapted Phy-ed teacher had gone to Walmart and bought sand-filled PVC piping for Matt's arm exercises with different amounts of sand for resistance to challenge his balance. He quickly said, "If there is anything else you think of, I'd be happy to go get it. He is doing so well with his paraprofessional in class, I don't need to be there with him." Scott, the TBI specialist from Mid-State had interviewed me prior to the meeting and discussed goals of Matt using his left hand more, including to lock and unlock his wheelchair brake. Matt proceeded to unlock then lock the brake to show everyone there he could do it—I was never so proud of him. He lifted his left arm over his head with his right hand to stretch, leaning back in his wheelchair at least four or five times during the meeting, causing everyone to smile. Yesterday, when I brought Matt to the truck to go home, he locked his brake with his left hand without me asking him too. I was so happy to see him do this. Scott asked me what Matt's plans were for after high school. I told him I didn't know, but I thought he'd take classes on-line or at St Cloud State for a year to transition, then go to Augsburg College, but we really have no idea when he'll be ready. Scott had interviewed Matt too and he said his plan was to stay at home with us after high school for a while. I was relieved to know Matt had the insight to know he may need a bit more time to transition into college, away from home. I know I won't be ready next fall yet—but with another transition year, it'll be amazing and I know Matt will be more than ready. The future is still completely in God's hands, but his blessings continue every day.

I know how much everyone enjoys Matt's sense of humor and couldn't wait to share this. Matt was working on going from sitting in his wheelchair to standing and then sitting again with Jenn, his PT. One trial, Matt pretty much flopped back down into his chair, versus controlling his sit. Jenn asked Matt if he broke his butt with the landing and Matt replied, "Well, it already has a crack in it." I was late for an appointment after bringing Matt home Thursday afternoon, so I told him I was going to change while he went to the bathroom. He only needed to void, so it didn't take long. When I came back and opened the bathroom door, Matt was standing at the grab bar with his clothes pulled up already. I said, "Holy Shit Matt!" He replied "I believe the saying should be Holy Piss." I couldn't stop laughing, as Matt had said this with a huge smile.

I have been so happy with Matt's progress using his left arm. He is now able to lift his arm up over shoulder height for "knucks." Matt worked so long on being able to straighten his arm even low towards the floor, then straight ahead to put on a shirt or jacket, and now can do this up toward the ceiling. He is able to shut off the facet in the bathroom, turn off light switches and the fan with his left hand too. Matt is using his left hand to stabilize paper to write, to hold cards, and to keep the page when reading a book. It's certainly an answered prayer as he continues to improve his function—one that I've been wanting for months. I have so much faith it will continue to get better. Matt has progressed from avoiding using his left arm due to the frustration (not neglect in my opinion) to wanting to use it and knowing he can. This is beyond HUGE in his recovery. Matt's Occupational Therapist, Joe, has been using electrical stimulation to "kick in" his interphalangeal thumb extensors (to straighten the tip of his thumb) to reduce tone (tightness) and increase his function. The goal is to be able to do a "thumbs-up" and use his thumb to pinch food and other items functionally.

Matt has been playing the cow bell in band and asking to play in pep band at volleyball and football games. One night Matt asked to play at the volleyball game at six-thirty pm, telling me he was supposed to be there at six-fifteen pm. I told him he had to let me know about this ahead of time. I was excited that he asked to go to the game on Tuesday morning this week for that night's game. Matt's short-term memory has improved one hundred percent. When I think back to when he was in the hospital and how difficult it was to remember what he had eaten for a previous meal and the doctor stating how impaired his short-term memory was. It literally brings tears to my eyes knowing how far he has come. He is now able to read a chapter at a time, versus a paragraph or page, and to remember what he has read. Thinking back to ICU and how the neurologist said he may read something and not be able to understand it, to look at a picture and not recognize who it is, and how devastated I was, it is a true testament to the power of prayer and healing.

Joyce Meyer wrote in her book that "As soon as we start wanting anything so much we try to take matters into our own hands to get it, we are asking for trouble. It takes a mature individual to be patient and wait on the Lord to work out things according to His perfect will and timing. Immature people rush ahead of God and end up frustrated. They don't realize nothing is going to work out right unless it comes from God and is carried out in the Spirit in accordance with His divine plan and purpose. She also writes to stop ruining today worrying about yesterday or tomorrow—neither of which we can do anything about. We need to stop wasting our precious "now" because it will never come again. I've thought about this and try to enjoy every little accomplishment Matt makes, every joke, every smile, every eyebrow raise. The future will continue to bring blessings and worrying about it will take away the joy of "the now." Look at your life and enjoy the gifts of "the now," versus looking at yesterday and tomorrow and wanting more. The peace and satisfaction of every day will be so much more plentiful as will your happiness.

Lindsey and Matt–"friends"

One year of miracles

—◊—

November 2, 2014

Yesterday was a day of mixed emotions for me—the one year anniversary of the accident. Matt has been angry lately with his physical limitations, having his friends at college without him, knowing the basketball season is starting without being able to play, etc., etc. In PT, Jenn asked Matt what he could have done better after practicing a transfer going from sitting to standing, and Matt replied, "Not to have gotten hurt in the first place." Last week, when Matt's football team won within the final minutes, I put my hands up and said, "touchdown." Bill did the same and I told Matt to also and he raised both hands straight over his head. I told him that was awesome and he yelled "But it shouldn't be awesome I can do that!" Bill explained to Matt how he couldn't move his left arm at all for two and a half months, so yes we do get excited when he does something new, or better. Matt did understand but was in a bad mood for days, even pointing versus talking at school—knowing the expectation is for him to talk. He did agree to talk to someone who had a brain injury for the first time—after offering him counseling several times before. I continue to remind Matt the only reason I nag so much about him using his left arm/hand is because I love and care about him and his future. He understands but I know is sick of having to try so hard to do everything. I really cannot blame him at all, as I have my days too, but need to continue to encourage him and remind him how far he has come.

When I think back to the first few days, then weeks after the accident, Matt and Abby's healing is such a miracle, and in a short time. Matt has progressed from being in a coma, unable to breathe on his own, control his body temperature, swallow, or open his eyes (with the left one pinpoint and the right dilated) for an entire month. Abby initially had fractured ribs, visual problems (unable to track vertically) balance impairments, pelvis instability, and jaw pain. She is now in the school play, jazz band, jazz choir, dance, ballet, youth group, church choir, art club, student counsel—you get the idea. Matt is diligently picking his fantasy football players, writing short essays, reading another book (in short intervals,) playing the cowbell in band, playing cards, saying jokes, walking with only one person, needing minimal assist, and continues to improve his left arm strength. It is incredibly above and beyond amazing. When I put it all into perspective and wonder how long our journey will last, I realize God's healing has been in warp speed and we will continue to have strength from God, as well as our family, friends, and even strangers I don't know. Yesterday I received several texts from friends, coworkers, family, our principal, etc., and a card from the youth group leaders letting us know we were in everyone's thoughts and prayers on this anniversary date It was so thoughtful and caring. Matt proudly wore a shirt that said, "I WILL NOT STOP" his aunt gave him for the anniversary date and we all went to a mass of thanksgiving for Matt and Abby's recovery yesterday.

Bill took Matt, Abby and Kami to the playoff football game last night while I stayed home with Brooke. They played pep band in the stands with many stairs, therefore Matt wasn't able to play his cowbell. I was very disappointed for him, but found out he did get to see Mark, the chaplain from the hospital, at the game. How ironic on the anniversary of the accident, for this connection of the one person who joined whole heartedly in our prayers and journey of faith. He asked if Bill and I would be interested in talking to other parents of children who sustain a brain injury. Of course, Bill's standard response was "Give Lynn a call." This confirmed my future plan to publish a book to help others who have a loved one with a traumatic brain injury—to give them strength, hope, and then faith through the power of prayer for God's healing. I had thought it'd be years down the road, but then realized "the first year" is such a critical and emotional time and there is such a need to help others understand brain injury and to find the faith for the journey.

My story wouldn't be complete without ending with a bit of Matt's humor. Thursday morning I was in a light sleep, dreaming of multiple random things–such as purple cats and hiding places (no doubt from watching Criminal Minds and Stalker before bed,) when Matt pounded on my bedroom door and literally yelled Get your ass out of bed!" Matt and Bill were laughing, as I sprung up to sitting with a racing heart, as Bill said "those weren't the words I told you to say." They are forever laughing at jokes, movie references, etc. the majority of the time at my expense, but as long as Matt smiles I'm totally okay with it. Today as Matt was standing, I looked up and puckered my lips as he smiled, then chuckled and wasn't quite sure what to do as he typically kisses me on the cheek. With encouragement from Bill, of course, he tried to lick my nose instead and did find this pretty funny. I love this glimpse of his humor, and for the record, I did get a kiss on the cheek too. Laura had her IQ tested in school last week and Matt instantly said "but you're a girl," and then teased her when a waffle fell off her fork one morning "how she couldn't eat a waffle even with her IQ." Laura of course loves it when Matt talks or teases her, often instigating it herself. Our dog had four puppies this week and when asked what he thought about this, Matt replied "Well, it's about time." There's subtle things Matt does, or doesn't do, that makes me aware of how he continues to change and heal. He no longer texts me when I'm home. As much of an improvement as this is cognitively, I kind of miss it—as it always made me smile.

We received flowers with a balloon yesterday that said, "Our God is an Awesome God." I believe the past year is a testimony to this without a shred of doubt. Thank you all again for the wonderful support we have received—giving us strength for our journey. You are all amazing.

I look forward to someday writing a sequel for the rest of Matt and Abby's journey. Until then, don't take anything for granted in your life and in trying times, remember the power of prayer—you will never be let down.

CPSIA information can be obtained
at www.ICGtesting.com
Printed in the USA
FFOW01n0009120116
20299FF

9 781498 455770